GREAT MOMENTS IN CURRIE CUP HISTORY

GREAT MOMENTS IN CURRIE CUP HISTORY

Wim van der Berg

PENGUIN BOOKS

PENGUIN BOOKS

Published by the Penguin Group
Penguin Books (South Africa) (Pty) Ltd, 24 Sturdee Avenue, Rosebank, Johannesburg 2196, South Africa
Penguin Group (USA) Inc, 375 Hudson Street, New York, New York 10014, USA
Penguin Group (Canada), 90 Eglinton Avenue East, Suite 700, Toronto, Ontario, Canada M4P 2Y3 (a division of Pearson Penguin Canada Inc)
Penguin Books Ltd, 80 Strand, London WC2R ORL, England
Penguin Ireland, 25 St Stephen's Green, Dublin 2, Ireland (a division of Penguin Books Ltd)
Penguin Group (Australia), 250 Camberwell Road, Camberwell, Victoria 3124, Australia (a division of Pearson Australia Group Pty Ltd)
Penguin Books India Pvt Ltd, 11 Community Centre, Panchsheel Park, New Delhi – 110 017, India
Penguin Group (NZ), 67 Apollo Drive, Mairangi Bay, Auckland 1310, New Zealand (a division of Pearson New Zealand Ltd)

Penguin Books (South Africa) (Pty) Ltd, Registered Offices:
24 Sturdee Avenue, Rosebank, Johannesburg 2196, South Africa

www.penguinbooks.co.za

First published by Penguin Books (South Africa) (Pty) Ltd 2010

ISBN 978 0 143 02685 3

Design and layout by Kevin Shenton, Johannesburg
Printed and bound Ultra Litho (Pty) Ltd, Johannesburg

Contents

CHAPTER 1

How it all Started

It started in 1889 – or so they say. The records would have it that Western Province won the first of their 32 Currie Cup titles in that year, even before South Africa had a Currie Cup to contest.

It may not sound important in the total context of the competition, but this is a contentious matter, given the often very animated fervour with which South African supporters argue the merits of their favourite team. For those who are not Western Province (WP) supporters, that first so-called Currie Cup title is hotly disputed and regarded as nothing more than a South African Rugby Board (SARB) title, acknowledged as such in the records. And so it is, yet that win in 1889 still counts towards Western Province's record number of 32 Currie Cup titles.

In fact, teams first played for the Currie Cup trophy in 1892, with a dominant Western Province by then already boasting the South African Rugby Football Board (SARFB) title won at the Kimberley tournament in 1889 where only four teams competed.

To add to the mini-controversy, Griqualand West have also added their plaque to the trophy as the 1891 winners!

This they arguably were, although there was no provincial competition of any kind in 1891 owing to the first international tour to South Africa which took place that year. The British touring team presented the trophy, now known as the Currie Cup, to Griqualand West as the best team they had encountered in their 20 tour matches, which included an unofficial match against Stellenbosch.

But more about that later.

The forerunner of the Currie Cup competition had its beginnings in 1884 when an inter-town competition was inaugurated, and then upgraded to an

Sir Donald Currie.

The first international game played in Kimberley, between the touring British side of Bill Maclaglan and South Africa.
The tourists won 2-0 on their tour in 1891.

inter-centre tournament in 1889. The then South African Rugby Football Board (some historians contend it was the South African Rugby Board) was established that same year, and donated a silver trophy to be presented to the winners of the tournament in Kimberley.

Western Province became the first winners, and the trophy today stands in the South African Rugby Museum in Cape Town. North of the Hex River Mountains, of course, everyone contends that was not the Currie Cup, and that Western Province can therefore lay claim to only 31 Currie Cup titles, not 32.

The magnificent Currie Cup trophy was donated by shipping magnate Sir Donald Currie in 1891, following his visit to South Africa in 1889. The story goes that Sir Donald instructed WE (Bill) Maclagan, the captain of the first overseas side to tour in South Africa, which retrospectively became known as the British Isles, that the gold cup should be awarded to the first side to beat the tourists.

There is, however, some conflict as to whether Sir Donald had also instructed that the cup should thereafter become a floating trophy for the provincial champions. Furthermore, there is no clarity on whether he had in fact instructed that it should be awarded to the team that performed best against the tourists.

According to Dr Danie Craven – rugby historian and the man who made such a mark in South African rugby as player, captain, selector and then President of the South African Rugby Board – Sir Donald's instructions were indeed clear that the trophy should go to the best team and then be donated to the South African Rugby Football Board.

Griqualand West, hub of hopes, iniquity and riches, became the first ever unofficial holders of the Currie Cup after their performance was deemed the best of the lot by the invincible tourists. The Griquas lost by only 3–0 to the touring side.

The famous Cecil John Rhodes was Prime Minister of the Cape Colony and the Member of Parliament for the Barkly West constituency near Kimberley at that time. Rhodes was also the underwriter of the British team's tour – or perhaps only the co-underwriter, as some historians have chronicled that Transvaal President, Paul Kruger, was the other. What is certain, however, is that Kruger officially entertained the tourists.

Rhodes also supported Griqualand West, and perhaps his ties with Kimberley and Griqualand West played a role in the trophy ending up in that rugby union's cabinet!

It is ironic that Rhodes and Kruger are linked to the tour. Seven years after the tour, Britain was at war with the Boer Republics, and before that, in 1896, Rhodes was forced to resign as Prime Minister of the Cape Colony owing to his apparent involvement in planning and assisting in the Jameson Raid.

During the South African War three years later, British troops would play a key role in entrenching the game of rugby throughout the country. Games among the Boer population in prisoner of war camps popularised the game further.

By then Griqualand West had duly presented Sir Donald Currie's trophy to the South African Rugby Football Board and the trophy had become the prize for the provincial competition, which had been dubbed the Currie Cup competition.

The inaugural Currie Cup tournament was held in 1892, with Western Province as the first winners.

However, before one looks at the Currie Cup, arguably the most famous and most sought-after trophy in South African sport, the socio-political and financial dynamics of the late 19th century must be understood.

It was with the arrival of permanent British control in 1806 that the Cape economy began to prosper. The cultural and political power of the British extended far and wide into the region, and a wide range of British cultural practices were introduced during the latter half of the 19th century.

British officers and settlers brought cricket and football to South Africa. The football was not the early form of what is today known as soccer, but instead a game of the Winchester Football variety, introduced by the Reverend George Ogilvie, who was appointed headmaster of the Diocesan College (Bishops) at Rondenbosch (sic) in 1861. It was a game Ogilvie had learned at his alma mater, Winchester College in Hampshire, England.

The first recorded match took place in 1862 'on the race course at Green Point', according to the *Cape Argus* of 21 August of that year, and was a match between the Officers and the Civil Service. A series of matches between scratch sides followed, with Town playing Suburbs, All Comers facing up to the Civil Servants, Home-born v Colonial-born, and the likes.

Then, in the 1870s, the accepted norm was rocked when a new club, Villagers, started playing a 'code' of their own, namely Rugby Football. This was despite the Winchester rules still being the preferred game for South Africa's oldest club, Hamiltons, which was formed in 1875, and for the Western Province Club. Rugby Football struggled to survive against Winchester Football and the oldest derby in the country, between Villagers and Hamiltons, was first played in 1876 under Winchester Football rules.

It was a former England international, William H Milton, who settled matters in favour of Rugby Football in 1878. He joined Villagers and supported and taught the Rugby code. By the end of 1878 this was the game played by most.

(It is interesting to note that Milton – later Sir William, the Administrator of Southern Rhodesia – represented South Africa at cricket in the late 1880s).

BEFORE THE CURRIE CUP

Representative rugby in South Africa goes back to the 1885 Grahamstown Exhibition when teams from Cape Town, Kimberley, Port Elizabeth and Grahamstown competed in what was known as an 'inter-town tournament'. Cape Town won.

The first South African Rugby Board tournament was held in Kimberley in 1889. The teams represented their regions, or centres, not their cities or towns. Griqualand West and Western Province shared first place on the log, but because Western Province had beaten the home team 6-2 earlier, they were declared winners even though they lost 2-5 to Transvaal.

Three of the four Versfeld brothers, Marthinus (Oupa) and Charles (Hasie) Versfeld, who both played for South Africa in 1891, and John, played in that tournament. The other one, Loftus, was also a fine Western Province three-quarter.

The inaugural Currie Cup tournament was played during the Kimberley Exhibition in 1892, when Western Province won all four of their matches to become the first holders of the famous trophy.

Western Province won the SA Board Trophy in 1889 at the tournament in Kimberley, which was the forerunner of the first Currie Cup tournament in 1892.

THOSE WERE THE DAYS

When Rhodesia beat Border by 31 points in the 1899 Currie Cup tournament in Kimberley, the losers presented a specially printed 'memorial' card to their conquerors. The wording was:

Currie Cup
Kimberley 1899
In Memory of the
BORDER TEAM
who met their death
August 24th, 1899
at the hands of
ROOD-DE-SEER
Aged 31 points.

For various reasons rugby was instantly accepted as a sport by the Afrikaners of the 19th century, being regarded as less imperialistic than cricket. By 1883, when the Western Province Rugby Football Union was established, the farmers and students of Stellenbosch had already formed a club. According to Dr Danie Craven, who wrote nearly 30 books on rugby, many of them on the history of the game and on Stellenbosch rugby in particular, the club in Stellenbosch was formed in 1880.

It was an era of growth. In 1884 rugby was established along the coast of the former Cape Colony. By that time inland and inter-town matches between Kimberley and Cape Town (1884) and Grahamstown and Port Elizabeth (1885) were already being played.

In 1886 the game had grown popular enough in the diamond fields for the Griqualand West Rugby Union to be formed.

HISTORY MAKERS

The members of the first team to win the Currie Cup, namely Western Province in 1892, were: B Duff (capt.), HT Jones, CJ Thompson, JH Anderson, AJ Munnik, EH Bisset, M Moffat, A Beswick, H Barnett, WM Bisset, BG Roscoe, FH Guthrie, M Versfeld, J Theunissen, BH Heatlie, NHM Cole, CG van Reenen, W Dowling, AM Mostert.

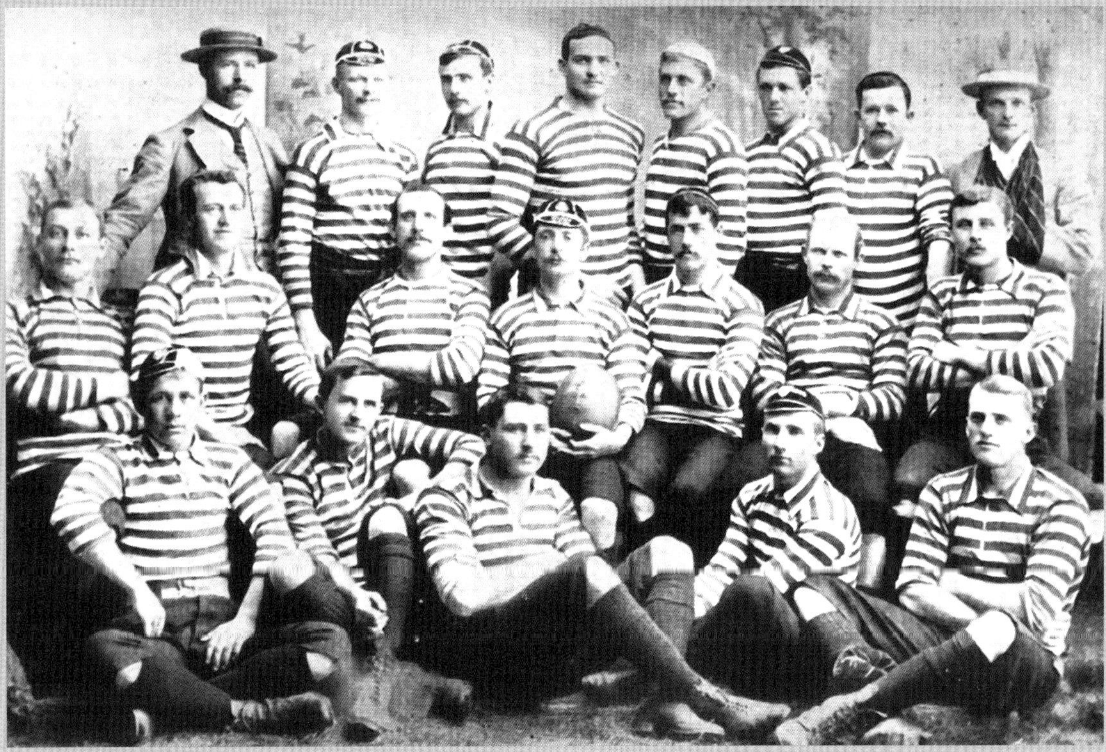

The game moved to Western Transvaal and then to Johannesburg and Pretoria, with the first inter-town matches between the latter two played in 1888. The Transvaal Rugby Football Union (TRFU) was formed in 1889. By the next year the code had also taken over as the leading sport from Association Football in Pietermaritzburg, the headquarters of the British Army, as well as in Durban.

It was this rapid expansion that led to the formation of the South African Rugby Football Board in 1889.

The establishment of the national body came about after Percy Ross Frames of Kimberley, only 24 years old at the time, and the 21-year-old Bill Bisset of Cape Town, agreed that something had to be done to end the lack of uniformity in rule interpretations and applications – very much as is the case today, some would say!

This discussion took place in 1888 after an inter-town visit by Kimberley to Cape Town. The SARFB was established the following year and its first meeting took place in the Craven Hotel in Kimberley.

Perhaps the name of the hotel was an omen of the future achievements of Dr Danie Craven, who was to

Barry Heatlie

THE FIRST CURRIE CUP ICON

Barry Heatlie, also known as Fairy or Ox, was the giant of his time, in physique as well as in stature.

As captain, Heatlie was peerless. He still holds the record for the longest captaincy of a provincial side. He captained Western Province from 1891 to 1904, with the exception of 1895, when Alf Richards was the skipper.

Heatlie was never on the losing side in his 28 Currie Cup matches in an era when Western Province won five Currie Cup titles between 1892 and 1898. This ties the record for the most consecutive Currie Cup titles, albeit not in successive years.

In all, he represented Western Province in 34 matches. That included five matches against British touring sides: in 1891, 1896 (twice as captain) and 1903 (twice as captain). Heatlie also captained South Africa twice – once against the British touring side of 1896 and once against the tourists of 1903.

Captaining South Africa against Mark Morrison's side in the third test of the 1903 British tour, Heatlie's name was engraved in South African history for leading South Africa to its first test win. This win also clinched South Africa's first series win, after the first two tests in the series had been drawn 8-all and nil-all.

Heatlie, a farm boy from the farm Glen Heatlie near De Wet in the Worcester district, was a big man for his time. He weighed 208 lbs (95 kg) and stood 6 ft 3 ins tall (1,91 m). He was taller and heavier than any player in the first Springbok side (that of Paul Roos) to tour the United Kingdom and France in 1906.

He first played for Western Province in 1890 as an 18-year-old in only his second season of rugby, and played test rugby the following year.

Yet Heatlie was not included in Paul Roos' Springbok side. By that time, he had left for Argentina, where he lived for 20 years to evade his creditors in South Africa.

His greatness as a forward is beyond dispute. The legendary Stellenbosch player and coach (and later national selector), Oubaas Markötter, said of him: 'I played with him and against him. Heatlie is the greatest all-round forward South Africa has produced. I am inclined to put him down as the best captain ever to lead a Springbok side.'

Those were early days, and by the time Markötter died in 1957, many more greats for South Africa had come and gone. It did, however, emphasise that Heatlie was something special.

Heatlie is also the man who is credited with giving the green jersey to South Africa's national teams. Until the third test of the 1896 series, the South African team played in either white jerseys or jerseys in the colours of the union/club hosting the test match, often with the badge of the local club on their jerseys.

'At the time I had on hand a supply of dark green jerseys, the colours of the defunct Old Diocesan's Club. It was decided to wear those jerseys at Newlands, and ever since South African fifteens have been clad in green,' he is quoted as saying in various chronicles.

The South African team for the fourth test of 1896 is pictured wearing these jerseys and Heatlie, as captain, is the only player with the Diocesan badge on his jersey. The caption to the photo in Dr Danie Craven's *Rugby Annuals 1891-1964* written for the SA Rugby Board, reads: 'The first South African side to wear a green jersey in an international match.'

In 1905 Heatlie fled South Africa and brought about the first 'high-level' contact between South African and Argentinian rugby. In Argentina he played for the Lomas Rugby Club. He then became captain and coach of Gimnasia y Esgrima, leading them to the national title in 1911 and 1912, by which time he had been playing top-level rugby for more than 20 years! He represented Argentina in two 'test' matches against an unofficial British touring side.

Heatlie was 43 when he retired in 1915, as a result of broken ribs. He died tragically – in South Africa – when he was 79.

The 1896 team of famous Diggers Rugby Club in Transvaal.

become South Africa's most influential rugby icon, even though the owners of the hotel were not related to Doc Craven at all.

The SARFB held the first provincial tournament in Kimberley that year, and fittingly the province where it all started, Western Province, won the four-team competition against Transvaal, Griqualand West and Eastern Province. Western Province didn't win that SARFB Trophy outright. They were tied with Griqualand West after suffering a surprise 5–2 defeat against Transvaal, who were regarded as little more than a scratch team.

This was Transvaal's only win, but it forced WP to rely on a count-out. As they had beaten Griqualand West in the round-robin stages, WP were declared the winners according to the tournament rules.

They repeated their win three years later in 1892 when they won the first Currie Cup to be played for. They also won it at the next four Currie Cup tournaments between 1894 and 1898 (no competitions took place in 1893 and 1896). The five consecutive wins are still a record – tied with the five finals Western Province won from 1982 to

Percy Ross Frames – first president of the SA Rugby Football Board.

The famous Newlands rugby ground in Cape Town when it hosted its first international against the 1891 British touring side.

1986. (There were also six consecutive wins from 1925 to 1936, but as two were shared with Border, this isn't considered a record.)

After five wins, Western Province relinquished their title in 1899. That was on the eve of the South African War, when they didn't take part and Griqualand West won the Currie Cup for the first time.

It was also Griqualand West that broke Western Province's second winning streak in 1911 after three more titles, with Transvaal winning in 1922 after a further two Currie Cups had gone to Western Province. It was Transvaal's first Currie Cup title and one they wouldn't repeat until 1939 in the first Currie Cup final. Prior to that, the team finishing at the top of the log was crowned the champions.

No Currie Cup titles were decided between 1915 and 1919 owing to the First World War, and only eight between 1920 and 1936.

By 1922 Western Province had won 10 of the 13 Currie Cup titles outright and then also added the next six, of which two were shared with Border in the years up to 1936. Their 16 titles, including the two shared, in the first 19 competitions gave WP a lead in Currie Cup wins it still holds today.

The league system to determine the champion side came to an end in 1939, when the first final was played. Transvaal beat the Cape side 17-6 at Newlands.

With the exception of the three tournaments in 1964 and 1966, as well as the one tournament decided over a three-year span from 1957 to 1959, all the other tournaments since 1939 have been decided with finals.

It is interesting to note that Western Province's dominance as Currie Cup winners faded after 1968, when play-offs and finals were introduced. Western Province have won only 15 of the 52 titles since finals were first played in 1939, sharing it twice with Northern Transvaal.

The Currie Cup was played for intermittently after the South African War, with gaps of three or four years in between. Only one Currie Cup competition – in 1936 – was played between 1934 and 1939. Then, due to the Second World War, there was another hiatus until the competition was resumed in 1946.

The Currie Cup was now contested more frequently, but another gap between 1956 and 1964 ensued. Only a single Currie Cup champion was crowned in that time and that was in a competition that took place over a

The Springbok brains trust of the 1937 Springbok side and all great contributors to the Currie Cup legacy. *From left:* Danie Craven, Gerry Brand, Lucas Strachen, Boy Louw and Philip Nel.

AT THE HEART OF THE GAME

It is impossible to do justice to Dr Daniel Hartman Craven in just a few hundred words. Many, many books and millions of words have been – and still are being – written about the man who was known as Mr Rugby throughout the rugby-playing world and beyond.

Craven fought many boardroom battles with the political leaders of South Africa and other countries to bring justice to rugby. In South Africa he battled to ensure that players of all colours were accepted into the South African rugby system, and developed to their full potential. Outside the country's borders he fought to retain South Africa's membership of the International Rugby Board.

He was not liked by all, but respected by most. He excelled as a player; as an officer during the Second World War; as an academic; as a coach at the very highest level; and as a rugby administrator. He often stood up to cabinet ministers and the Broederbond and worked hard to unite the South African Rugby Board and the South African Rugby Union – South Africa's two strongest rugby bodies.

Doc Craven viewed the Currie Cup as the lifeblood of rugby and the benchmark against which a player was measured. In 1931–1932 Craven became one of the first players to be selected for a Springbok side without having first played Currie Cup rugby. To his last days that was something he treasured.

He was a member of the Western Province team that won the Currie Cup and shared it (twice) with Border in 1932 and 1934.

He played Currie Cup rugby for Western Province and later for Eastern Province (EP), captaining both these teams. He also captained Northern Transvaal in 1938, when there was no Currie Cup competition.

He became head of the Physical Training Battalion during the Second World War and had a huge influence on rugby in Griqualand West when he was stationed there.

In the days when specialisation was paramount, Craven, who perfected the dive pass and tactically exploited it to the hilt, was first and foremost a scrumhalf. However, he also played flyhalf, centre and even no 8 for South Africa in test matches.

His aim, as quoted by Ted Partridge in his book *A Life in Rugby*, was to 'devote the rest of my life to improving the relationship between the races in whatever way I can. I think that sport will always be the catalyst for true permanent change ...'

Craven, who was a true amateur but very much aware that the advent of professionalism in rugby was unavoidable, predicted most of what has happened since players and officials started to be paid: a faster game played by fitter men at the top level; the demise of club rugby and this level as a feeder for the top system; the loss of the camaraderie that was so much part and parcel of the game in years gone by, and for many the reason why they preferred it to any other sport.

Rhodesia first played in a Currie Cup tournament in 1889. Above is that year's side that finished third in the tournament in Cape Town.

three-year period between 1957 and 1959.

Western Province won that 'three-year title', which was effectively played over two years, as the fixtures for 1958 were suspended because of the first tour by France to South Africa. These visitors, led in the two tests by caretaker captain Lucien Mias, inflicted the first test series defeat in the 20th century over the Springboks.

The format of the Currie Cup competitions, with many variations, developed over the years from a round-robin format in the early years to a structure of strength versus strength in the second half of the 20th century.

Only five teams – Western Province, Transvaal, Border, Griqualand West and Natal – participated in the inaugural Currie Cup tournament in 1892 in Kimberley. In those early days, the matches were played in a round-robin format at a central venue over a period of a week to ten days, with the log winners crowned as champions. This structure remained in place until 1920.

In 1922 the Currie Cup competition was extended to eight teams, with Western Transvaal (established in 1918) making their debut. The Orange Free State, North Eastern Districts, Rhodesia and South Western Districts had all played in one or more of the tournaments since 1894, but of those, only the Free State competed in 1922. By now matches were played on a home and away basis over the duration of the rugby season. Transvaal won in that year, but Western Province continued to dominate in the next six competitions from 1925 to 1936, with two titles shared with Border.

By 1939, the tournament had grown to 12 teams, split into Northern and Southern regions. The winners of each section faced each other in what was to be the very first Currie Cup final. Transvaal beat Western Province 17–6 to record their first-ever Currie Cup win at Newlands in Cape Town. The next Currie Cup final was to take place seven years later, in 1946, after the end of the Second World War. Western Province again qualified for the final but again they were beaten, this time by Northern Transvaal, in Pretoria. The score was 11–9.

Western Province won their first final in 1947 when they took revenge against Transvaal (16–12); Transvaal beat Northern Transvaal in Johannesburg in 1950 and then they also won against Boland in Wellington in 1952, courtesy of a Natie Rens drop goal.

Over the years various so-called Currie Cup golden eras stand out in a competition that is the oldest of its kind in the world. Five sides, in particular, can each lay

Western Transvaal joined the Currie Cup fray in 1920.

claim to such a golden era, namely Western Province, Northern Transvaal/Blue Bulls, Transvaal/Lions, Natal/The Sharks and Orange Free State/Free State Cheetahs.

Below is a summary of their golden years, which will be discussed in detail later in this story of the Golden Cup.

- Western Province, leaders on so many terrains of the Currie Cup competition discussed above, hold the record for the most successive wins. Their two golden eras came in the time when the competition was still held as a tournament (1892–1898) and after the introduction of finals (1982–1986). The latter is the only instance of the Currie Cup being won in five consecutive seasons. (Western Province also won six consecutive titles between 1925 and 1936, but two of those titles were shared with Border.) To achieve the five wins in five years, they beat Northern Transvaal three times and also accounted for Natal and Transvaal in the other two finals. Since then, by their proud standards, they have had lean time of it, sharing the Currie Cup once (in 1989 with Northern Transvaal) and winning it in the finals of 1997, 2000 and 2001.
- The first golden era of Northern Transvaal, who first played Currie Cup rugby in 1939 and have since dominated the competition, started in 1968 when Buurman van Zyl was appointed the Light Blues' first coach. Over the next 14 years Northern Transvaal played in 12 finals, won the title nine times and shared it on two occasions – every time

The 1959 *South African Rugby Annual*, edited by Ron Aldridge, carried this enlightening note:

A tournament was organised at Kimberley by the Western Province Rugby Union in 1889 with the following results:

	P	W	D	L	F	A	Pts
Western Province	3	2	0	1	13	9	4*
Griqualand West	3	2	0	11	1	11	4*
Eastern Province	3	1	0	2	7	9	2
Transvaal	3	1	0	2	12	14	2

* As Western Province beat Griqualand West in the match between the two teams they were considered winners of the tournament.

Stellenbosch Rugby Club, over the years probably South Africa's leading club, won the Grand Challenge competition for the first time in 1896.

with Van Zyl as their coach. Only in 1970, when Griquas beat Northern Transvaal 11–9 in Kimberley, did they fail to win a final under Van Zyl. Eastern Transvaal and Transvaal (1972) and the Free State and Western Province (1976) prevented Northern Transvaal appearing in 14 consecutive finals. The second golden era for the Blue Bulls, as they were by then officially known at Currie Cup level, followed a rather lean period in the 1990s. In the early 21st century, however, they played in seven of the eight finals from 2002 to 2009, missing out only in 2007 when the Free State beat the Lions in Bloemfontein. Of those seven finals, the Blue Bulls won four (2002–2004 and 2009), shared the title once (2006) and lost two finals against the Free State (2005) and Natal (2008). What really clinched this as a golden period in the history of the Bulls/ Northern Transvaal were the Super 14 titles they won in 2007 (the first by a South African side) and in 2009 when the Bulls and Blue Bulls franchises became the first side from the same union to hold both the Super Rugby and Currie Cup titles. In another lesser era of excellence, the Blue Bulls played in six of the seven Currie Cup finals from 1986 to 1991, winning three and drawing one.

- Transvaal, later the Gauteng and Golden Lions, have won the Currie Cup nine times. Their golden period was the years between 1991 and 1996 when the side of semi-professionals – a forerunner to the professional era that really started in 1996 – played in five finals in six years. Four of these finals (1991–1994) were consecutive and included two back-to-back wins against Natal in 1993 and the Free State in 1995. The 56–33 win in Bloemfontein is still a Currie Cup final record score. They also won the Lion Cup and the Super 10 title in 1993. In the five Currie Cup finals between 1939 and 1950, the Rooibontes as they were called because of their red and white colours, were represented four times and were the winners on three occasions. They also vied for the title in three of the four finals between 1971

ALMOST UNBEATABLE

Western Province won 101 of their first 110 Currie Cup matches. Until the end of 1932, they had lost only six and drawn three. The Cape side scored 2 088 points and conceded only 271 in those 110 matches. Transvaal, in their first 109 matches, won 73, lost 28 and drew 8.

and 1974, winning one, losing one and drawing one under the most peculiar circumstances (which is a story in itself).

- The Sharks struggled for 100 years before winning their first Currie Cup in 1990, their centenary year. It was the first of four titles in the 1990s, with the others coming in 1992, 1995 and 1996. They were also finalists in 1993 and 1999, when the Lions took the honours. However, Natal was undoubtedly the team of the 1990s. Previously they had been in two finals, namely those in 1956, when they lost in the last minutes to Northern Transvaal at the Kingsmead Cricket Ground, and in 1984, when they lost to Western Province at Newlands following the strangest semi-final win in the competition's history. Their golden years coincided with the era of Ian McIntosh as coach after they had struggled for five years to gain promotion to the elite competition from the so-called B Section of the Currie Cup. McIntosh later went on to become a Springbok coach and also a Springbok selector. Playing as the Sharks, the former Natal have contested two more finals since the 1990s, winning in 2008 when they beat the Blue Bulls, and losing in 2003 to the same side.

- Free State played in five finals in six years between 1973 and 1978. They won their first title against Western Province in 1976 by what was then a record score of 33–16. This followed the dramatic and heart-breaking try by Pierre Spies (Snr) the year before, which robbed Orange Free State of success when they were within seconds of sharing their first Currie Cup title. Since then they have done much better; in the six years between 2004 and 2009 Free State have been in five finals, winning two and sharing one. They have played Northern Transvaal/ Blue Bulls in nine finals.

The five unions above may have had their golden eras in regard to playing in and winning finals and titles, but other teams too, have sometimes performed well throughout the early years, the amateur days and the days of professionalism. Of them, only Border, with two shared titles in 1932 and 1934, and Griquas, with three titles, including a shock win over Northern Transvaal in Kimberley in 1970, have tasted success. The others, however, have in no small way contributed to the glory and mystique of the Currie Cup and to the many tales and legends that follow.

THEY LOOKED UNBEATABLE ...

The Western Province team of 1932 would have been favoured to beat most international sides. Among the players who turned out for the Cape team that year were Bennie Osler, Gerry Brand, Danie Craven, Pierre de Villiers, Boy and Fanie Louw, JC and Ponie van der Westhuizen, George van Reenen, André McDonald, Alfie van der Merwe, SP van Wyk, Frank Waring, DO Williams and Morris Zimerman.

They shared the Currie Cup with Border that year. and in 1934.

In 1932, when the teams competed on a league basis, Border beat WP 8-3. They played 7, won 6, lost 1 (12 log points) and scored 81 points against 37. WP played 7, won 6, lost one, scored 159 points and conceded 26.

WP RUGBY
NORWICH
BANKFIN
SA PO
E HERE

CHAPTER 2

Changing the Format

Over the years the format of the Currie Cup competition has often been a surprise packet for competitors and supporters alike, and on a number of occasions the self-interest of rugby unions determined the system that was used.

The format changed from a simple league system with five sides competing, through various phases of unbelievably complicated and amateurish systems to the present format that has been in use since 2003 (with a small refinement brought about in 2004).

Initially, transport constraints were a major factor in the decision to centralise competitions where the Currie Cup winners were decided after a round-robin format over a period of a week to ten days, with the trophy awarded to the log leaders. Only five teams participated in the inaugural Currie Cup tournament in 1892, which was won by Western Province, with Griquas second.

This structure remained in place until 1920, with a varying number of teams participating. In 1899, with the South African War looming large, only four sides competed.

The venues used in the tournaments before 1920 also changed regularly.

In 1904 seven sides, including Border, competed, and in the next tournament, that of 1906, Rhodesia also took part. North Easterns joined in 1908, and by 1911 there were ten teams when South Westerns were present.

In 1920, the tournament took place at two venues, Bloemfontein and Kimberley, but as the winner was determined over the same period of time as before, it turned into a logistical nightmare.

In those early years the competition was not played annually. International tours took preference, and there were disruptions during wartime. In the 1950s

Danie Gerber, brilliant Springbok centre whose international career spanned 13 years from 1980–1992, in action for Western Province.

there was a five-year break because of unhappiness with the system.

The centralised league competition was relinquished as a format in 1922. From then on eight teams entered, and each union's seven matches were played on a home and away basis over the duration of the rugby season. Transvaal, who had four away matches and three at home, won in 1922.

Then Western Province, who had dominated by winning ten of the first 13 Currie Cup competitions, again exerted their dominance and won four of the next six tournaments. They notched up four outright wins (1925, 1927, 1929 and 1936), and shared the trophy twice with Border (in 1934 and 1936).

By 1939 the tournament had grown to 12 teams, split into north and south regions. The winners of the sections played one another in the very first Currie Cup final. Transvaal beat Western Province 17–6.

Because of the Second World War, the next Currie Cup final only took place seven years later, in 1946. Again Western Province qualified for the final, but again they were beaten, this time by Northern Transvaal at Loftus (11–9).

However, it was third time lucky and Western Province won their first final when they beat Transvaal 16–12 at Newlands in 1947. Transvaal clinched their third title when they beat Western Province in 1950 and then beat Boland in Wellington in 1952.

In 1954, the Currie Cup structure was changed again. Fifteen teams were divided into three sections, and semi-finals were played for the first time. Northern Transvaal and the Free State met in what was called a semi-final, with the former winning the match. They were then pitted against Western Province, who won the Currie Cup with an 11–8 win at Newlands.

Northern Transvaal were victorious in 1956 after they beat Natal 9–8 at Kingsmead Cricket Ground, the side's first final appearance. Natal had had to take the long route in the so-called semi-final for the honour to meet Northern Transvaal; the Light Blues were given the right to advance to the final without a play-off.

In one of the two most ridiculous competition formats used in the Currie Cup competition, the 1957 Currie Cup was played on a league basis over two seasons – 1957 and 1959. There were no Currie Cup matches in 1958 because of the first visit to South Africa by a French side. By the end of 1959, Western Province had gathered one more league point than Northern Transvaal, and the trophy returned to Newlands. No final was played.

Unhappiness over this system led to the Currie Cup being cancelled for five years, until 1964.

Then, in an attempt to give every side affiliated to the South African Rugby Board a chance to win the Currie Cup, the competition was divided into five sections of three teams each. The five section winners went through to a further league competition. Western Province finished top of the standings and were crowned winners. They repeated this success in 1966, when the same system was used.

A French tour once again halted Currie Cup proceedings, and no competition was played in 1967. In 1968, the number of teams in the competition increased to 16 and they were divided into two pools. Northern Transvaal won their third title after beating Transvaal in the final.

Since 1968 the Currie Cup has been contested every year, with the winner always determined after a final. In four instances, however, the finals were drawn and the trophy shared: in 1971 between Transvaal and Northern Transvaal at Ellis Park (14–all); in 1979 (15–all) and 1989 (16–all) in two Newlands finals between Western Province and Northern Transvaal; and in 2006 when the Free State Cheetahs and the Blue Bulls drew 28–all in Bloemfontein.

In consequence of this final it was decided that the Currie Cup would not be shared again and that a winner had to be determined if sides were still tied after extra time.

Since 1968 a number of formats have been used to determine the finalists.

In the 1970s, the top 15 (and later 16) sides played for the Currie Cup, while the Paul Roos competition was introduced for the other unions and the Natal Country and Transvaal sub-unions. The Currie Cup sides were divided into sections, and on occasion even one big league.

In the early 1980s, in an effort to keep the sides of the B Section interested in the competition to its very end, the two top sides in the B Section played the two

THAT'S WHAT FRIENDS ARE FOR ...

There were the days when the grass on the Highveld was hard and yellow in the middle of winter – when even the ground on the King's Park Stadium field was hard, and the grass was not as green, throughout the year, as it is now.

Those were also the days when all the unions in South Africa played in the Currie Cup competition and when the glamour sides with their Springboks had to get on a bus and travel to faraway places like Burgersdorp.

Eben Olivier, mercurial Springbok centre of the Maties, Western Province and Eastern Province tells the story:

'We mostly travelled by bus, sometimes by train, and only the long trips were by plane.

'I clearly remember our trip to Burgersdorp in 1971, where we had to play a Currie Cup fixture against North Eastern Cape. 'The spectators came from the whole region and packed out the field, sitting right onto the touchline. There wasn't a blade of green grass and the little grass there was on the field was yellow. The field was bone-hard – and on those hard fields you would find the home side pumping the balls extra hard so that they would bounce higher than usual. As Northern Transvaal captain Thys Lourens said about that tactic: "The ball bounces either way!"

'If anyone of the visitors didn't have the guts to take the home side's frequent up-and-unders, they were literally caught on the rebound when they gathered the high bouncing ball coming down!

'Hannes Marais captained North-Eastern Cape that day in Burgersdorp. We were team mates for the Maties, Western Province and the Springboks; we toured together many times. In fact, we were good friends and still are,' Olivier says with a laugh, 'although I don't know why! In that match Hannes' instructions to his centres were simple: "Flatten them, with or without the ball!". And that is exactly what Droes van Vuuren who opposed me that day did!'

'I won't forget that day as long as I live! And we had to play Northern Transvaal in the Currie Cup final the next week!' Olivier says those bone crunching tackles were always the highlights for local crowds who knew their teams had no chance of winning. 'The referees were also not always of the best, so it was really tough.'

But afterwards, the opposing sides would mix, laugh about these incidents and become good friends.

top sides in the A Section in semi-finals. This is why Natal played in the 1984 final against Western Province at Newlands, after beating Free State, the A Section's second-placed side, in such a semi-final.

In the 1980s it was decided to give the log leaders a direct route into the final without a play-off, while the second and third-placed sides had to fight it out in a 'semi-final' for the right to play the log leaders in the final.

There was also the format whereby four sections of three teams each played one another, with two semi-finals following. In 2002, the top two from each section played in a new eight-team league, and the top four sides of that league played in the semi-finals.

The top six sides were also put into a single section in a particular year, with the top two teams then meeting in the final.

Nothing was certain from year to year, as the unions' self-serving interests dominated decisions on the format to be followed in a particular year.

Eventually, however, some measure of consistency was achieved, and since 2003 the Currie Cup has reverted to a strength-versus-strength system, with a Premier Division of eight teams and a First Division of six teams. A double round of matches has since been played, with play-offs then determining the winner.

But even after 2003 there was a change. Whereas in 2003 only the two top sides played in the final, the top four of each section have since contested semi-final play-offs – probably because this meant more money in the coffers.

The elite strength-versus-strength competition proved a huge success and was confirmed for five years. It is to be hoped that this will be re-endorsed, with the B Section sides annually having the chance to qualify for the following year's A Section through promotion-relegation play-offs.

Points Systems Through the Years

When the first British team, led by Bill Maclagan, visited South Africa in 1891, a try was worth a single point and a goal worth three points. Up to 1889, the only way to win a match was to score more goals (i.e. converted tries) than the opposition, as an unconverted try counted for nothing when the result of a match was determined: it was merely the route to a goal.

A drop goal netted a team three points, while a penalty counted two points and a goal after a mark counted three points.

By 1894, when the second Currie Cup competition was held, the try had increased in value to three points, a conversion was still worth two points, and a drop kick would have had players like Morné Steyn and Naas Botha smiling broadly, as it then counted four points. A penalty counted three points.

This scoring system remained in place for the Currie Cup competitions until 1939 – the last one before the outbreak of the Second World War.

In 1946, when Currie Cup rugby was resumed, the drop goal had been devalued to three points.

No other change to the scoring system took place for the next 26 years. Then, in 1972, in an attempt to encourage more tries, its value was increased from three points to four. Scores soared as a result: when Diggers, in a 1971 pre-season friendly, beat Newcastle at Arbor Park in Northern Natal, the star-laden visitors scored seven tries, and won 42–12. A year before, it would have been a much more respectable score of 35–11.

The next change came in 1992, when the try became five points (and the above score of 35–11 would have been 49–13).

Changing the Laws

The laws, of course, have changed over the years; in fact, they are still evolving. Over time, this has had a big effect on style of play, game plans and the physical attributes required from players in particular positions.

The 'job descriptions' and responsibilities for particular playing positions changed with the laws. It was something entirely new when Western Province's HO de Villiers changed the game by regularly running from the fullback position in the late 1960s. At national level, Gysie Pienaar further refined this new fullback art. Now fullbacks are routinely selected as much for their skills under the high ball as for their speed, and kicking for the line is only one among many skills in a fullback's armoury.

As the entertainment value of the game became increasingly important, the laws were continually adapted to make for more open play and bigger scores. Whereas it was quite common for combined scores in a match in the 1960s and 1970s to total 10 or 15 points per match, scorelines of 38–33 are now the order of the day.

Professionalism

Many books have been written about the advent of professionalism in rugby. Officially (or openly) this came about only in 1996, but individuals had flaunted the rules long before then. Louis Luyt used incentives quite openly to strengthen the Transvaal sides of the late 1980s, and this played no small part in their golden era in the 1990s.

In fact, payment for play was nothing really new.

The effect of professionalism on Currie Cup rugby, in particular, has been huge. The Super Rugby series and Tri-Nations rugby were (rightly) regarded as more important than the Currie Cup, which is therefore now contested in the absence of the best players in the various provinces.

The top players are often involved with Tri-Nations tests and at times rested at the request of SARU before the end-of-the-year tours to the UK and Europe.

To a very large extent, the absence of Springbok players made for a more exciting Currie Cup competition as provinces like Griquas, in particular, were more competitive.

In addition, it also gave the major provinces the opportunity to blood their young players and stars of the future.

In 2006, with 24 contracted players from both teams withdrawn from the competition to rest them for the 2007 World Cup, there was the wonderful 28-all drawn final between the Free State Cheetahs and the Blue Bulls in Bloemfontein. At the time Andy Colquhoun, SARU's communications manager, wrote that the Currie Cup competition 'comfortably survived' the absence of the big stars.

Professionalism, however, has had its negative effects as well. Court cases about contracts, money ruling over loyalty, the acquisition of players by affluent unions instead of building an own reserve strength, and top players succumbing to the lure of the pound and euro are just a few of them.

According to leading sports scientist Professor Tim Noakes, there are too many matches at provincial and national level, resulting in a high injury toll that is a direct result of too much rugby and not enough rest. Furthermore, caps are dished out quite liberally – another drawback of so much money being poured into the game. Add to that the virtual demise of club rugby, and the picture is far from rosy.

One of the more serious legacies of professionalism in South Africa is that many of the players who either don't make the grade at professional level, or those finishing after years in the game at the highest level, are not trained for any other profession.

This is a major problem, says Piet Heymans of the South African Rugby Players Association (SARPA). He points to the position of players in Australia and, to a lesser extent, in New Zealand in this regard, who are being put through academic courses to prepare them for the future. Although this is happening in South Africa to some extent, very few of the top players have any academic qualifications, or have been prepared for life after rugby.

Heymans, who was appointed as CEO of SARPA when it was founded in 1998, captained the South African under-20s in 1987, with François Pienaar and Joel Stransky in the side.

Legal contracts between unions and players remain a source of great concern and exasperation for SARPA, and Heymans makes no bones about the fact that some of the unions are, after 13 years of professionalism, still struggling to come to the realisation that the amateur days are gone.

Strength and Apparatus

In the old days, rugby players did not go to gym. When gyms began to flourish in the late 1960s and 1970s, coaches were reluctant to use them, or to instruct their players to train in them. To a large degree, it wasn't necessary. The bulk of the Springboks were from the country districts. Many of them came from farms, and they had a natural strength.

Springbok captain Wynand Claassen tells this delightful story of the huge Springbok lock Louis Moolman in the 1970s:

> 'Oom Buurman (van Zyl) told us that those who wanted to, could attend a gym. John Borland was known to us and Louis pitched up at his gym in Hatfield.
>
> 'Most of the guys there were weightlifters, and big Louis, not having a clue what it was all about, simply walked in, picked up one of the bigger stacks of weights and lifted it above his head without any ado or preparation!
>
> 'There was a quiet air of disbelief.
>
> 'But then, Louis was a strong fellow and a builder to boot, and obviously didn't need the artificial strengthening.'

Until the 1970s there were no floodlights for training. The players – at club and provincial level – honed their skills with the ball for an hour or so and then did a little running in the late dusk or dark. Most provincial teams only gathered once a week to prepare for their fixtures on the weekend.

Doc Craven, always thinking and planning for the game he loved so much, designed his own 'practical gym' in the 1960s. Benches, tree trunks, big stones from the Eerste River next to the Coetzenburg sports field in Stellenbosch, and apparatus built for strength and stamina as well as to improve jumping, throwing into lineouts and handling skills, were used. The proof of that particular pudding was the way in which the Maties dominated club rugby for years (as they still do at university level).

Doc Craven's 'practical gym' at Stellenbosch, where stones from Eerste River and homemade equipement were used to enhance strength and skills.

Training

Deon Oosthuysen, the Springbok wing and sevens player, and later also the Springbok sevens coach, tells of how players and coaches of his era – not even 20 years ago – did not have enough time to train properly to meet the requirements of matches that were becoming increasingly demanding.

'We had to do a lot of training and preparation ourselves; work on our weaknesses; sharpen our speed; our defensive play; lineout throws; moves.'

The man who played 140 matches for Northern Transvaal tells of an ambitious player at the Department of Correctional Services who, in an effort to improve his tackling, defied all the regulations and used prisoners to assist in sharpening up his defence!

Captaincy

Until the advent of professional rugby, the captain had to make the decisions on the field and at half-time. No coaches were allowed on the field during the three-minute half-time break, and any changes to the game plan or tactics were up to the man on the field.

Wynand Claassen, legendary captain of Natal and a fine leader of the Springboks, says that in his day a captain was sent onto the field with a guideline. 'Thereafter he had to adapt as the game unfolded,' he says.

But, he added, he always consulted with senior players in his side on how they felt about the way the game was going. 'I valued the input of guys like [later Springbok captain] Divan Serfontein and, with Natal, of a player like Mark Loane, who was a former Wallaby captain.'

In the modern game, messages are sent onto the field with doctors and physios who tend to injuries, and the coach has ten minutes during half-time to transmit any change in game plan to the team as a whole.

Travel

Altitude has always been a problem for sides visiting the Highveld. Among the various theories of how to beat the effects of overcoming this disadvantage, is flying up from the coast on the morning of the match.

But it wasn't always that way.

Elsewhere in this book, former Springbok flank and Transvaal captain Piet Malan tells of how it took Transvaal's players away from work for a full week to play Western Province in Cape Town.

That was as recently as the early 1950s. They travelled by train.

In the early days of provincial tournaments, before the first Currie Cup competition in 1892, and for years thereafter, it would take days for a team to travel to the venue.

There is the instance of Kimberley, on their first visit to Cape Town in 1884, who travelled for three days on a mule-wagon to reach De Aar, from where they caught the train to Cape Town – a five-day trip in all!

Bill Maclagan's British team played 20 matches on their tour of a little over two months, and just how taxing it was cannot be imagined, with large portions of their travel by horse-drawn cart and the rest by train. As the young Scottish student Peter Clauss remarked when they arrived back in Britain: 'It was all travel and champagne!'

One can only imagine the shock for the Brits, coming from the soft yielding fields of Scotland and England, when they first experienced the hard ground of Kimberley and those on the Highveld. The huge distances must have been an eye-opener for them as well.

The British tourists of 1891 had five days between matches, when they had to move from one district to the other, and with most of that time spent on a train or horse-drawn cart, the matches on the hard grounds probably came as a welcome relief!

After their match against Grahamstown, for example, they travelled by boat from Port Elizabeth, to take on the Natal side in Pietermaritzburg. There they found themselves amid a shambles of note, as other teams had also converged on the Natal capital over the same weekend, resulting in a series of fixture clashes. In fact, the curtain-raisers to the main match between the tourists and Natal were used to decide which players would represent Natal against the British side!

Former Springbok and also international Sevens player and coach Deon Oosthuysen tells the story of how prison inmates were used to sharpen up a team mate's defence.

Other Factors

There are so many other factors that changed the thinking about and attitude towards the game over the years: the system for appointing referees; increased fitness levels; the replacement principle that has changed selection policies; the impact of the coach on the game; the clothing that makes it more comfortable and safer; lifestyle and many, many more.

However, the frenzy and fervour before a big match, support for the union the supporters have sworn allegiance to, and the ideal to win that Currie Cup, will remain as strong as in the very early years, throughout the period of 118 years since 1892 (during which time the temporary resting place of the Currie Cup has been decided 71 times), and for long after the 2009 season has run its course.

CHAPTER 3

The Winning of the Currie Cup

When Peet Smith kicked that penalty of 53 metres in Kimberley in 1970 to win the Currie Cup final for the Griquas against Northern Transvaal, it made him an instant hero. Of course it was the result of a team effort that provided one of the biggest shocks in Currie Cup finals and became part of South African rugby's folklore.

There were many other such instances – some that led to victory and celebrations in finals, others in the lesser league games and for lesser sides, for whom a win was just as important.

Some of the outstanding feats didn't even lead to victory, but were memorable in their own right, or were overshadowed by the outstanding examples discussed below.

There was, for example, the great try by Western Province wing Carel du Plessis, set up by his brother Michael, in the Currie Cup final against Northern Transvaal in 1989; Naas Botha's drop goal in 1979 that squared the game against Western Province at 16–all, also at Newlands; or the brace of tries by Des Mclean in the semi-final for Natal against Free State in 1984, courtesy of which they progressed to the final from the B Section.

And what about Natie Rens' drop goal in 1952 that denied Boland in their only final, and gave Transvaal their second successive Currie Cup? There was also Uli Schmidt's try for Transvaal against Natal in 1993 that saw them win 21–15 at Kings Park.

Some of the scores were decisive, some controversial and some decisive and controversial, such as the winning try by Northern Transvaal against Natal in 1956, when Schalk van Dyk scored right at the end to win the match for the Light Blues 9–8.

The great Frik du Preez on the run with another Northern Transvaal captain Piet Uys up in support.

Frik het Gedrop, Geplace en Gescore!

When older people talk about the Currie Cup and the players of their time, nine unforgettable minutes in 1969, when Loftus Versfeld's favourite son almost single-handedly won the Currie Cup for Northern Transvaal, will more often than not be part of the discussion.

They will talk about Frik du Preez. There is so much he left from his playing days at the top: his deeds on the field of play; some of his funny sayings on the field and off; and many little anecdotes of the man known in Pretoria and far beyond as Ou Frik.

Perhaps, in the context of the game's development and the changing laws, he was not really the best South Africa has had, but he surely is right up there with the top players, and the choice of Frik du Preez as South Africa's Player of the Millennium was accepted by almost every South African fan (although not a single living person had seen the other contenders like Japie Krige, Fairie Heatlie and the like).

Honours were bestowed on him like on few other South African players. One, it is said, was even for 'wasting' a try that should have been! That was against Western Transvaal, when Frik du Preez burst through, storming to the tryline in inimical fashion with the heavy leather ball clasped in one huge hand.

As Frik turned towards the posts, Albie Bates, who was later to captain Northern Transvaal but was playing for Western Transvaal at the time, was hot on Big Frik's heels. He had clearly not given up the chase. Then, as the Northern Transvaal and South African icon prepared to plant the ball, Bates coolly grabbed it from his hands and dotted down. The ball was dead!

At the end of the season, Frik was honoured by Western Transvaal by presenting him with an honours tie for his 'contribution to Western Transvaal rugby.'

The measure of the man's magic is explained in the way in which the Newlands crowd gave him a standing ovation after his last match at South Africa's Home of Rugby, and carried him off the field in the days when spectators could still run onto the field.

Perhaps the big man – not as tall as locks even in his days used to be – who could outjump any forward in the world, and did so on numerous occasions, could have done a little more work in the tight loose. Perhaps he could have been a little fitter.

But Better? Hardly!

Of his many great deeds, the outstanding one was undoubtedly in the Currie Cup final against Western Province on 4 October 1969.

The great Frik had been dropped from the Springbok side for the last two tests against Greg Davies' Wallabies. The man replacing him was André de Wet, a young Matie lock also renowned for his lineout work in the days when barging was not allowed but happened, and lifting was penalised.

There was an outcry in Pretoria when Frik du Preez was dropped, and the general refrain from the fans was: wait until Frik gets his hands on De Wet! De Wet, they said, would be shown a thing or two.

Not that Frik du Preez was a dirty player. He had too much class on his side to turn to underhand tactics. Far from it. But he did admit afterwards that it probably was a good thing that De Wet had to withdraw from that final. 'I don't know what I would've done,' Du Preez said. De Wet was replaced by another Matie, Teddy Hoffman.

At two tries apiece, with both Province's tries coming from Springbok wing Gert Muller, and André van Staden and Piet Brand scoring for Northern Transvaal, the home side was 16–13 ahead at half-time.

And so it stayed for the next ten minutes.

Enter Frik du Preez. Captain Piet Uys threw him the ball. The penalty was more than 60 metres out after a Western Province scrum transgression; Frik had to try and stretch the slender lead.

He did so, with a drop kick that went true and straight, and easily soared over the cross bar.

Amidst the wild scenes on the stands that followed, the national selectors had to reflect on their folly in dropping the great man from the last two tests as they were heckled by the supporters.

But Frik wasn't finished. For his next act, shortly after the restart, he had an ally. His great – and enormous! – friend Mof Myburgh was that man.

Myburgh broke through a lineout. Not normally known for his handling skills, he off-loaded the perfect pass as Du Preez came storming through on his shoulder. On his run of more than 30 metres, Du Preez left two defenders in his wake because they couldn't keep up. Another, HO de Villiers, was simply ignored as Du Preez ran over him to score.

The game had been won. But Big Frik still had one more arrow to fire at the selectors.

Northern Transvaal were given a penalty inside their own half, and with the crowd demanding it, captain Uys again passed the ball to Du Preez.

It seemed impossible, but this time he took his time as he meticulously placed the ball. Straight and true it went.

Frik du Preez had won the Currie Cup for Northern Transvaal in those nine golden minutes when, as Mof Myburgh summed it up afterwards: 'Ou Frik het gedrop, geplace en gescore!'

The final score was 28–13 to Northern Transvaal, and Western Province had again been denied in a final.

As they did for Mannetjies Roux the following year, the crowd chanted to see their big hero, and in a province where the wins and losses are those of the team as a whole, the Northern Transvaal president Fritz Eloff, this time, made an exception. Frik was loudly cheered as he appeared on the balcony to wave to the hundreds of spectators still on the field.

Two years later, when he scored three tries and kicked a penalty drop at Newlands to help his side to a 21–9 over Western Province at Newlands, Frik du Preez was cheered for minutes afterwards, carried off the field, and had the whole of the Newlands main stand on their feet to greet the big man for a last time.

A Break for Engelbrecht

The north-south feeling of respect that sometimes manifests as near-hatred is virtually unique in world rugby. Perhaps the North and South islands of New Zealand have – or had – the same measure of competitiveness.

Anyhow, down in the Cape, they regard the rugby Northern Transvaal played in the 1970s as conservative and unintelligent. Up north, however – and that's not only in Pretoria! – the Western Province approach was jeered at. Touch rugby, they said; rugby only played against the Baa-baas, where running is everything and the basics are neglected.

The above views are, to a large extent, still relevant today.

Reciprocal respect for one another there certainly was, but in Northern Transvaal in particular, it remained difficult to understand why Western Province would, more often than not, provide the Springboks even when Northerns were winning the Currie Cup!

And so it was in 1964. Jannie Engelbrecht, in particular, was seen as overrated and too 'soft' because of his many injuries. His hands were poor, he couldn't tackle, they said. Northern Transvaal's Johan Fechter and Corra Dirksen, who was first capped against Australia in 1963, were better.

From a Currie Cup point of view, the year 1964 brought a resumption of the Currie Cup competition. The previous Currie Cup had been won by Western Province and led to a fair amount of unhappiness among the unions. It was played over two seasons, 1957 and 1959, with no fixtures in 1958 because France toured South Africa that year.

The unhappiness brought about a near-boycott of the competition, which was only resumed during the next French visit in 1964. The Currie Cup would once again be decided on a league basis and without a final, which suited Western Province to a tee.

After all, they had won 14 and shared two of the 19 Currie Cup league competitions before the first final was played in 1939. Their success rate then plummeted to one title from five attempts, including three losses from the four finals contested.

Northern Transvaal had trounced Western Province 29–5 in the friendly at Loftus Versfeld earlier in 1964. In those days, when the Currie Cup or the play-off teams were often decided over a single round and in some cases only three or four league matches, friendlies were as close to the real thing as could be found, not like today – mere warm-ups for the Super Rugby competitions, and no record of the score or scorers is kept.

Northerns scored seven tries in the friendly, to the one

CUP FINALS AT UNUSUAL VENUES

Only three Currie Cup finals have been played at venues outside Cape Town, Pretoria, Johannesburg, Bloemfontein and Durban. The picturesque Boland Park Stadium in Wellington, the De Beers Stadium in Kimberley, and the PAM Brink Stadium in Springs are the exceptions.

Transvaal featured in two of those finals, beating Boland 11–9 in 1952 and Eastern Transvaal in 1972. The home team triumphed, however, when Northern Transvaal defended the Currie Cup in Kimberley in 1970; Griqualand West won 11–9 that day.

Seventeen of the 49 Currie Cup finals, up to the end of 2009, have been played at Loftus Versfeld in Pretoria; 11 at Newlands in Cape Town; six at Ellis Park (now Coca-Cola Park) in Johannesburg; six in Bloemfontein (five at Free State Stadium/Vodacom Park, and one at Springbok Park); six in Durban (five at Kings Park and one at the Kingsmead Cricket Ground in 1956); and three elsewhere.

The first Currie Cup final was played in 1939 at Newlands, when Transvaal beat Western Province. That was the last time Western Province lost a final at Newlands. Province have won eight of the Newlands finals, two have been drawn, and then there was the defeat in 1939 against Transvaal.

The Blue Bulls (and Northern Transvaal) have won 14 of the 17 finals at Loftus Versfeld.

Natal have won the Currie Cup final five times, but only one of those victories has been at home – against Western Province in 1995. They have lost four home finals.

Of the 49 finals the home team has won 28, the away team 17 and four have been drawn.

The venue for the final used to be determined by seniority, or by where the final was last played between the two teams involved. Now the team that finishes higher on the log gets the final.

In the four draws to date (1971, 1979, 1989 and 2006), the trophy was shared. That has now changed, and extra time of ten minutes each way is played in the event of a draw. If the teams are still drawn at the end of extra time, the Currie Cup will be awarded to the team that ended highest on the log.

by Province. The Light Blues provided only three members for the Springbok side that lost 8–6 to France in Springs, and Western Province seven.

It was against this background that Western Province arrived in Pretoria for the Currie Cup encounter.

Ernst du Plessis was selected as the Northern Transvaal left wing. He had arrived from Free State that season and showed tremendous form in club matches for Oostelikes, setting a series of new Carlton Cup records.

He was a surprise inclusion in place of Corra Dirksen, who was dropped by Northerns after playing in the test against France the previous week.

Du Plessis was therefore the man to mark Jannie Engelbrecht.

Early in the match Northern Transvaal captain Louis Schmidt got hold of Engelbrecht. He took him by the collar and literally threw him into touch. It was a legal tackle, but certainly not pleasant!

In fact, it was so unpleasant that when Engelbrecht got up, he found that his collar bone was broken. It was another injury for the man they called soft and injury-prone. There was only one thing to do: he had to leave the field.

But Province captain, the great no 8 Doug Hopwood, would have none of that.

'You stay on!' he instructed. 'We need you!'

They did, indeed. There were no replacements in those days, and Engelbrecht's departure would have necessitated moving a forward out to the back to cover the man-over in the backline.

The two sides went into the break with Northern Transvaal 6–3 to the good.

There are few things as painful as a broken collar bone. The pain must have been excruciating, and Engelbrecht, during the break, once again indicated to his captain that he was crying off.

'No, you're staying,' instructed Hopwood, and added that the tall winger was not to show his pain to the opposition, lest they exploit his injury on that side of the field.

Just three minutes after the break the unsympathetic Hopwood was vindicated. Gertjie Brynard joined the backline on the blind side, broke through and sent Engelbrecht on his run.

Broken collar bone and all, Engelbrecht rounded fullback Martin Grundlingh and dotted down near the posts. With the conversion good, Province led 8–6.

Northern Transvaal won the battle up front hands down. However, for those in the south who said they cannot play thinking rugby, this match was fuel on their fire. Northerns kicked the ball away, took wrong options on the break when they had overlaps, and in general simply squandered opportunities. Yet they remained in command on the field, and eventually André van Tonder put the home side ahead.

Northern Transvaal were on their way to another Currie Cup title, it seemed, although this was only a league match.

Northerns drove the visitors back to their own quarter. From the scrum, Western Province's Springbok scrum-half Dirkie de Vos, who later played many matches for Northern Transvaal, broke around the right side of the scrum. Northern Transvaal's Louis Schmidt was in his way, but De Vos popped the ball into the injured Engelbrecht's hands, and from 60 metres out the Springbok wing pinned his ears back …

Ernst du Plessis gave chase. Engelbrecht and Du Plessis were amongst the fastest wings imaginable, and it was a wonderful race. However, the winger from Koekenaap in the Cape won the race, and he scored with the knowledge that the match was won, and the Currie Cup probably retained.

The best team had lost, and Engelbrecht had proved to every doubting Thomas in Pretoria that he was good enough for the green and gold.

Schmidt, father of Uli, who later played for South Africa as a hooker, was dropped after that match. Perhaps it was because of perceived deficiencies in his captaincy, or perhaps because he didn't get hold of De Vos in time to prevent the pass to Engelbrecht.

Whatever the reason, he decided to call it a day at the young age of 27, thereby forfeiting many more tests that could and should have come his way, apart from the two he had earned against the 1958 French side and the British Lions of 1962.

The Currie Cup isn't Won in May …

Naas Botha was undoubtedly the greatest match-winner in the history of South African, and possibly, world rugby.

That is not a statement: it is fact, as far as South African rugby goes, anyway. Statistics bear it out, but at the same time, they cannot tell the whole story of his ability to influence the course of a game tactically and territorially.

At international level, he proved himself to be the greatest drop kicker in history, with 18 drop goals in 28 tests and another 12 in 40 matches in the Bok jersey.

His three most memorable performances were in wet playing conditions. That is not to say that he was a kicking flyhalf only. This is borne out by testimonies from two of the greatest rugby writers from the Cape, from where most of the criticism was levelled at the blonde flyhalf, namely Chris Greyvenstein and AC Parker in the booklet *Naas Botha: Rugby's Golden Boy* (Don Nelson), which was first published in 1989.

Dr Danie Craven described him as a rugby genius, and in the wake of what was probably his greatest performance, in the 1987 Currie Cup final at Ellis Park, Craven made the statement that Hendrik Egnatius Botha was the greatest rugby player, in any position, that South Africa has produced.

One of his greatest matches was arguably in 1981, in the third test against the All Blacks in New Zealand. On that tour he showed how adept he was at the running game too, something he had been given little credit for in South Africa. The statistics show that in Botha's tenure as flyhalf, South Africa had the highest try strike rate by backs in the country's test history (although changing laws make this a rather unreliable way of comparing players).

It was nevertheless a fact that the greatest performances that Naas will be remembered for was as a kicker.

In 1985, at Newlands, where they loved to hate him, he single-handedly demolished Western Province in a Lion Cup semi-final. The way in which he 'attracted' the ball was uncanny. On a day when running was impossible, Botha was there to field the slippery ball wherever Province kicked it, in muddy conditions as bad as it could be at Newlands.

It was a display of absolute genius, and showed Botha's feel for the game and his kicking skills as had never been seen before.

Two of his greatest kicks came in tests in 1980 and 1985.

In the third test against the 1980 British Lions, Botha first set up a corner try with a lovely diagonal kick. The conversion to win or lose the test and the series, in the wet conditions and with a typical Eastern Cape wind, was over. And he repeated the dose in the first test against the Cavaliers in 1986.

Then, two drop kicks and the corner kick for Carel du Plessis to dot down near touch made this a superlative performance in his first test as Springbok captain. It was even greater when he slotted the conversion in the most treacherous conditions imaginable.

But those were only a promise of what he was really capable of.

His best match was the Currie Cup final in 1987 at Ellis Park. Botha says so himself. That was the day when he silenced most of his few remaining critics.

It was also the year in which Transvaal, with the first batch of 'imports' for a super team that their president Louis Luyt was putting together, were rampant in the early rounds of the Currie Cup. They had played in the 1986 final but lost to Western Province, but now had an even stronger team and were on a roll.

The Johannesburg (and other) critics, as early as May, started punting the Rooibontes from Johannesburg as Currie Cup champions. Botha, not known for outstanding diplomacy, as was also evident after Natal's shock final win at Loftus in 1990, cautioned with the now-famous statement in 1987: 'The Currie Cup isn't won in May.'

He could well have added 'or in the first half of a final'.

Botha dominated the second half of the 1987 Currie Cup competition with outstanding displays, and the now prophetic words must have started casting doubt into the minds of the Transvaal players and coaching staff as Northern Transvaal climbed out of Currie Cup obscurity to reach the final.

On a day, and in a match, that started in sunshine, the rain and hail and, at times, a tricky wind which soon appeared, made playing conditions less than ideal. Transvaal were soon ahead in that final, and dominated to the extent that they were nine points ahead at the break.

By then the rain was pelting down, and the hail hit spectators and players alike, driven on by the wind.

The half-time talk for Botha was an easy one. 'Give me the ball,' he told his players.

They did. And with Adolf Malan's magnificent play in the lineouts leading the way by turning even Transvaal's lineout throw-ins into Northern Transvaal possession, the platform was set for Botha. He kicked for territory, he kicked for pressure, and Transvaal started making more and more mistakes as they wilted under the onslaught. And he dropped.

The match will ultimately be remembered for Naas' four drop goals – a Currie Cup final record – and four penalties, as he scored all his team's 24 points in their 24–12 win. There will also be the vision of Wahl Bartmann's despairing face as he charged down on Botha in the second half, with the flyhalf coolly jinxing to the inside to slot another one; and the equally despairing cry from a Transvaal supporter on the main stand's northern ramp long after the match: 'Naas Botha is a *&%**&' and the echoing response from elsewhere: 'Nee, Naas is koning!'

Naas rates this as his best performance. After all, it was for the Currie Cup that had eluded Northern Transvaal since 1981.

How great Botha was on that day was summed up later by Freek Burger. The experienced test referee was in

CHRIS BURGER AND OTHERS

The first player to be killed in a Currie Cup match was Western Province fullback Chris Burger in 1980. His death in the Universitas Hospital was the result of a fatal neck injury sustained in a ruck in the Currie Cup match against Free State.

Ironically he had told the administrative head of the Western Province Rugby Union, Joey Enslin, in the week before the match that he would retire at the end of that season. Furthermore, 90 minutes before the incident that cost him his life, he was part of a guard of honour for Rampie Stander, the Free State and Springbok prop who had collapsed from a stroke on Thursday while preparing for the match that claimed Burger's life.

Burger's death prompted Morné du Plessis, the Western Province captain in that match, and his team mates to found the Chris Burger Fund.

In 1989, Petro Jackson, a young player from Kylemore in Stellenbosch, was killed during a rugby match, prompting SARU to found the Petro Jackson Fund.

Unity in 1992 resulted in the two funds amalgamating to become The Chris Burger/Petro Jackson Players' Fund. The aims and objectives of the fund are to raise money for the benefit of past, present and future rugby players at all levels, irrespective of colour or creed, who may be the victims of misfortune.

In 1987 the fund purchased the leasehold rights to a specially designed suite in the Danie Craven Pavilion at Newlands Rugby Stadium exclusively for the use of disabled rugby players.

The fund runs the Power of Prevention programme through which it has established the SpineLine, a 24-hour emergency response service for rugby injuries, the Rugby Medic Club, which trains hundreds of club and secondary school medics annually, and the Coaches Logbook, a practical aid for coaches with advice on conditioning, safety, techniques and more.

The fund hosts an annual banquet and golf day through which it raises much needed funding for its activities. As SARU's official Social Responsibility partner, the fund receives a generous annual grant from the governing body.

Ockert Brits, Transvaal's no 8, died of a heart attack after the match against Northern Free State in Welkom in 1984. His death was, however, not related to injury sustained in the match; Brits collapsed at half-time and died on his way to the Welkom Hospital.

The first recorded death in South African rugby was in 1884 when A Schlemmer of West End was tackled on his way to the tryline in the first final of the Grand Challenge competition in Kimberley against Beaconsfield. He died in hospital a week after the match.

In another freak accident, Walter Wright died as a result of an injury during a rugby match in 1907. Described as a talented Pirates three-quarter, he apparently crashed into one of the bulky flagpoles that were used those days. The tragedy occurred on the B field of the old Wanderers club.

charge in the first of his five Currie Cup finals. He later summed it up as follows when he reminisced about his career:

'In 1987 at Ellis Park we had four seasons in one day. The sun shone, the rain fell, then hail fell and then the wind blew. That day Naas Botha dictated the game as I have never seen any other player do in any game anywhere.'

Botha's four drop goals are the most in a final. They were scored in a season when he came close to his Currie Cup record for a season, as he kicked 19 (the record of 20 drop goals was set by Botha in 1985). He eventually held the record of 135 Currie Cup goals in his career, an average of more than a drop in every Currie Cup match.

Natal wing Tony Watson on the run.

The Centenary Try

Perhaps it was not quite as spectacular as the try by Pierre Spies 14 years earlier when he clinched the title for Northern Transvaal against Free State, but in the context of the Currie Cup competition as a whole, and for Natal in particular, the try by Tony Watson that brought the province its first Currie Cup title in its centenary year was hugely significant.

It was also more than just a significant try, it was an outstanding score which put Natal up there with the big ones. Also, with the ice having been broken, Natal continued to make the 1990s a truly memorable decade.

It was a try set up from good forward play, but somehow came against the run of play as Northern Transvaal were in control after they had started poorly.

The ball went to the narrow side of the field, and Watson was given a perfect pass by later Springbok Jeremy Thomson.

Watson said to Albert Heenop, author of the book *Natal Sharks: Team of the 90s*: 'Jeremy chose to give his best pass of the season, truly the perfect pass, just at the right moment.'

The man Watson beat with speed and, let's not forget it, power, was Theo van Rensburg, who was to become the Springbok fullback two years later when South Africa were readmitted into international rugby.

Van Rensburg was playing at centre that day because Northern Transvaal's Pieter Nel was injured in the tunnel as the Light Blues took to the field. Van Rensburg was selected as fullback but did remarkably well if one considers that he had not trained with his unexpected centre partner, Jannie Claassens.

Watson described the try as one for which he needed extra speed. Perhaps that helped to deceive Van Rensburg, affecting the timing of his attempted tackle. Watson dropped a shoulder, and Van Rensburg was left stranded on the ground. The try and conversion took the score to 15–12, which meant that Northern Transvaal were still in it.

However, referee Freek Burger gave a penalty against Claassens who had kneed Watson on the head after his try, and Joel Stransky made the difference six points with a successful kick from the centre spot. The score then stood at 18–12, which meant that the home side needed a converted try to win.

But Natal held out.

The significance of that try spoke from the size of the parade through Durban's streets and the many, many words written on that final and that season. It was a day in which Natal rugby had come of age, Natal coach Ian McIntosh said afterwards.

It's Like Kissing Your Sister!

Sakkie Sauermann was to become an unlikely Currie Cup hero. It wasn't because of his proficiency as a rugby player or a prop forward, but stories of props scoring winning or score-levelling tries are few and far between.

He did so in the very last seconds of one of the toughest matches played in a Currie Cup final. That was on 9 October 1971, and Ellis Park was the venue.

Currie Cup finals are very important matches – that goes without saying. This one was even more so for Northern Transvaal, who left Pretoria for Ellis Park that morning on a mission. They had lost the 1970 final to Griquas and wanted the Currie Cup back where they felt it belonged: in a cabinet at Loftus Versfeld.

For the great Frik du Preez and his close friend Mof Myburgh, it would also be their last match for the Light Blues.

'I don't want to go out like Piet (Uys),' said Du Preez about the other member of the triumvirate, who captained the side in the 1970 loss to Griquas and retired after the 1970 season.

The lead-up to the final was dramatic in its own right. In the days when scrumming machines were far from as sophisticated as today, the Northerns forwards scrummed one to pieces on the Monday before the final.

There were also the boardroom games that Transvaal played when their president negotiated a reprieve from the mid-week play-offs his team had to play. The Currie Cup final was postponed to give Transvaal more rest between their matches.

This meant that Northern Transvaal had four weeks without any game time, and they hastily arranged a friendly against Rhodesia to try and compensate.

There was also unhappiness with the referees for the match. Cas de Bruyn was one of the three Northern Transvaal could select from, but that in itself was a decision criticised in Johannesburg. De Bruyn had not awarded a try to Transvaal in his previous match, and as members of the TRFU felt that it should have been awarded, they didn't want him on the panel.

Transvaal were annihilated in the first scrum, and Sauermann and company were on the retreat. They were in trouble for some time but somehow held out. Northerns should have led by more than the 5–3 following a dominant first half, but didn't.

And then the tide changed. Transvaal went onto the attack after half-time, and Tobias du Toit was put over following a Gert Schutte break, for an unconverted try. Jannie van Deventer then added another penalty to his first-half effort, and the home side were 9–5 up.

Northerns came back, as is their wont in tight matches, and started to control territory. Flyhalf Dudley Gradwell put over two drop kicks during this spell of territorial dominance, and the game was now played mostly in the Transvaal half.

Time had expired when the Transvaal backs were caught off side. Referee Gert Bezuidenhout awarded the penalty, and Chris Luther made no mistake.

Northerns were home and dry!

Or so they thought, together with hundreds of spectators who had streamed onto the field.

Officials and the police restored a semblance of order, and the restart was ordered. According to referee Bezuidenhout, there was time left for another play.

'We weren't in position yet,' Frik du Preez recounted later, when he described what had gone wrong.

The Transvaal forwards, however, secured the ball and Gert Schutte, the Transvaal scrumhalf who somehow

HELPING THE REF

Scrumhalves – especially the smaller variety – can be likened to wicketkeepers. They're forever chirping the opposition and, in rugby, often get on the wrong side of the bigger guys on the other side, and often, also of the ref.

Craig Jamieson, captain of Natal when they won the Currie Cup in 1990, was one such scrumhalf. The story is told how the cocky Natal hero – and cocky he was indeed! – 'assisted' the referee with advice on how the game should be reffed.

Eventually, Ian Rogers, who was handling the match, turned to Jamieson and said: 'Craig, who's reffing this match? Me or you?'

Jamieson immediately shot back: 'At the moment, ref, neither of us!'

Free State scrumhalf Barry Wolmarans on the break with his Free State flyhalf De Wet Ras on hand to assist against Transvaal.

missed out on Springbok colours, made his second telling break of the match. He passed to his captain, Piet Greyling, and from there Sakkie Sauermann was put into possession.

With Northerns' forwards still disorganised after the kick-off, the Springbok prop drove over – and everything then depended on Van Deventer's conversion.

Transvaal need not have worried. It was over, and the scores and match were tied at 14–all.

It was Northerns' own fault, some said. Others pointed to what they had seen as a knock-on from Greyling in receiving from Schutte, and still some others felt that Sauermann had lost the ball in driving over.

But the ref is always right, and the score of 14–all denied Northerns a Currie Cup for the second year in a row, although they at least had a share of it this time.

But as Frik du Preez, who captained Northern Transvaal in what was to be his last match following a famous career, quipped afterwards: 'The best team drew today!'

And he is also remembered for his other utterance after the disappointing result: 'To draw a game is like kissing your sister!'

Sakkie Sauermann – his real name is Theo – played in five tests and 11 matches in all for the Springboks between 1971 and 1974 and didn't score a single point in those matches.

But when it counted, that day at Ellis Park, he did what every prop dreams of. He won the Currie Cup – or at least a share thereof – for his team.

Ninety-Four Seconds and Thirty Players

In the Free State people will always hark back to the 1976 final in Bloemfontein, when their team won their first Currie Cup title after 82 years as a union. And when they do, the name of Edrich Krantz will always come up. This winger, who later became a Springbok and also played in a Currie Cup final for Northern Transvaal, scored a memorable try in that match.

Western Province, beaten 33–16 in the match, had their backs to the wall, recounts Herman le Roux, who was then with the *Volksblad* and later became sports editor of *Beeld.* Their no 8 and captain, Morné du Plessis, decided on a tap kick when they were awarded a penalty. He passed to Springbok scrumhalf, Divan Serfontein, out it went to Dawie Snyman, and under pressure he kicked diagonally, where the ball was collected by Free State's Gysie Pienaar near the touchline and on his own 10-metre line.

And there he went. He avoided Snyman and Springbok wing Chris Pope, running across the field towards the main stand. Hennie Bekker dived desperately, and had a measure of success as he caught Gysie's ankle and caused him to stumble.

The ball went loose. Dirk Froneman picked it up. Out it went to prop Martiens le Roux, who went over the advantage line before he passed to Gerrie Sonnekus on his right. Krantz was there to the left of Sonnekus. He in turn passed to Barry Wolmarans, and out it went to De Wet Ras who kicked high with his left foot. Bekker retrieved, and after a maul, he passed it to Serfontein who again gave it to Snyman, who turned around to feed Christo Nel who was running behind him.

Nel kicked the moment Froneman tackled him, and Free State wing Gerrie Germishuys stopped the ball from going into touch. As he was tackled, he got the ball away to Pienaar who passed back as Nel tackled him.

After beating a few Province players, Germishuys passed to Jansen, who was caught, and a ruck formed around him.

Western Province won the ball back, but Chris Pope was then halted by Wouter Hugo. Another ruck, and this time the ball emerged on Free State's side. Martiens le Roux got it away to Jansen, who beat Peter Whipp and Johan Oosthuizen but was tackled by Nel. He passed to Klippies Kritzinger who sent Ross van Reenen on a run. He was stopped by Serfontein, and as the ball rolled loose, Sonnekus was there to gather and feed to Krantz.

The wing beat a defender on the outside, swerved to the inside, passed Bossie Clarke and beat Whipp before crossing with Tiny du Plessis up in support.

It was one minute and 34 seconds since Morné du Plessis had started the move with the tap kick, and 30 players from both sides handled the ball in that time.

It was the Free State's third try and took the score to 33–16 – at that time a Currie Cup record winning score.

There was, of course, also the try by Tewis de Bruyn against the Lions in 2007, which overturned the visitors' lead three minutes before time, to give the Free State Cheetahs victory by 20–18, as well as Meyer Bosman's try against Northern Transvaal at Loftus in 2005, to see his side take the spoils 29–25.

Good? Yes. Winners? Yes, but not nearly as spectacular as that effort that Krantz had the honour of rounding off.

Spies Gets the Bounce of the Ball

They say athletes can't play rugby. It's a generalisation, of course, and probably devoid of most truth. One only has to look at the successes of South African rugby players, at provincial and international level, who were also outstanding athletes, to realise that athletes from field or track can indeed excel at the fifteen-man game.

Just think of men like Andy van der Watt, Gert Muller, Warren McCann (all three of them sprinters), Poens Prinsloo (pole vault) Kerneels Cronje (110 m hurdles), Gert Potgieter (440-yard hurdles world record holder) and Reg Marchant (hammer throw), to name just a few.

And, of course, the late Pierre Spies. That is Pierre Spies senior, of course, father of the present Bulls and Springbok no 8.

Tall, rangy, and with a high knee action, Spies was the South African champion in the short hurdles. He was also a Springbok athlete, and could count himself unfortunate not to have played rugby for the Springboks as well.

After all, in those days of amateurism – or by then already shamateursim – there was enough time to excel in more than one sport, as cricket Springbok Lee Barnard did in playing rugby and cricket for both Transvaal and Northern Transvaal.

Spies dominated Northern Transvaal's scoring in the seasons that he played for them in the 1970s. A very high percentage of his tries came towards the end of matches, after Northern Transvaal had completed their softening-up process of the opposition pack.

They called it unimaginative rugby outside the borders of the Northern Transvaal Rugby Union (NTRU), and in fairness, it was a rather predictable game based on kicking for territory and mauling and grinding the opposition forwards into submission.

Even under the changed laws of today, that is to a large extent still the game plan used by the Bulls.

It was with this selfsame game plan that Northern Transvaal prepared for yet another final under Buurman van Zyl in 1975. Free State would be the opponents and the venue would be the Free State Stadium in Bloemfontein.

It had not been an easy year. Northerns had lost a preseason friendly against Western Transvaal and scraped through, after coming from behind against Natal. But slowly they got into their familiar stride – if that is the right word for a Northern Transvaal team!

But then they lost their league fixture to Free State, and that, it was said later, was probably a good thing from a motivational point of view.

The Free State, and most of South Africa, who were hoping for the Light Blues' stranglehold in the competition to be broken, used that last league win by Free State as a guideline for the final.

Northern Transvaal had little good possession from the lineouts in that match, but felt that they had been let down by the referee who had not patrolled that facet properly.

Masters of the psychological battle, and with their loyal press in support, Northern Transvaal made their unhappiness known in no uncertain terms. When they selected Dr Justus Moolman of the Eastern Province, who was a Grey College old boy, as referee for the final, they made it abundantly clear that they trusted his interpretation in the lineouts.

Springboks John Williams and Louis Moolman, two of the best that South Africa had fielded, were the Northern Transvaal locks. In the final analysis, their work in the lineout, where the Free State locks were not allowed the illegal latitude of their previous encounter between the

Big, strong Maties, Western Province and Springbok wing Gert Muller was a sprinter of note and represented WP in the national athletics championships.

The try that broke Free State hearts in 1975. Northern Transvaal wing Pierre Spies dots down to deny the home side a share of the Currie Cup.

two sides, pulled Northerns through to their first hat-trick of Currie Cup wins.

Northern Transvaal's jumpers took 14 Free State throw-ins in the lineout. From that position of strength in possession, flyhalf Len Gerber dictated territorial play, on a day that suited Northern Transvaal more than Free State, who wanted to run.

The wet ball and the muddy field put a damper on Free State's hopes to run with the ball. The underfoot was soft and rather muddy because the curtain-raisers had proceeded as normal.

Everything considered, this was not the dry, hard field that Free State, with their dangerous backs and mobile pack, had wanted.

Northerns, predictably, did little running. They kicked and drove, kicked and mauled and took Free State's lineouts even when the Light Blues' kicks went out and Free State had the put-in.

It simply wasn't Free State's day. De Wet Ras, one of the best kickers in South Africa's long Currie Cup history, had an off day and missed four very kickable penalties. Keith Thorreson, on the other hand, kicked two penalties for the visitors.

There were no tries scored, not until the very end.

Then, with two minutes to play, Free State centre Pikkie du Toit broke through and scored under the posts. With Ras' conversion, it was 6–all, and Free State at least had a share of the spoils, after 81 years of toiling in the Currie Cup league matches.

Big men hugged one another, a few wiped their tears of joy, and hats and rain coats were thrown into the air, some of them never to be retrieved again.

But it wasn't over. Gerber kicked off. The ball was mauled up, taken to the blindside and forward again.

MEN WITH THE WHISTLES

Neutral referees in Currie Cup finals were first used in 1973 when Piet Robbertse from Eastern Transvaal was appointed to officiate in the match between Northern Transvaal and Transvaal at Loftus Versfeld. That was his second appearance in a final, having handled Eastern Transvaal's home final which they lost against Transvaal at the PAM Brink Stadium in Springs the previous year.

The advent of neutral referees came about after the chaotic circumstances in which Transvaal's Sakkie Sauermann scored an equaliser in 1971. (See main text for the full story.)

With referees in South Africa now contracted to the South African Rugby Union, the principle of 'neutral' appointments is outdated. This has been taken even further at Super 14 level where, since 2009, referees have been in charge of matches involving teams from their own country.

However, a lesson can be taken from the very first Currie Cup final in 1939. The Springbok vice-captain of the previous year against the British Lions, Boy Louw, handled the final between Transvaal and Western Province. He was a former WP player, and Transvaal were captained by his brother Fanie, who was also Boy's fellow-prop in many test matches, the last being against the British Lions the previous year. Transvaal won the match, but there were no complaints in Cape Town about Boy Louw's handling of the game.

Incidentally: Boy Louw was the only ex-Springbok to handle a Currie Cup final.

It has always been an honour to referee a Currie Cup final. It has also not been the sole prerogative of test referees. In earlier years, the visiting team was given three names from which to select their preferred referee for the final. Currie Cup finals were sporadic from 1939 to 1968 (since when there has been a final every year). Because of the infrequency of the finals, only 24 referees have, to date, officiated in the highlight of the South African season since 1939. André Watson's seven finals top the six of Free State's Steve Strydom and the five of Freek Burger and Jonathan Kaplan.

Watson handled six consecutive finals between 1996 and 2001 and is the only referee to have officiated in two World Cup finals. Jonathan Kaplan refereed his fifth Currie Cup Final in Pretoria in 2009 after having refereed his first final in 2002, when the Golden Lions played the Blue Bulls. He missed out only in 2007 due to his World Cup duties.

Eddie Hofmeyr, Chris Ackermann, Ralph Burmeister, Bertie Strasheim, Gert Bezuidenhout, Piet Robbertse, Steve Strydom, Justus Moolman, Johan Gouws, Freek Burger, Stef Neethling, Tappe Henning, André Watson, Jonathan Kaplan, Shaun Veldsman and Mark Lawrence were all test referees who have also officiated in a final.

Referees who refereed in a final but not in a test were: Jimmy Smith-Belton, Boy Louw, Carl Basson, Albie Henkes, Bowden Coombe, Fonnie van der Vyver, Ben Calitz and Cassie Carstens. (Carstens did however officiate in test matches while stationed in France.)

The following is the list of referees in Currie Cup finals (home teams first):

1939: Western Province v Transvaal:
Boy Louw (Western Province)
1946: Northern Transvaal v Western Province:
Carl Basson (Northern Transvaal)
1947: Western Province v Transvaal:
Albie Henkes (Western Province)
1950: Transvaal v Western Province:
Eddie Hofmeyr (Transvaal)
1952: Boland v Transvaal: Chris Ackermann (Boland)
1954: Western Province v Northern Transvaal:
Ralph Burmeister (Western Province)
1956: Natal v Northern Transvaal:
Bowden Coombe (Natal)
1968: Northern Transvaal v Transvaal: Bertie Strasheim (Northern Transvaal)
1969: Northern Transvaal v Western Province:
Fonnie van der Vyver (Northern Transvaal)
1970: Griqualand West v Northern Transvaal:
Ben Calitz (Griqualand West)
1971: Transvaal v Northern Transvaal:

Gert Bezuidenhout (Transvaal)
1972: Eastern Transvaal v Transvaal: Piet Robbertse (Eastern Transvaal)
1973: Northern Transvaal v Transvaal: Piet Robbertse (Eastern Transvaal)
1974: Northern Transvaal v Transvaal: Steve Strydom (Orange Free State)
1975: Orange Free State v Northern Transvaal: Justus Moolman (Eastern Province)
1976: Orange Free State v Western Province: Gert Bezuidenhout (Transvaal)
1977: Northern Transvaal v Orange Free State: Jimmy Smith-Belton (Eastern Province)
1978: Orange Free State v Northern Transvaal: Gert Bezuidenhout (Transvaal)
1979: Western Province v Northern Transvaal: Steve Strydom (Orange Free State)
1980: Northern Transvaal v Western Province: Steve Strydom (Orange Free State)
1981: Northern Transvaal v Orange Free State: Johan Gouws (Eastern Transvaal)
1982: Western Province v Northern Transvaal: Steve Strydom (Orange Free State)
1983: Northern Transvaal v Western Province: Johan Gouws (Eastern Transvaal)
1984: Western Province v Natal: Cassie Carstens (Northern Transvaal)
1985: Western Province v Northern Transvaal: Steve Strydom (Orange Free State)
1986: Western Province v Transvaal: Steve Strydom (Orange Free State)
1987: Transvaal v Northern Transvaal: Freek Burger (Western Province)
1988: Northern Transvaal v Western Province: Jimmy Smith-Belton (Eastern Province)
1989: Western Province v Northern Transvaal: Jimmy Smith-Belton (Eastern Province)
1990: Northern Transvaal v Natal: Freek Burger (Western Province)
1991: Northern Transvaal v Transvaal: Freek Burger (Western Province)
1992: Transvaal v Natal: Freek Burger (Western Province)
1993: Natal v Transvaal: Freek Burger (Western Province)
1994: Orange Free State v Transvaal: Stef Neethling (Boland)
1995: Natal v Western Province: Tappe Henning (Northern Transvaal)
1996: Transvaal v Natal: André Watson (Eastern Transvaal)
1997: Western Province v Free State: André Watson (Gauteng Falcons)
1998: Blue Bulls v Western Province: André Watson (Gauteng Falcons)
1999: Natal v Lions: André Watson (Gauteng Falcons)
2000: Natal v Western Province: André Watson (Falcons)
2001: Western Province v Natal: André Watson (Falcons)
2002: Lions v Blue Bulls: Jonathan Kaplan (Boland)
2003: Blue Bulls v Sharks: Shaun Veldsman (Boland)
2004: Blue Bulls v Cheetahs: André Watson (Falcons)
2005: Blue Bulls v Cheetahs: Jonathan Kaplan (Boland)
2006: Blue Bulls v Cheetahs: Jonathan Kaplan (Boland)
2007: Cheetahs v Lions: Mark Lawrence (Mpumalanga)
2008: Sharks v Blue Bulls: Jonathan Kaplan (Western Province)
2009: Blue Bulls v Free State: Jonathan Kaplan (Western Province)

Note: Since 1998 referees are no longer members of a union but of SARU, and reference to their union after that date is an indication of where they lived in the year of their Currie Cup appointment.

NUMBER OF FINALS (49)

7 André Watson
6 Steve Strydom
5 Freek Burger, Jonathan Kaplan
3 Gert Bezuidenhout, Jimmy Smith-Belton
2 Piet Robbertse, Johan Gouws
1 Boy Louw, Carl Basson, Albie Henkes, Eddie Hofmeyr, Chris Ackermann, Ralph Burmeister, Bertie Strasheim, Bowden Coombe, Fonnie van der Vyver, Ben Calitz, Justus Moolman, Cassie Carstens, Stef Neethling, Tappe Henning, Shaun Veldsman, Mark Lawrence.

And when Louis Moolman plucked it out and passed to scrumhalf Tommy du Plessis, he let it out to Gerber.

The flyhalf in turn passed to Christo Wagenaar, who received an opponent from an offside position and the ball at the same time. He had no option: time had expired.

Wagenaar kicked it to the right, high and into the no-man's land. It bounced very high for a wet field that had often seen the ball stop dead in the run-up to this moment.

With his high knee action, Spies had chased after the kick. The bounce eluded him – or did it?

Reaching up at full pace, the tall winger got his finger tips to the ball, tapped it and caught it, without losing even a semblance of a stride. Free State no 8 Kleintjie Gobbler's despairing dive had no chance, and Spies' opponent Gerrie Germishuys could do little but look on as Spies hared over in the corner. Thorreson's conversion mattered none, but he slotted it for a wonderful win – deserved, but also lucky.

Northern Transvaal wing and fullback Chris Luther, who wasn't in the team for the match but had played in the curtain-raiser, watched this win from the temporary stand, to the right of the main stand, in the Free State Stadium.

'When Pierre scored, I looked to the crowd behind me. It was as if 3 000 people had all lost a close relative,' Luther said afterwards.

Two men who didn't see the try were the president of the South African Rugby Board, Dr Danie Craven, and the Free State Rugby Union's president, André Volsteedt. They were on their way through the tunnels that led to the field, where Volsteedt would have received the golden cup on behalf of co-winners Free State.

But it was not to be, and in the first year of television in South Africa, this try was screened over and over again. The two rugby bosses therefore had ample opportunity to see how the Cup was won, and a share of it lost.

CHAPTER 4

Western Province

Over the years the ongoing banter between supporters of Western Province and Northern Transvaal/Blue Bulls has been a battle won hands down by the people from the Cape.

The facts are on their side: they hold the record for the most Currie Cup titles; for the most consecutive wins when the competition was still decided by league competitions; and for the most consecutive wins after the introduction of finals. Furthermore, they can boast a proud record of having lost only one of their ten finals at Newlands.

In fact, the only argument the Blue Bulls supporters have when the Currie Cup is brought up, is that they have won it most since Northern Transvaal became an independent union in 1938.

At the end of 2009, Western Province had won the Currie Cup competition 31 times, including the four times they shared it. (Of course, they also won the very first provincial tournament in 1889, taking home the South African Rugby Football Board trophy.)

Of those 31 wins, 16 titles (including two shared) came during the 19 Currie Cup competitions decided by league systems in various formats until 1936, and three more in 1957–1959, 1964 and 1966. Only 12 titles (including two shared) have been won in 49 competitions where the Currie Cup winners were decided by means of a final.

It seems as if the play-off system does not agree with the team from the Cape.

The first competition for the Currie Cup was played in Kimberley in 1892. Western Province duly won the first tournament in which five teams – Western Province, Griqualand West, Transvaal, Natal and Border – took part. They then

At last! In 1982 Western Province won their first outright title since 1966 after a drought of 14 Currie Cup competitions when they beat Northern Transvaal 24-7 at Newlands. The two teams had shared the 1979 title. In the picture captain Divan Serfontein and a very happy president Jan Pickard share the moment.

THE GREAT MARKÖTTER

Oubaas Markötter (or August Frederick Markötter, to use his real name) was arguably the greatest coach in South African rugby history. He got the nickname 'Oubaas' in his schooldays, and at Stellenbosch and throughout South Africa, he was referred to as Oubaas Mark.

He was the man who took Stellenbosch University from a very good and competitive side to four Western Province Grand Challenge titles in the five years between 1903 and 1907. During this period he captained the Western Province Country team that beat Mark Morrison's Lions 13-7 at Newlands - the first non-test side to beat a Lions team in South Africa.

It was, however, as a coach, and particularly a coach with an eye for spotting and developing young talented players, that Markötter will be remembered. Virtually until his death in 1957, Oubaas Mark's identification of players and his coaching produced many, many Maties for Western Province sides who dictated at provincial level and especially in the Currie Cup, from the competition's inception until 1936.

It was under Markötter that the Maties developed into the foremost talent factory in the country. Paul Roos' 1906 Springbok squad to Britain included 11 players who had developed under Markötter at Stellenbosch, and had played their part in Western Province's Currie Cup successes in the first decade of the 20th century.

Markötter captained the Maties in 1903 and also played for the clubs Paarl, Villagers and Wellington. His coaching methods were uncompromising, but built on basics, and his often dour disposition hid a fine sense of humour that made him a popular and much respected figure, though one not to be trifled with.

He was also dictatorial, or let's rather call it undemocratic (as was his protégé Danie Craven, who was later known as Mr Rugby throughout the rugby-playing world; he had obviously learnt his lessons well!).

There is also the story told of how Markötter 'elected' members of the Stellenbosch Rugby Club's committee at an AGM. As chairman of the meeting, he stood up and announced: 'I propose Kockie de Kock as secretary and Herman Steytler as his assistant. There are no further proposals.' When Springbok loose forward André McDonald was proposed as club captain at the same meeting, Markötter said: 'André McDonald has been proposed. Who dares propose against him?'

De Kock, Steytler and McDonald were elected without a murmur, it is said!

Markötter graduated in 1898, and established his legal firm Kriege & Markötter in 1900.

But by then it had already become clear that the man who only started playing rugby at the age of 16 in 1893 would spend more time on the rugby field than in his chambers. In a letter to a friend he wrote: 'I definitely decided to dedicate the rest of my life to rugby football.'

The Maties, Western Province and also South Africa, reaped the benefits of that decision.

stacked up a remarkable sequence of wins, namely 45 consecutive matches, before Griquas beat them 12-0 in the 11th Currie Cup tournament at Newlands in 1911.

That was Griquas' second title. They also won the 1899 title when Western Province didn't take part because of the impending South African War.

It was quite understandable that Western Province dominated rugby in those early years. They were the 'teachers' of the game, as it were. The first established clubs, the first competitions, the first official structure, namely the Western Province Rugby Football Union in 1884, gave them a huge advantage when inter-city rugby first started.

The Western Province dominance was increased by the large number of top-class players that were developed under these conditions.

They have not had the same fortune of late, however. This is how things go in the world of rugby (and all sport, for that matter). The wheel turns. Western Province supporters have had a lean time of it for eight years, with their team last challenging for and winning the title in a final in 2001, the year when the Blue Bulls suffered their third successive Currie Cup campaign without making the final.

It was so very close for Western Province in 2009, when Morné Steyn of the Blue Bulls broke the hearts of the Newlands faithful with a huge pressure penalty three minutes from time in the semi-final at Newlands.

The Blue Bulls denied Western Province a place in their first semi-final since 2006 when the visitors pinched two consecutive lineouts in the dying minutes when they seemed to be out for the count.

That was the season when Western Province lost only four of their 14 Currie Cup league matches, and their refreshing running approach helped them to a second place on the log, behind the Sharks. Their success was built around their often controversial captain Luke Watson, who has since succumbed to the lure of the pound, the return to his forming province of hard-working lock Anton van Zyl, and the scrummaging strength that was immeasurably improved by Tiaan Liebenberg's decision to return to the Cape after a spell overseas.

The running and kicking of Joe Pietersen from the back and a number of new faces in the pack added lustre to a year that promised much for the future. The first signs of a step up in their growth towards becoming a great side were also noticeable in the Stormers' 2010 Super 14 performances.

Following the record five consecutive Currie Cup final wins from 1982 to 1986, the last 20 years have not been easy for Western Province after sharing the title with Northern Transvaal in 1989.

Just a single title came their way during the 1990s, a decade when they played in only three finals. They lost the first of those against the Sharks in Durban in 1995 (25–17); beat the Free State 14–12 in Cape Town in 1997; and narrowly lost the Loftus final against the Blue Bulls the following year (24–20) when a pass to Chester Williams which would surely have won the game, was controversially judged to have been forward.

Two titles in 2000 and 2001 made it a barely more acceptable five finals and three titles in the 20 years from 1980 to 2001.

After the 2001 win until 2009 they reached the semi-finals of the Currie Cup competition on only four occasions. Of those they lost the first two to the Free State Cheetahs in 2004 and 2005, and their two semi-finals in 2006 and 2009 were won by the Blue Bulls.

There is a concern in Western Province that the outstanding young talent of the region, which boasts probably the country's top rugby schools, does not manifest at junior national level. It is also felt that the continual flow of talent through to the provincial side has not been as strong as in years gone by.

Of course, in the early years the school system did not supply such a stream of talent, and the strength of the provincial side was a complement to the region's clubs and structures.

From those clubs, from the army and from overseas, bringing with them vast experience of the game as it was played in Britain at the time, came players like Biddy Anderson, Ben Duff, Charles Vigne, HH Castens, Alf Richards, Fairie Heatlie and Japie Krige, to name only a few.

Griquas were the early main rivals, as one would expect in view of the influx of people to Kimberley after the discovery of diamonds in the 1870s. They occupied second place in the first three tournaments won by Western Province. Transvaal, third in those three tournaments, then swapped places with Griquas in the fourth tournament.

However, Transvaal dropped to fifth place as they forfeited their match against Eastern Province in the following tournament in 1898 to attend the funeral of their international teammate Davie Cope, who was killed in a train accident on his way to the tournament.

Western Province went through the 1898 tournament without a single point being scored against them in their four matches, and notched up 62 points themselves.

Only 24 points in their first 22 Currie Cup matches were put past Province as they unquestionably dominated the first five tournaments from 1892 to 1898.

If anything, Western Province's dominance after the South African War seemed even more pronounced. The

Continuing Western Province's dominance of the Currie Cup competition were famous 1906 Springbok captain Paul Roos, left, and the 1906 touring team's vice-captain Paddy Carolin, right. Together with 1906 team manager Cecil (Daddy) Cardin from Eastern Province they formed the 1906 team management.

influence of Stellenbosch University in no small way added to this, as the first of the hundreds of provincial players this institution produced over the years started making their mark.

In fact, as early as 1891, the first four of the long list of Springboks that had received their rugby grounding at Stellenbosch played against Bill Maclagan's team: Japie Louw, Arthur de Kock, Robert Shand and Jim McKendrick. They were key members of the Western Province sides that laid the foundation for the union's success at Currie Cup level.

The real Maties stars, however, were those of later years: Japie Krige, Bob Loubser, Paul Roos, Jan Stegmann and Boy de Villiers.

Krige, Stegmann (who incidentally scored the first try by a Springbok on tour), Loubser and De Villiers were known as 'The Thin Red Line' when they played for Western Province and later overseas.

They were 'made' by Oubaas Markötter, and Mr Mark, as the genius coach was addressed by all, coached Loubser into a great player within a year of the youngster's first run on a rugby field.

Loubser was selected for South Africa in 1903 – also his first year of Currie Cup rugby – and he played for Western Province until 1908. He also played for Transvaal for two years.

Even in today's game of big centres, Loubser would have held his own. He was immensely strong, a big man, and exceptionally quick. In fact, Loubser came very close to being selected as a sprinter for the South African Olympic side.

The future Member of Parliament was plucked from obscurity as an athlete, even though he had not played rugby before, to partner Japie Krige whose speed was such that he left his teammates behind. They were the perfect foil for one another, and also became good friends with a special mutual admiration.

Loubser, who scored 24 tries on the first Springbok tour to the UK in 1906, gave much of the credit for his many tries over the years to Krige. It was false modesty, however, as he showed in the great Western Province side of 1908.

Krige had by then retired – and Loubser was the hero of the 5–0 win over Transvaal, who played with only seven forwards to try and curb the attacking danger of the Western Province backs. Sommy Morkel and Duggie Morkel were the two men who alternated to assist their backs on the defence.

John Gainsford

In their own quarter, Transvaal used both Morkels at the back, with a six-man scrum.

Transvaal had a huge and very effective pack, and Western Province an outstanding backline. Their form up front had prompted the Transvaal decision to play with only seven – or even six – forwards.

It was a must-win encounter for Western Province (who eventually scored 190 points in their nine matches without conceding any) after they had drawn 0–0 with Griquas.

In the last five minutes Loubser received the ball after a well-constructed backline movement. Thanks to his blistering pace, he squeezed through between the two

FAILING A YEAR IS A VIRTUE!

Boys will be boys, and students of those years were renowned for their fun, even if it was at the expense of a fellow student or his parents.

Doc Craven, in his book *Die groot rugbygesin van die Maties*, tells the lovely story of the great Japie Krige.

Syd Harvey, later to be a lecturer in physics at Stellenbosch University and a man who was secretary of just about every club at his alma mater, was on his way back to his koshuis (residence) Wilgenhof when he heard the song 'For he's a jolly good fellow' ringing from the quad. He saw a group of students with the great Japie Krige on their shoulders, and on enquiring what it was about (the rugby season had run its course and it was now near the end of the year and time for exams), Harvey received the jolly answer: 'Japie has failed and he'll be back next year!' What Krige's parents thought of the additional cost of this year-to-be-repeated is not known!

Quick as lightning, Krige was a genius at centre – so described by the great Oubaas Markötter. Krige was so fast that he had problems finding a wing who could keep up with him, until the day that coach Oubaas Mark tried sprinter Bob Loubser. Even quicker than Krige, Loubser was a big and very powerful man, but knew nothing of rugby. Oubaas Mark coached him, coaxed him and made him work at his game – and the rest is history.

Krige and Loubser became good friends and got to know one another's game inside out. They were a match-winning combination for the Maties, Western Province and South Africa of a calibre arguably not seen since.

Morkels and beat fullback Billy Stoll. Even Loubser's former teammate Anton Stegmann was left for dead.

It was just another league match, but as important as a final, as was often the case in those early years when Griquas were the opponents. Loubser, on the old Newlands field where the touchlines were orientated differently from how they are now, had a special corner in front of the Malay stand. Within a year after his first match for Western Province it was called 'Bob's Corner'.

Furthermore Loubser's speed earned him the nickname among those fervent rugby supporters of the Cape. He was called the Wit Rooiblits (the White Red Lightning), referring to his white skin and the reddish maroon jerseys of Stellenbosch.

The highlight of 1908 was followed by Western Province's first defeat in a Currie Cup match and competition. Griquas beat a very good Western Province team away at Newlands. The score was a comprehensive 12–0, and the win was based on a good pack and some outstanding defence.

The last tournament before the Great War was in 1914, and the best Western Province side between 1904 and 1914, according to former Bok captain WA Millar, regained the Currie Cup in no uncertain manner.

Western Province won all nine of their games in Durban and scored 193 points to 6. They also comprehensively beat Griquas 16–0 in their encounter. Transvaal were second, and were beaten 10–0 by Province.

That was the year that Western Province used seven Morkels in the tournament. It was also the first time that the orthodox halfback position as we know it today had been adopted by Western Province – until then they had played with a scrumhalf and two inside backs.

'There was not a single weak link in that side ...' Millar wrote in his book *My Recollections and Reminiscences*.

Transvaal had given notice before the First World War that they were on the up, and only an unlikely and scoreless draw with fledgling Western Transvaal (which had broken away from their mother union, Transvaal, that very same year) denied them a joint first place and share of the 1920 Currie Cup.

That was the last tournament to be held at a centralised venue and, fittingly, it was at Kimberley, where the first Currie Cup tournament had taken place 28 years before.

Two of Western Province's greatest, Phil Mostert and Bennie Osler.

In 1922 the first Currie Cup competition with teams playing home and away matches took place. (The fixtures were quite haphazard, and saw Transvaal awarded six home games and only three on tour in 1927.)

In 1922, the men from the Reef managed to draw with Western Province who had lost to Griquas (9–6). The invincibility of Province was being questioned, and many described this as 'a good thing for rugby'.

However, 1925 (with Free State's second place indicating a rise in their rugby standard), 1927 and 1929 showed that Western Province was truly boss, and it took also-rans Border to bring them some way back to earth with their two shared titles in 1932 and 1934.

It was no mean feat to share the Cup with Western Province, who had all-time greats like Bennie Osler, Danie Craven, Pierre de Villiers, Boy and Fanie Louw, André McDonald, JC van der Westhuizen, Mauritz van den Berg, Alfie van der Merwe, George van Rooyen, Frankie Waring, Dai Williams, Maurice Zimerman and Koffie Hofmeyer in their squad of 35 who played Currie Cup rugby in that year.

They were all Springboks of South Africa's outstanding international era between 1930/1931 and 1938, and most of them were members of the great 1937 side to New Zealand.

By the end of that 1932 tournament, Western Province had won 101 of their 110 Currie Cup matches – well ahead of Transvaal who had 73 wins from their 109

LIKE FATHER, LIKE SON

Morné du Plessis was one of South Africa's greatest rugby players and captains, with an international career stretching from 1971 to 1980.

Like so many other great players of his era, the former Grey College pupil who made his mark as a provincial and international player at Stellenbosch was limited by politics to only 22 test appearances.

He followed in the footsteps of his father Felix, who led the Springboks in three of their four tests in the whitewash of the All Blacks in 1949, the first series after the Second World War.

Morné, too, was a natural leader of men, and like his father 37 years before, he led the Boks to a series win over the All Blacks, when South Africa won the 1976 series 3–1.

The Du Plessis are the only father-son combination in Springbok history to have captained the national side.

Morné made his debut as Springbok no 8 in 1971, in a three-test away series to Australia. It was the first and only unbeaten tour by a Springbok side (led by Hannes Marais), during which they won the three tests 18–6, 14–6 and 19–11.

It was another three years before the Boks played test rugby again. This time captain Marais was in charge of a Springbok side that lost the series against the British Lions 3–0, with the last test at Ellis Park drawn.

Morné du Plessis played in the first two tests, with losses of 12–3 and a record 28–9 inflicted on the Springboks. It led to the selectors' panic in a four-match series, where they used 33 players (before the years of replacements!). Only three players played in all four tests.

Through the rest of his 22-test career Du Plessis would play in only two more losing matches.

Du Plessis made his debut as captain when France toured South Africa in 1975, and the Springboks won 38–25 in Bloemfontein and 33–18 in Pretoria.

Then came the All Blacks. The Boks won the first test 16–7, lost the second 15–9, and won the last two tests 15–10 and 15–14. In 1977 the Springboks played a World XV in Pretoria and won 45–24. After that Du Plessis led the side to wins over South America in 1980 and then the British Lions in the same year.

In October 1980 the Springboks toured South America but Du Plessis played in only one of the two tests, leading his team to a 30–16 success against the Jaguars in Santiago. His final test was a November clash against France in Pretoria.

Morné du Plessis played 22 tests for South Africa and was on the winning side 18 times. He captained the Springboks in 15 matches, winning 13 times and losing only twice.

In 1995, Du Plessis managed the victorious Springbok team in the World Cup held in South Africa.

Du Plessis is a founding member and chairman of the Chris Burger/Petro Jackson Players' Fund that provides assistance to rugby players who have sustained serious rugby injuries.

His stature in the world of rugby, and in sport in general, was recognised by the Laureus World Sports Awards. Morné serves on the World Sports Academy – a group of 42 world-renowned sportsmen and women who act as the electoral college for the Laureus World Sports Awards and promotes the use of sport for social change throughout the world.

It is ironic that one of South Africa's greatest players and captains never had the honour of holding aloft the Currie Cup as a sole winner. Du Plessis was captain in 1979, when Naas Botha's drop kick in the final move of the game gave Northern Transvaal a share of the trophy.

After the match, Du Plessis added to Frik du Preez's famous quote following the controversial draw between Transvaal and Northern Transvaal in 1971 when Frik remarked: 'It was like kissing your sister.'

Morné's view was that it was like kissing your cousin – after a while it became quite pleasant!

Du Plessis' mother Pat, like her husband and son, also captained South Africa at international level – in hockey. Two of his uncles, Horace and Norman, played soccer for South Africa, and Horace also captained South Africa.

Du Plessis and Dawie Snyman (also born in 1949)

Felix du Plessis

were recognised as the Maties' 100th Springboks when they were selected on the same night.

Du Plessis mostly played fullback for his school and didn't make the Free State schools side for the Craven Week. At Stellenbosch, however, he was immediately put into the under-19 A side and eventually captained Western Province well over 100 times. He also played Currie Cup cricket for Western Province.

matches, and Griquas who had 63 from 112.

Border, who shared the Currie Cup again in 1934, were only seventh in the rankings after 1932, with a mere 35 wins from 100 matches and a winning record of less than 40 percent.

However, class was not to be denied, and in the next competition – in 1936 – Western Province went through unbeaten, the only blemish on their record being a scoreless draw against Griquas in Kimberley.

The next tournament (in 1939) was the first time the Currie Cup was decided by a final. Since then only three tournaments – 1957–1959 (played over the two seasons of 1957 and 1959), 1964 and 1966 – have been decided in other ways than through a final.

Western Province were involved in the first final in 1939, but lost the match 17–6 to Transvaal. In ten finals at Newlands, this was the only time that Western Province did not get at least a share of the spoils. They have shared the Currie Cup twice in Newlands finals and won seven times; this partly compensates for their away record in finals (played 10, won two, shared one, lost seven).

Because of the Second World War, Currie Cup competitions were suspended until 1946, when Western Province lost their second final, and Northern Transvaal won their first Currie Cup in Pretoria (11–9).

Province won their first Currie Cup final in 1947 by beating Transvaal 16–12 at Newlands in front of a crowd of 29 000 fans.

It was not easy. The two sides boasted the core of the Springbok side that played against the All Blacks in 1949, and the game was very much in the balance as the two teams had their half-time break.

The match was won by Western Province after Otto van Niekerk scored one of his many famous tries in 'Otto's Corner' at Newlands, eluding a desperate do-or-die tackle by Hennie Muller.

The see-saw battle with Transvaal continued in the next final in 1950, when Transvaal won 22–11 at Ellis Park.

In 1954 Western Province beat Northern Transvaal for the first time in a final, something that was not to be repeated until 1982 after a further 15 Currie Cup finals had come and gone, and during which time Western Province

Dawie de Villiers, who later played for Diggers and Transvaal.

lost the 1976 final to the Free State in Bloemfontein 33–16; drew 15-all with Northern Transvaal at Newlands in 1979; and lost 39–9 to Northern Transvaal in 1980 (still the biggest score difference in a Currie Cup final).

In 1956 there was the disappointment of Western Province's 11–10 loss to Natal in the semi-final – the first time Natal had won at Newlands. This competition, like the year before, was played in three sections, with two section winners playing for the right to meet the third in the final. It was an unsatisfactory arrangement, to say the least, but also one that was at times used after the advent of annual finals in 1968.

It was in the 1970s that Western Province's huge reservoir of talented players of colour got their first break in the top tier of South African rugby when they started playing in competitions of the SA Rugby Board, the only one of many South African rugby bodies recognised by the International Rugby Board (IRB).

In 1978 two teams from the so-called 'coloured' SA Rugby Football Federation, established in 1959, took part in the Sport Pienaar Cup competition, as did two teams of the SA Rugby Association (SARA).

The Western Province League team fared well, but the other three sides, namely SWD League, SARA West and SARA East, found the competition too tough a challenge and struggled against teams of average strength.

These three teams decided not to take part in 1979 and went ahead in the Golden Cup competition, in which white teams of semi-provincial strength played.

Western Province Federation, however, proved that they could become a strength in South African rugby. Consisting of star coloured players, they ended joint fourth in Section 1 of the Sport Pienaar competition, and gave a good account of themselves by winning four of their seven matches.

Against the Western Province Currie Cup side, however, it was obvious that, despite some outstanding talent, the depth was not quite there yet and the Western Province Federation lost 51–0.

The national SARA team replaced the two regional teams in 1979, and the combined team's rugby was of a marked higher standard. Names like Morgan Cushe and Timothy Nkonki became well-known among South African supporters.

The Federation was represented at first-class level by the WP Federation, with players of the calibre of Cuthbert Loristen, Abe Williams (later to become a Springbok assistant manager), John Cupido and Dougie Dyers (later a national selector).

Eight Federation players were included in the SA Barbarians' side for the 1980 tour to the UK. They were Errol Tobias, who in 1981 became the first non-white player to represent South Africa; and Hennie and Turkey Shield, Nicky Davids, Charles Williams, Louis Paulse, Hanne Meyer and Pompies Williams.

The team was coached by Dougie Dyers.

Tobias' road to the Springbok team had been through the Federation team and later via Boland, which he represented in the 1980 Currie Cup competition.

Playing a barbarian-style game with free running whenever possible, Avril Williams and Wilfred Cupido made it to the Western Province provincial side in 1982, and more were to follow with regularity.

Williams played for the Springboks in the series against the 1984 England tourists and Cupido played for the national under-23 side, the Gazelles.

In 1985 the Western Province League team, as they were now called, missed out on promotion to the Currie Cup when they were beaten in the final by Vaal Triangle who went on to win the promotion matches against Boland.

But before the introduction of players of colour to South Africa's major rugby competitions in the 1970s, and following their 1954 Currie Cup win over Northern Transvaal, Western Province added three more Currie Cup titles to their record.

They won the league competition that was played over the two seasons of 1957 and 1959 (there was no Currie Cup rugby in 1958 due to the first visit to South Africa by France).

In 1964, Province again won the league, and repeated this feat in 1966.

The highlight was probably their win against Northern Transvaal at Loftus 1964. Although it wasn't a final, the win nevertheless ensured that Northerns would be out

SETTING THE TREND

Western Province were fortunate that when they lost Morné du Plessis to retirement at the end of 1980, they had a future national captain in Divan Serfontein to take over the reins in 1981.

Despite a rather poor season that year when they struggled to come to grips with the loss of one of South Africa's greatest captains, as well as some other senior players, there were signs that a few good years were just around the corner for Western Province.

And so it proved, as Serfontein led the team in its first three years of their record spell of five successive years as Currie Cup champions between 1982 and 1986.

Not only that, he also captained the team to 51 unbeaten home matches and became the first Western Province captain to play more than a hundred matches for his province.

The little scrumhalf, now an orthopaedic surgeon, first made his mark at Maties. He also played for Defence and made his debut for the Springboks in 1980 when he was selected to partner Naas Botha against the British Lions.

Together they became an outstanding halfback pairing and were part of probably the best backline the country has boasted.

He was South African Rugby Player of the Year and was also a Player of the Year nominee in 1981 and 1983 and was a nominee for South African Rugby Young Player of the Year in 1976.

The scrumhalf, one of the best South Africa has produced, played in 19 tests. He also played in seven tour matches and accompanied the Boks on the tour to South America in 1980 and New Zealand and the United States in 1981.

Serfontein captained the Springboks in his last two tests in 1984 against the combined South America and Spain side. He was 30 when he retired.

of the running and Western Province were on their way to the title.

Northern Transvaal had earlier that year given Western Province a drubbing of note in a friendly at Newlands (27–5). They were firm favourites, and the result seemed a mere formality when the Springbok great Jannie Engelbrecht suffered a broken collarbone in the first half.

In the end, forced to stay on the field by his captain, Doug Hopwood, the man the Northerns fans regarded as injury-prone and not a real quality player, scored two outstanding tries despite the pain, as described in Chapter 3.

In 1968 it was decided that the Currie Cup would be contested every year, and that a final would determine the winner of the competition.

In 1969, Western Province had a close 13–11 semi-final win at Newlands against neighbours Boland under the captaincy of Springbok captain and former Western Province skipper Dawie de Villiers. That set them up for their final against Northern Transvaal in Pretoria. This was the day when the great Frik du Preez demonstrated his versatility when he dropped a huge penalty goal, placed a penalty goal and scored a try to deny Western Province (28–14).

In 1970 Griquas beat Western Province and won all their other Currie Cup fixtures while Northern Transvaal eventually lost the final in Kimberley against Griquas 11–9.

In 1971 Western Province were in the throes of an administrative refinement of their systems to ensure that players of better quality and with greater skills progressed from the club system to the provincial sides.

Coach John Gainsford was happy with what had been achieved 'with the available talent'. Western Province easily won their 1972 Currie Cup matches against the weaker sides in their section: SWD (76–0, a Currie Cup record), Griquas (30–10), South West Africa (51–6), Western Transvaal (19–10) and NW Cape (63–12) were beaten. However, Province lost the matches that mattered against Transvaal at Ellis Park (21–9) and Free State in Bloemfontein (33–6). They ended third in their section because of those two defeats and were out of Currie Cup contention.

Schalk and Schalk Burger, one of the ten sets of fathers and sons that represented South Africa at rugby. Schalk Jnr was also an outstanding cricketer at school. Both played for Western Province.

In 1973 the rebuilding of the provincial side started showing dividends. In the ridiculous four-section Currie Cup competition of that particular year, each of the five sides in a section had to play four matches.

Western Province beat NW Cape 38–10, accounted for Transvaal 18–7 (both matches were at Newlands) and beat Western Transvaal and Far North away.

They also convincingly beat Northern Transvaal in a friendly at Newlands.

In the Cape it was hoped that it would be Western Province's year, but then Free State – and Western Province's own ineptitude – stood in their way.

Playing before their home crowd and in wet weather on a muddy field, everything was in Western Province's favour, but somehow they contrived to let this one get away as they played 'fancy' rugby on a day when a dour approach probably would have brought victory.

Instead it was Free State who played the dour rugby, and won 15–9, which earned them another crack at the Currie Cup. Once again Northern Transvaal would be their opponents in the final.

Looking back over the previous six to seven years, one of the major problems identified in the Western Province team was a lack of good, solid forwards who were prepared to do the donkey work.

In 1974 Dr Cecil Moss (who also assisted the Springbok side with coaching, although he was never appointed the national coach, as has become the norm after unification in 1992) started working on this aspect of Province's play, and there was a noticeable improvement during the season.

Once again an incomprehensible system for the Currie

THE ENFORCER WHO TOOK WP TO THE TOP

Over the years there have been many stories (some better left untold) of funny moments on and off rugby fields.

One of the characters of the 1950s was former Western Province captain and Springbok lock, Jan Pickard. He was involved in many an incident on and off the field, and provided as much amusement to his supporters as he did indignation to opponents and their supporters.

One of his favourite tricks was to pick an opponent who was on top of his game in a particular match and to put the referee onto him. So it was when Western Province were playing Natal, and big lock Lappies Labuschagne (unlucky never to play for the Springboks) proved a real thorn in the collective Western Province side.

When a little flare-up occurred during the match, Pickard instructed his scrumhalf, Aubrey Luck, to drop to the ground.

When Luck did so, Pickard called to the referee: 'Mr Ref, look what Labuschagne has done to our scrumhalf!'

On another occasion, when Province were playing Border, Pickard's Province team were given a lesson by a Border strongman.

Pulling his head out of the scrum, Pickard addressed the ref: 'Please talk to Edwards. He's not fit and he's spoiling the scrums.'

Pickard wasn't the only player in the side to try to influence referees. Doc Craven described him as a 'great footballer' in his book on Matie Springboks.

'Of that there can be little doubt, and that he played some outstanding games cannot be denied. However, he probably did not reach the heights he should have. He had so much potential,' wrote Craven.

'What I can say without hesitation is that he was an outstanding captain. Not only will his teams do well, but Pickard always set an example for his teammates.

'I think his success in business points to him being firstly an individual. Perhaps that was our mistake, as coaches and selectors, that we did not give him enough freedom. I am convinced with more responsibilities he would have reached greater heights.

'However, he will live in South African rugby history long after players who were preferred to him are forgotten.'

In the pre-tour pen sketches of the players for the 1956 Springbok tour to Australia and New Zealand he was described as a 'bullocking player with amazing strength.'

Just prior to that tour, Pickard was involved in an altercation with the appointed captain for the tour, Salty du Rand, which cost the latter the tour captaincy.

Both the locks made their mark for Western Province and South Africa after receiving their grounding at Stellenbosch University under Doc Craven and Oubaas Markötter. Du Rand played his first test against the 1949 All Blacks of Fred Allen. By then he had moved to Rhodesia, and became the first Springbok from the neighbouring country to play Currie Cup rugby in those years (with their players being eligible for Springbok selection).

Pickard made his test debut against the 1953 Wallabies after (like Du Rand) touring the British Isles and France in 1951–1952 without playing in any of the tests.

His fitness, which was often not of the desired standard; his image as an enforcer, which today would probably have seen him off the field as much as on it; and his penchant for standing in the backline, were 'weaknesses' held against him by many a selector.

Pickard was an established businessman, even before he went on the 1956 tour to Australasia as a 29-year-old. He played only four test matches in three series; but those first years as a businessman saw him grow his own business to eventually control no fewer than 13 listed companies on the JSE.

Pickard's liquor companies were the foundation of his empire; Sportsman's Warehouse comes from his stable; and Comair, Rennies and KIC were others in which his influence was noticeable.

As president of the Western Province Rugby Union from 1981, he turned around Western Province's average performances since 1936, leading his executive and the provincial team to a record five consecutive Currie Cup final wins from 1982 to 1986. Before Pickard succeeded Hannes Pretorius, Western Province had won only two finals and shared one, out of the 19 times from 1939 that the Currie Cup was contested in a final. Their three other successes in that time came in 1954,

WP president Jan Pickard with the Currie Cup and the Percy Frames Trophy won by Western province in 1982.

1957–59 and 1964, when there were no finals to decide the Currie Cup titles – a total of six titles (one shared) in 22 competitions.

Pickard was also, in no small way, behind the resurrection of the ageing Newlands into a modern stadium, which he ran like a business.

His grandson François Louw, flank of the Stormers and Western Province, was capped for the Springboks in 2010.

Cup was used. The A Section of seven teams played six matches against the C Section that had six teams, while the B Section (seven teams) played six matches against one another.

Western Province finished second in the C Section after losing to the only real quality side in the A Section, Transvaal (36–22), at Ellis Park after an earlier win in a friendly at Newlands. Transvaal went out to play in the final against Northern Transvaal.

The steady improvement in Western Province's rugby manifested itself in 1976 when they advanced to the Currie Cup final in Bloemfontein.

However, Western Province that day in 1976 found a Free State side more determined than ever awaiting them at Free State Stadium. Free State had lost their second final the previous year when Pierre Spies' famous try for Northern Transvaal denied them 12–6.

Free State were rampant, and beat Western Province 33–16 – at that point the biggest loss suffered in a Currie Cup match, beating the 15-point margin recorded when Northern Transvaal triumphed over Province 28–13 in 1969.

Western Province had advanced to the final despite an unlikely loss against Western Transvaal (22–17) at Potchefstroom and also against Transvaal at Ellis Park (30–16). The Free State's two defeats in the other half of the cross-section competition came against their opponents in the final. Western Province beat them twice: 21–12 in Bloemfontein and 21–7 at Newlands.

The great Springbok captain Morné du Plessis captained Western Province in that 1976 final and again in the 1979 final.

But first there was 1977, another year of so-near-yet-so-far for Western Province when they lost only two matches: against Rhodesia in Salisbury, now Harare (18–9), and Northern Transvaal (15–13 at Loftus). In the first round Western Province had beaten Northerns 16–14. With two sections of five teams each, Province ended with eight wins from 10 matches in the double round of cross-section matches, but Free State (yes, Free State again!) had denied them by beating Rhodesia and losing only to Northern Transvaal. Once again it was Northern Transvaal and the Free State in the final.

Dawie Snyman, an outstanding Springbok and the only man to have coached a side to five successive Currie Cup titles.

SNYMAN COACHES WP TO A RECORD FIVE

Dawie Snyman is one of a few players who was selected for South Africa before playing provincial rugby. He was also one of South Africa's most successful Currie Cup coaches. The former Grey College scholar was selected for Hannes Marais' 'Invincibles' to Australia in 1971, after making his debut for the Maties as a 19-year-old.

Injuries curtailed his career and in the end forced him into retirement, but before that, he had played rugby that caused his mentor Doc Craven to say of him: 'He is so gifted that he didn't know how much effort to put into his play.'

In fact, Craven had such a high regard for the Matie who came to him as an under-19 player that he had earmarked Snyman as his successor as coach at Stellenbosch. 'In fact, I think he can take it further,' wrote Doc in his book *Die groot rugbygesin van die Maties*.

And, as so often with so many things, Doc Craven was right in this instance as well. Snyman coached Western Province to a record five successive Currie Cup titles won in finals. That equalled the record of five successive titles in the last decade of the 19th century which were won in league competitions at tournaments. Those titles weren't in successive years, however, nor in finals, and the achievement by Snyman and Province from 1982 to 1986 was therefore a second Currie Cup record for Western Province.

Dawie Snyman became the youngest coach of a winning side in a Currie Cup final. He was only 33 years, 89 days old when Province beat Northern Transvaal in 1982. Rassie Erasmus became the youngest successful final coach 23 years later, at 32 years, 351 days, when Free State beat the Blue Bulls in 2005.

Snyman also had a stint as coach of Transvaal, after Louis Luyt's initial success in buying players to win the Currie Cup petered out, with no succession planning done once the players retired or moved.

Snyman coached the Lions in 1997 and 1998, but when he didn't bring home the goods, he followed the same path as a large number of other unsuccessful coaches of the Luyt era.

At the time of Snyman's appointment there was talk that Luyt had earmarked him as the man to take over as national coach from Carel du Plessis. Whether it was true became irrelevant when he was fired as Lions coach.

Snyman played in ten test matches and 12 tour matches. His elder brother Jackie was also a Springbok and played in three tests. They played together in only one test, the second test against the British Lions at Loftus Versfeld in 1974, when Dawie came on as a replacement.

He made his debut against England in 1972 in the test lost 18–9 by the Springboks at Ellis Park.

Dawie Snyman's brilliance as rugby player was probably suppressed by his versatility that saw him play at flyhalf and fullback.

The 1977 season will be remembered in the Cape for the controversial decision by test match referee Ian Gourlay of Natal to penalise Province captain Morné du Plessis for a tackle on Naas Botha, the young Northern Transvaal flyhalf, which he judged to be dangerous. Botha slotted the penalty, and Northerns won 15–13. A win in that match at Loftus would have made a season's difference to Western Province.

However, the season had seen the best rugby in many years from Western Province and the future looked rosy. They had a largely new team, and Du Plessis' captaincy played a big part in their top performances that saw the side also do well in their friendlies.

Free State beat Western Province twice in the 1978 Currie Cup competition on their way to a third successive final. First Province lost 21–16 at home and then got a 43–15 hiding in Bloemfontein.

Their forwards had improved, but back play, and especially their defence, were problems, and once again the union looked at the club system as a reason for the downward curve.

After two years as captain/coach Morné du Plessis decided that he couldn't handle the two jobs in tandem and Dr Apies du Toit from Maties was appointed Province coach for 1979.

At last, they sighed in Cape Town and surrounds when Western Province made it through to a Newlands final for the first time since 1954. It was also only the third final Province would contest since their loss to Northern Transvaal in 1954.

Northern Transvaal's experienced captain Thys Lourens had to cry off before the 1979 final because of a shoulder injury and Daan du Plessis, who was to become a Springbok prop the next year, took over the captaincy in his sixth Currie Cup final.

Northerns had gone through to the final after a hard slog in wind and rain against Eastern Province, while Western Province had come from 15–3 behind at the break against Griquas for the honour of playing the Currie Cup final which took place at Newlands.

In that final Northern Transvaal dominated the lineouts with Theuns Stofberg and Louis Moolman at lock, while the struggle for the loose ball was even. Western Province were nevertheless in the lead until literally the last move of the match.

The ball came Northern Transvaal's way from the Railway Stand on the west side of the stadium. Time was up and Province were leading 15–12 when Naas Botha decided to drop. It was over, and Botha, not for the last time in a final, had scored all his side's points with three penalties and two drop goals, while Province had the satisfaction of a Peter Whipp try.

In 1980, it was the turn of Western Province captain Morné du Plessis to withdraw before the final and Hennie Bekker captained the side in the final at Loftus. It was a season during which their rugby had varied between outstanding and poor, and which will be remembered for the death of their fullback Chris Burger after a serious neck injury.

Transvaal were beaten 37-0 in one of the highs; Northern Transvaal were the conquerors in their three clashes with the 39-9 drubbing in the final the lowest point of the playing season for Western Province.

Northern Transvaal and Free State contested the 1981 final as Province again lost outright at the end. Western Province lost a play-off to Free State 21–18, and Free State then beat Eastern Transvaal in the semi-final to meet Northerns in the final.

Divan Serfontein was the new captain, and he held the Currie Cup aloft in 1982 after a comprehensive defeat of Northern Transvaal at Newlands.

At last heeding the need for a tight five that worked hard in the loose, Western Province had a team that gradually started believing in themselves as they moved towards the title. With outstanding backs and a tight five who were all selected for the Springbok tour to New Zealand in 1981, the season was arguably Western Province's best yet.

One loss from 12 Currie Cup matches, including the semi-final and the final told the story of total dominance. This is underlined by their 52 Currie Cup tries against only 13 conceded, and 341 points against only 131.

Three brothers, the Du Plessis Springboks Willie, Carel and Michael, played in the final – the only time since finals were first played in 1939.

Western Province wing Carel du Plessis dots down for yet another try, this time against Transvaal.

With the 1982 title, Dawie Snyman became the youngest coach of a Currie Cup side to win the Currie Cup.

What Western Province and the rest of South Africa didn't realise was that this was the first of a new record of five successive wins in a Currie Cup final. Western Province had achieved this before, namely from 1892 to 1898, and again from 1925 to 1934 (of which two were shared with Border), but this was under the league system.

Northern Transvaal also won five consecutive titles (1977–1981), but had to share the 1979 Currie Cup with Province.

The manner in which Western Province won the 1983 Currie Cup title was almost as impressive as the previous year's performance as they moved relentlessly to the semi-final. They first had to play the second-placed team in the inferior B Section, namely Natal in Durban, before again accounting for Northern Transvaal in the final, this time at Loftus (9–3).

Western Province's points total and try tally were not

as impressive as in 1982, but Western Province coach Dawie Snyman pointed out that defending a trophy was probably more difficult than winning it.

The season was also notable for two things in particular: the Currie Cup win came in Western Province's centenary year, and Province won their first match at Loftus Versfeld since 1964.

If 1983 had been a successful year, 1984 was the best in history. Province scored 53 Currie Cup tries and conceded only seven; and their points breakdown in the competition was 361 for and only 124 against.

Coach Dawie Snyman's stated objective to get the players to play an adventurous type of rugby was also achieved.

Captain Divan Serfontein called it a day after the 1984 final after eight seasons with Western Province and three consecutive Currie Cup titles in his four years as captain since 1981.

In 1985, Theuns Stofberg took over the reins as captain, but it was Springbok prop Henning van Aswegen who was in charge in the final against unlikely opponents Natal.

The team from Durban, led by Wynand Claassen, defied all predictions and a lot of logic when they lost the play-off for promotion from the weaker B Section but then comprehensively beat Free State, the number two side of the A Section, to advance to the final at Newlands.

Western Province had to work hard for their 19–9 win after an early defeat to Free State and two close wins against Northern Transvaal. Yet they moved into top gear, winning the last four matches before the final by more than 50 points, and were overwhelming favourites to win the their third consecutive title.

It wasn't a good final and Province played one of their poorer matches of the season.

It was not a season of good rugby for Province, although they retained the Currie Cup for the fourth consecutive season. Many injuries to key players presented coach Dawie Snyman with what he later admitted was his most difficult season in charge.

Four matches were lost (to Northern Transvaal, Transvaal and the Free State) and Western Province ended second on the A Section log to Northern Transvaal. They met in the final at Newlands and Western Province's new-found belief that they were as good or better than Northerns manifested again as they won 22–15.

It was a tough final with little running rugby and too many handling errors. Western Province were worthy and deserving winners, with their forwards grinding Northern Transvaal down, especially in the rucks and mauls.

In the lineouts Northern Transvaal again dominated with Louis Moolman and Adolf Malan just too good for Hennie Bekker and Schalk Burger at lock. Province also fielded another Schalk Burger at no 8 in the final.

In a final only the final score is relevant, but the fact is that Province scored two tries through Hennie Bekker and Neil Burger, while Northerns again had to rely on Naas Botha's boot. He scored all 15 points through two drops and three penalties.

South Africa's most impressive and sustained Currie Cup golden era ended in 1986 with a 22–9 Western Province win over Transvaal at Newlands. It was a victory for running rugby over the conservative pattern employed by Transvaal.

Dawie Snyman, who was persuaded to continue after retiring as coach the previous year, in 1986 again faced the challenge of bringing his side together following the tour by the New Zealand Cavaliers, which split the season into two halves.

Snyman also lost the services of eight internationals and three more of the previous season's stalwarts. That he was an outstanding coach is an undoubted fact. That he was never asked to coach at national level is unfathomable.

Western Province were not quite finished yet, though. In 1988 they lost the final by a single point at Loftus, 19–18.

Western Province had to play B Section winners Northern Free State in the semi-final, and after an impressive league phase, went into the final as favourites, especially as Northern Transvaal had a break of four weeks between their last league match and the final. Three penalties and two drop kicks, and an immaculate tactical kicking display by Northerns' Naas Botha, put paid to another Province title.

Chester Williams played in the 1995 World Cup final won by South Africa.

In 1989 Northern Transvaal were in command and minutes away from another Currie Cup title, and Western Province seemed certain to suffer their second defeat in a final at Newlands, when they were trailing the Light Blues 16–11 at Newlands.

Again, it was a Western Province wing, this time a left wing, that denied Northerns as Jannie Engelbrecht had in 1964.

Carel du Plessis, arguably the best left wing South Africa has produced, was the man who rounded off sustained pressure by Western Province when his brother Michael switched play from a ruck with a long pass to the left.

Carel cut through Northerns' defence to go over in the corner. The Currie Cup was at least shared. It was up to inexperienced Western Province flyhalf Riaan Gous to bring the Currie Cup back to Newlands.

His kick was good, but swerved at the very last moment to pass the right-hand upright – and the two great old foes shared the cup for the second time after Naas Botha's drop had saved his side in 1979.

In 1995 Western Province lost the final 25–17 in Durban against what were now the Natal Sharks, but made amends when they won in 2000. In between there was the final against their old nemesis, now known as the Free State Cheetahs, in 1997, won 14–12 by Western Province; and the near win against Northern Transvaal in 1998 when Chester Williams' last-gasp try was disallowed.

The 2000 final was won 25–15 by Western Province against the Natal Sharks in Durban.

The winners exploited the fact that the Sharks were on the rebound. They had lost icons such as Gary Teichmann, André Joubert and Henry Honiball, and other stalwarts like Shaun Payne, Steve Atherton and Adrian Garvey. Ian McIntosh had also finished as coach after nine years in this position.

In 2001, Western Province, after dispatching the other opposition in the Currie Cup, won their 12th final (two shared) and their 31st (four shared) Currie Cup title. They beat the Natal Sharks 29–24 at Newlands with Braam van Straaten equalling Naas Botha's 24 points in a final.

Western Province scrumhalf Bolla Conradie prepares to kick against the Lions.

Wildeklawer

CHAPTER 5

Griquas and others …

To some, the outstanding performance of Griquas in the 2009 Currie Cup competition might have come as a surprise. After all, Griquas weren't one of the so called 'Big Five'.

However, their track record over the years, since the inception of competitive rugby in South Africa, should have been a warning: never underestimate Griquas!

The role that Griqualand West played in the development of the game in South Africa can never be over-emphasised. After all, they have three Currie Cup titles to their credit, as well as two semi-finals, and they've won a number of Sport Pienaar and other national competition trophies over the years. Both Currie Cup semi-finals were played in Kimberley: Western Province won 20–15 at the De Beers Stadium in 1979, and repeated the dose at Hoffe Park in 1998 (27–11).

Along with Cape Town, Kimberley was the unofficial headquarters of South Africa, and according to available records, the first inter-town match in South African rugby was played when Kimberley travelled to Bloemfontein on 22 July 1881. The match was played on the grounds of the Bloemfontein Cricket Club, approximately where the Shimlas now have their fields, and was won by Kimberley, who scored five tries and kicked a drop goal.

Matches against Beaconsfield kept the Kimberley team in shape, and in 1884 the diamond fields team accepted an invitation from Western Province to come to Cape Town for a tour of seven matches. The 24-man team travelled by mule-wagon to De Aar, where they arrived 60 hours later. From there they would proceed by train.

The following morning the team's first training run was attended by just about every soul in De Aar. Then followed another day by train to Cape Town, which

Bjorn Basson, prolific Currie Cup try scorer and Griquas' newest Springbok in 2010, has help on hand as he is tackled by the Blue Bulls' Wynand Olivier.

The Griquas team that won their first Currie Cup in 1899 at the tournament in Kimberley.

gave them the remainder of that Wednesday and the Thursday morning to relax or train for the match on Thursday 7 August 1884. The opposition was picked from the civil servant players in the region.

Two days later, the Kimberley side was beaten by Villagers before a huge crowd. Villagers' points consisted of a goal and a try (four points).

Matches against a combined side, Woodstock/Gardens, and a colleges side followed, and then came the main match of the tour: against Union on 16 August. This was the highlight of the tour, as Union was selected from 11 clubs.

Kimberley had to use reinforcements because of injuries sustained in their previous matches. In the end, they gave a good account of themselves before narrowly losing what was effectively the first provincial match in South Africa.

One more game, against the first winner of the Grand Challenge Trophy, Hamiltons, followed, with the oldest club in South Africa winning by a goal to a try (3–1).

Griquas were present at the first inter-district tournament, held during the Grahamstown Show of 1885. This time Port Elizabeth and Grahamstown joined Kimberley and Cape Town in the fun, and four sides contested the forerunner of the Currie Cup.

All the above was organised and happened before the formal establishment of the Griqualand West Rugby Football Union (GWRFU) on 6 February 1886 at the Central Hotel.

In the first final of Griquas' Grand Challenge Competition, the trophy was awarded to West End, despite complaints by the losers, Beaconsfield, to the GWRFU committee about the validity of the only try in the game. The committee ruled that the result should stand.

The final also brought South Africa's first known rugby death, after A Schlemmer of West End was tackled on his way to the tryline. He died in hospital a week after the match.

It was during the 1888 visit of Kimberley to Cape Town that Percy Ross Frames suggested that a national body be established to control rugby in the whole of South Africa, and that a regular competition between provincial sides should be instituted.

The SA Rugby Football Board was consequently formed in 1889 at the Craven Hotel in Kimberley, and

IT'S TOUGH AT THE BOTTOM!

The glamour of playing in a Currie Cup final belongs to only a few, and winning it to even fewer. The build-up, the expectation, the enthusiasm of supporters and talk in clubs, pubs and at work turn this competition's final into the special event that it is – probably the highlight of any rugby season. South Africa's in-bred provincialism sees to that!

Many unions have never had that privilege. Some, like Border and Boland, have come close. Some, like Natal, have been there and have stayed at or near the top, while others, like Griquas, have been there but have sunk back to relative obscurity, although they always present a threat to the more glamourous sides.

However, the Currie Cup belongs to more than those chosen few. It also belongs to the players in the B Section – and for many years before the B Section was devised, also to all the rugby players from what were, at one stage, 22 separate unions.

Natal, relegated in 1981 to the B Section of the Currie Cup, where they languished until 1986 (it took a Board decision to bring them back to the big time) found out just how difficult it was to play in the less glamorous lower half of the competition. They lost their first play-off for promotion to the A Section to Eastern Transvaal – last in the A Section – in Springs. Then Northern Free State proved too much for them. And so it went for five frustrating years.

New coach Koos Beukes, tasked with trying to and rescue Natal from ignominy, summed it up as reflected in Reg Sweet's book *Natal 100 – Centenary of Natal Rugby Union*: 'We will have to go flat-out to achieve the type of fitness it will require to stay on top of the pile in the B Section. It is the right type of fitness we will be needing most.'

Injuries were Beukes' main worry. Rugby in the B Section was tough and hard. It was simply another rugby world, and the refereeing was not what it should be or what the players were used to in the A Section.

The undisciplined approach of the B Section sides made it more difficult to play against them and plan for them than teams in the A Section, Beukes said, as they were more destructive in their play.

It was very much what the top teams had experienced in former years, when all the teams played in the same competition, with cross-section matches or leagues determining who would be in the play-offs.

The lesser unions would go all out to prove a point to their more illustrious opponents, and bets that Springboks in particular would finish without injury were not clever. Some of South Africa's greatest players have been on record that they would rather field a rolling ball against the might of Northern Transvaal than go down on a loose ball in, say, Kimberley, Springs or Upington.

Currie Cup war horses Thys Lourens of Northern Transvaal and North West Cape stalwart Herklaas Engelbrecht share a joke.

A case in point was the third-round Lion Cup match between South Eastern Transvaal and Western Province in Witbank in 1983. It was to become what was called the 'dream year' of Province rugby. They were defending their Currie Cup title and went on to win it that year, as well as for the next three, in a record run of five consecutive Currie Cup finals won.

Home side South Easterns were relegated to the B Section at the end of the previous season. They knew the aversion of A Section sides to playing on the hard Witbank field and wanted to use it to their advantage.

That they did. With Albie Kruger, a wily old fox, leading the way, South Easterns started watering the field the Sunday before the Lion Cup fixture against Western Province. In pursuing the hardest surface possible, they used a heavy roller that would have made cricket captains green with envy. It was as hard as concrete when Western Province took the field on 4 June, and the balls were pumped to near maximum.

Coming from softer grounds, with the cold and rare Highveld air and the yellow-brown surface awaiting them, the Western Province players were not too keen to compete with an abrasive and uncompromising side that boasted some hardy, and also some very good, players. Western Province lost 24-19 to South Easterns. Players from the home side relate with some glee how the ball would bounce nearly 20 metres after striking the hard ground from an up-and-under.

(South Eastern Transvaal lost their next game, the semi-final, against Free State in Bloemfontein 41-6. Free State went on to clinch the final against Transvaal 24-12 at Ellis Park).

The Border team that shared the Currie Cup with Western Province in 1932.

Percy Ross Frames became the first president by virtue of the agreement that the union where the meeting was held would appoint the chairman.

The new chairman proposed that a Board competition be held in the same year, and so it happened that Griquas, Western Province, Transvaal and Eastern Province contested the first provincial trophy in the country.

The first match was between Western Province and Eastern Province, and was played in Kimberley on 28 August 1889 – a little more than a month after the trials were held to select the Griquas side for the tournament.

The first of the many matches between Western Province and Griquas was played on the third day of the tournament and was won by Province (6–2). Although the two sides were tied at the top of the log, this result gave the first official trophy in South Africa to Western Province according to the rules of the tournament.

An interesting aside to the first Currie Cup in 1892 – also held in Kimberley – was that Transvaal challenged Griquas for the golden trophy that was handed over to Griquas in 1891 by Bill Maclagan's touring British side. Griquas were adjudged the best side that the British side had played against on their 20-match tour.

In the 1892 Currie Cup round-robin, a courageous Griquas side was denied by Western Province, who were regarded as runaway favourites. The score was 5–2, and the first Currie Cup title went to Western Province, who would retain it for the next five tournaments.

It was very close in 1894, however, and Province, who were under the cosh for most of the match, had to rely on a planned interception by Percy Jones that saw them regain the Currie Cup at Newlands by a close 8–6 win over Griquas.

The following year, Griquas were again beaten into second place by the 5–0 league defeat against Province, and 1897 was a repeat in the log standings.

By now, Griquas' strength and depth were dwindling and the team was not as good as in earlier years. Many players had migrated to the Witwatersrand in search of the riches there. Griquas lost to Transvaal (3–0) who, in turn, bowed out to Province by the same margin. For the fourth time in succession, Western Province were the holders of the Currie Cup.

Although the home of the Currie Cup in those days was determined by centralised tournaments at one venue, there was a slight deviation in 1898.

Rhodesia had entered the tournament that would again take place in Cape Town. To break the long trip from Bulawayo to Cape Town, they stopped over in Kimberley where they played their Currie Cup fixture. Griquas won 13–8 and the two teams travelled together to the tournament at Newlands.

Western Province took the honours again, and Griquas were second again – this time after a 38–3 drubbing from Province.

After five consecutive titles, and amid severe criticism from their press and fans, Western Province (like Transvaal) decided not to play in the 1899 Currie Cup tournament in Kimberley in 1899. The impending South African War was the reason given by the two absentees.

Rhodesia, and three sides from the Cape Colony, namely Griquas, Border and Eastern Province, were the only participants, and Griquas won at a canter despite a nil-all draw against Rhodesia.

It was the first time Griquas were the 'real' winners of the Currie Cup, but some of the gloss was taken off by the withdrawal of Province and Transvaal from the tournament.

After the war, the Currie Cup rivalry continued in 1904, with East London hosting the tournament. Western Province recovered the trophy after beating Griquas14–3. And so it was in 1906 and 1908, until Griquas turned the tables to take their second title.

Good performances in friendlies played in 1910 pointed to great deeds ahead, and so it turned out in 1911, when the tournament was played in Cape Town at Newlands and at Green Point.

Free State held Griquas to a draw and then the men from Kimberley beat Natal, North Easterns, Transvaal and ultimately Western Province to secure the trophy for the second time.

In context, it was just as impressive and important to Griquas rugby as the 1970 win against Northern Transvaal in Kimberley, when Griquas were again not given a snowball's chance to win.

In pouring rain, they beat Western Province 12–0; the first loss for Western Province in 46 matches which also included two draws.

It was the first time Province lost a Currie Cup tournament in which they had played. However, the single breakthrough for Griquas was just that: a solitary win. They followed it with a sequence of average and even poor placings in the next five tournaments. A slight resurgence saw them recover to third place in 1929, but then they faded and ended last of eight sides in 1934 and second from the bottom in 1936.

Griquas' next great performance, an unforgettable day in their history, came in 1970.

It followed a building process of eight years after the former Griquas Springbok Ian Kirkpatrick, who had played his final international rugby match the year before, returned to Kimberley from Bloemfontein. A year after retiring as player, he started the road to glory. The 1964 competition started off in the absence of a number of players who had either moved to other centres or had retired. Griquas lost their captain and other stalwarts to injury, and had to be content with the Sport Pienaar Trophy, contested by the second-placed teams in the five Currie Cup sections.

Kirkpatrick, one of South Africa's greatest coaches of all time, was the man behind the selection of his former Springbok team mate Mannetjies Roux for the side. Roux's presence was immediately felt, and the revenge sought year after year for the loss of their

Springbok and Griquas flank Piet van Deventer gets the ball away against Eastern Transvaal.

players to Transvaal was exacted in a 12–8 win over the Johannesburg side. Then Boland succumbed, and in the first final for the Sport Pienaar Trophy, Eastern Transvaal were beaten 18–9 in a match dominated by Griquas.

In 1966, Griquas drew with eventual Currie Cup champions Western Province, but achieved little more in the competition, and in 1968 (the first year of what would now become an annual competition for the Currie Cup) Griquas again won the Sport Pienaar Trophy. By then Piet Visagie, who had become a Springbok against the French in 1967, was a difficult customer, both with his general play and as an exceptional kicker. In the Sport Pienaar final against Boland, Visagie played against his Bok halfback partner and national captain Dawie de Villiers. Griquas won the match 22–9.

In 1969, in another strange competition structure, Griquas were beaten in a 'revenge' game by Boland (13–0) and eliminated from a semi-final play-off against Western Province. That relegated them to the Sport Pienaar competition, and they won the competition for the third time when they beat Natal 16–3 in Kimberley.

Griquas were not yet one of South Africa's top sides. They threatened and they won, but not with the sort of consistency needed to make them a feared side. Nonetheless opponents were wary of them, of that there was little doubt.

The harder you work, the better your luck, or something to that effect.

Close and sometimes fortuitous wins helped Griquas through the year in 1970. First, they scraped through against Natal at Kings Park in Durban; East London was the venue of their 15–11 squeaker against Border; North Western Cape and North Eastern Cape were easy prey.

They were on track for the Currie Cup, and if they didn't always look convincing, their win against Western Province in Kimberley made the critics really sit up and take notice. The score was 22–18, and a 43–16 win against Eastern Transvaal reinforced that Kimberley was not a friendly city!

To add to Griquas' earlier bits of fortune, Transvaal drew with Natal. A Transvaal win would have meant a play-off match for the Kimberley side.

To retain their sharpness and work on teamwork, in the years when distance made training more than once a week a luxury, Griquas played Free State in a friendly. The positives of the match were overshadowed by the fact that Mannetjies Roux, the heartbeat of the side and the kingpin on whom their slim hopes as rank outsiders rested, was injured in the friendly.

Griquas centre Koos Waldeck on the break against Natal.

Springbok and Griquas flyhalf Piet Visage was a prolific points scorer for both the national and provincial teams.

One of the un luckiest men ever to be denied Springbok colours was scrumhalf Gert Schutte, in action here Griquas.

A record Currie Cup final win was predicted for Northern Transvaal for that big day in Griquas' Currie Cup history, namely 26 September 1970.

Roux was declared fit. It was his 44th match for the union where he had grown up, but represented only late in his rugby life. It was also his 25th match as captain of the side.

On the Northern Transvaal side captain, Piet Uys, had also come to the end of his rugby road. The Light Blues admitted afterwards that they were perhaps a little overconfident. Also that the best team had won. They were also uncomplaining about the 53-yarder that the Griquas no 8, Peet Smit, lofted through the uprights four minutes before full time.

Griquas' referee Ben Calitz was the man in the middle, in the days when the home side still provided three referees from whom the visitors could pick their man, but there were no complaints from Northerns on the issue of the referee.

Frik du Preez, according to Johan Volschenk's *Die Ligbloues*, had said to his old friend and room-mate Mof Myburgh, just hours before the match: 'This is not how one feels before a Cup final.' There was a looseness, a lack of focus, noticeable among the Northerns players.

Brothers Peet and Tos Smith both played for Griquas in the 1970 Currie Cup final win against Northern Transvaal, and Peet slotted the winning penalty.

Griquas led for most of the match, but it seemed unreal to the 16 000 or so spectators who had packed the De Beers Stadium. They knew that the might of Northern

MANNETJIES – GENIUS WITH THE VALUABLE AUTOGRAPH!

It's no wonder that a young collector of autographs once asked one of South Africa's former state presidents to sign his name five times; he wanted to trade it for one of Mannetjies Roux!

That is one of the lovely stories about Mannetjies Roux, one of South Africa's greatest of all time, and a spectator favourite through the years of Springbok and Currie Cup rugby.

Former sports commentator Jan Snyman was the author of a biography of Roux, which he named *Groete van Mannetjies Roux*. Herman le Roux wrote the following about the book:

'Just as Dr Danie was my rugby personality of the previous century; Frik du Preez was nominated as the player of the century; and Naas Botha was undoubtedly the greatest points scorer in the Springbok jersey, I will remember Roux as the player who most captured the imagination of fans.

'I was privileged in my career of more than 40 years as a sports journalist to report on 23 of Roux's 27 test matches. He had pace, a staggering swerve, and he could, like no other player, pick up the ball from the ground with one hand.

'But above all it was his flair and unpredictability that made him one of the best attacking players of his time.

'His solid, fearless defence should however not be forgotten. That played as big a role as the gaps he took or created for his fellow backline players.'

When the name of Mannetjies Roux is mentioned, writes Le Roux, one remembers the young Matie who played for the Junior Springboks after only one match for Western Province, and made his test debut after only two provincial matches; his memorable try for the Springboks in the fourth test against the 1962 British Lions in Bloemfontein, when he left defenders groping fresh air as he weaved through from his own half to finish off with an acrobatic dive; and Roux's great contribution to the surprising Currie Cup final win of Griquas over Northern Transvaal in Kimberley in 1970.

In that same year, Roux was a stalwart in the Springbok side that won the test series against the All Blacks in South Africa. Roux represented South Africa as a wing and centre in 27 tests between 1960 and 1970.

In 1962, Roux made headlines with a tackle on the brilliant British Lions flyhalf Richard Sharp, whose cheekbone was fractured in the match against Northern Transvaal at Loftus. The tourists' manager, Commander Brian Vaughan, accused Roux of dangerous play.

Dr Craven described Roux as a rugby genius, and said a player of his quality can be forgiven for squandering tries because he will also score tries no other player could: 'With Mannetjies in your team, you can take on the world.'

Craven also had high praise for Roux's captaincy in Griquas' Currie Cup win over Northern Transvaal.

'Mannetjies, more than anyone else, was responsible for a relatively small union like Griquas winning the Currie Cup from defending champions Northern Transvaal,' Craven said.

Roux, a sheep farmer on the farm Noblesfontein near Victoria West, had to make an 800-kilometre return trip

Transvaal would deny them. After all, they had done it so often before against other sides, when they came back from the dead!

Mannetjies Roux's involvement with Griquas had done wonders for the team's confidence, strategy and experience level, and he also acted as a sort of decoy. Opposition teams would concentrate on him and forget about the other good Griquas backs.

Two great breaks by the home side's centre Koos Waldeck, and scrumhalf Joggie Viljoen – who became a Springbok the next year – put Buddy Schwartz through for two unconverted tries in only his second match for Griquas. After the first 30 minutes, Griquas were 8–0 to the good. Waldeck had broken through on the halfway line and the ball went to his captain, Roux, who sent Schwartz over.

Up front, the home side were under tremendous pressure throughout, although the efforts of their pack, in their quest to keep the Light Blues at bay, played a huge part in the victory. Springbok Piet Visagie turned the visitors around with smart tactical play and pin-point kicks, but the crowd remained a little disbelieving as half-time arrived with Griquas 8–3 ahead.

Northern Transvaal reverted to their proven tactic of

Mannetjies Roux, Griquas Currie Cup hero and also a Springbok legend.

to Kimberley to play for Griquas. He caught the train from Biesiespoort station late on Thursday evening to attend the team practice on the Friday afternoon, before the home match the following day in Kimberley.

For away matches, the sacrifice was, of course, even bigger.

François Du Toit Roux was born at Victoria West on 12 April 1939. He attended the Somerset West Primary School and Paarl Boys High, and then played centre and wing for the Maties under-19s. He became an air force pilot after finishing his university studies, and subsequently a Harvard instructor. He became a legend during his career.

Roux made his debut in Wales in 1960 as a wing, and was moved from centre to wing for a number of his 27 tests. Doc Craven, however, was adamant: Mannetjies Roux must play at centre. At one stage he said: 'We have weakened our Springbok sides by playing Mannetjies on the wing.'

The nickname Mannetjies is probably derived from his youth when the rough little fellow played on the farmhouse stoep, which was fairly high from the ground. He was often warned by the housekeeper: 'Mannetjie (little man), beware that you don't fall off!' The Mannetjie, over time, probably had the 's' added to make it Mannetjies, and that is what he became famous as, and is still called.

Roux has donated much of the memorabilia he gathered in his playing days to charity. In his lounge he still displays the ball used in the 1970 Currie Cup final. In contrast, he no longer has the ball that found the target when he aimed it at a demonstrator in Coventry on the 1969/1970 Springbok 'demo' tour to the British Isles! He does, however, still have the shoe that found the backside of another demonstrator that interfered with play on that tour.

And that autograph of his is still as valuable as in the years when it was traded for five autographs from a State President.

driving up-field, and Griquas were under the cosh and against the wind after half-time. Northern Transvaal wing Chris Luther slotted his second penalty, and then a charging try by Frik du Preez made the nightmares come true for the home crowd. Their team was 9–8 behind, and the Light Blues were in command.

Until four minutes from time, when a penalty was awarded and Roux called up his veteran no 8, Peet Smith. It was now or never, and it was against the wind. The kick was struck beautifully, and flew as straight as an arrow. 'I just hoped; prayed that it would have the length,' hero of the moment Smith said afterwards, and added he was confident of success as he had kicked longer penalties in his time.

Big men cried when the final whistle went. In the changing room there were also tears in the eyes of Griquas' captain Mannetjies Roux and other Griquas players as their achievement began to sink in.

Long after the final whistle, Griquas supporters were still milling about in front of the main stand, and their chants of 'we want Mannetjies, we want Mannetjies' were eventually answered when the famous Springbok came to the balcony clad only in his shorts.

Ian Kirkpatrick (who as coach at Griquas in the 1970s

Johan Claassen Western Transvaal's pride and a Springbok captain and selector.

Former Griquas and Springbok coach Dawie Theron is now the Griquas head coach.

also played a major part in realising Doc Craven's vision of discovering and developing black players, and later became a coaching icon at Doc's beloved Stellenbosch) must be lauded for what he did with a team regarded as no-hopers. He worked with them for only 10 or 12 training sessions in a year, when many of them would travel hundreds of kilometres to play their Currie Cup matches. The training was done on Friday nights, the only session since the match before.

Kirkpatrick admits that the win was the culmination of a golden period in Griquas rugby, if only for the fact that the union retained the services of many of its stalwarts, unlike previous years when many would move to other centres for more lucrative job offers in days when direct payment of players was not allowed.

Kirkpatrick held trials annually. Clubs nominated players to attend the trials, and this policy of inviting all newcomers ensured that nobody worth his salt would fall through the net.

The winning of the Currie Cup brought with it a certain amount of prestige. Kirkpatrick later admitted that they were not aware of how important that Currie Cup title was. Perhaps this was was just as well, as it kept the players relatively calm before the match.

A mere five years later, Griquas were back in the Sport Pienaar competition. The best players, as in the years gone by, had been lured away to greener pastures, and the pressure to keep their place in the Currie Cup series took its toll.

Kirkpatrick resigned in 1972 after an unhappy relationship with the selectors over the selection of the provincial side came to a head. He returned as coach, but left Kimberley in 1973.

Piet Visagie took over the coaching in 1973, but was replaced by former Springbok hooker Charlie Cockrell. This brought a measure of stability to the team's performances, and the rebuilding had started.

In the mid- to late 1970s, however, Griquas found that regaining one's place in the elite competition was no easy matter, a reality that also confronted Natal a few years later. In 1979, however, Griquas were back in the Currie Cup competition after beating Eastern Transvaal 34–10 in the promotion-relegation match.

Skip Henderson of Eastern Transvaal wins the lineout battle against Transvaal. He captained the Red Devils in the 1972 Currie Cup final.

In 1979 Griquas headed the B Section log in the Currie Cup competition, and in so doing earned the right to play the second-placed team in the A Section, Western Province, in the Currie Cup semi-final. The match was played in Kimberley and Griquas were 15–3 ahead at the break. They eventually lost to a star-laden side with loads of experience, as Western Province scored 17 points in the second half to win 20–15.

There was another semi-final and some shocks in the years to follow.

The highlight of 1970, to a large degree (but unfairly so) overshadows the performances of the 1998 team under André Markgraaff. This was probably Griquas' best year yet, and it showed up in the 1998 numbers:

Biggest Curie Cup win: 87–14 v Border
Highest Currie Cup score: v Border: 87
Most tries in a Currie Cup match: 4: Jearus Nicholas, v North-West (tied with Dave Prins, v Eastern Province in 1978)
Most conversions in a Currie Cup match: 11: Boeta Wessels v Border
Most team points: 1 428 (32 matches)
Most team points Currie Cup: 489 (14 matches)
Most points by a player: 361, Gaffie du Toit
Most team tries: 210 (32 matches)
Most team tries by a player: 24, Robert Markham
Most Currie Cup tries: 11, Robert Markham
Most conversions by a player: 98, Gaffie du Toit
Most drop goals by a player: 7, Gaffie du Toit

Players who played in that era also set a number of career records. Edrich Lubbe, who played for the Springboks against the 1997 Lions the previous season, scored 719 points for Griquas between 1995 and 2001; Jearus Nicholas scored 61 tries (1998–2002), and Lubbe slotted 133 conversions and 91 penalties in his Griquas career.

Griquas won the Vodacom Cup in 1998, 2005, 2007 and 2009.

The expected high of 1999 didn't materialise. Coach André Markgraaff had been called up to do the coaching duties at the Cats. Griquas were good, but not as great as expected after the heights and promise of the

Jonathan Mokuena, who captained Griquas in 2009 when they topped the Currie Cup log at the end of the first round. Mokuena is a former Springbok sevens captain.

previous year, when they won the Vodacom Cup for the first time.

Always good and always dangerous but not quite good enough was the tag Griquas carried around with them until 2009 when the team, now coached by former Springbok prop Dawie Theron, who had taken over as head coach in 2006, showed what can be done without the huge budgets of the more glamorous unions.

Kobus van der Merwe left for Western Province midway through 2005, and his successor at Griquas, Gysie Pienaar, lasted less than a year.

Before that, there were the odd surprise Currie Cup wins for Griquas, notably the 26–18 win over the Blue Bulls in 2007 in Kimberley, and the 21–20 win over Western Province in 2008 and 33–22 in 2009, both in Kimberley.

Under Theron, the team added their third and fourth Vodacom Cups, but, more importantly, did the union proud with their success at Currie Cup level in 2009. They led after the first round and missed out on a semi-final because of a lack of depth as the top unions' Springboks returned from Tri-Nations action.

Too many of the Griquas players had played too many matches through the season. After five wins from their first five Currie Cup matches, they counted the scalps of franchise unions Free State Cheetahs and Xerox Lions (both away), and Western Province at home. They lost by a single point to the eventual champions, the Blue Bulls, in Kimberley, after a last-gasp try denied them, and ended the season as a proud side that could stand with the best Griquas had yet produced. Points differential eventually denied them a place in the semi-final.

As in 1998, when Markgraaff had nearly taken Griquas to the top, Springbok colours were the reward for a number of the players of 2009 who did so well under the leadership of former Springbok Sevens captain Jonathan Mokuena.

There were glimpses of promise from the smaller (or should one say less affluent?) unions who made it to the semi-finals. Of course, there were also unexpected wins in league matches, but these were few and far between.

In 1969, Western Province sneaked in by a single conversion at Newlands, when they beat Boland in the semi-final for the right to play Northern Transvaal at Loftus for the title. Five years later, Transvaal were far too good for Eastern Province at Ellis Park and won the semi-final 30–6, but lost the final to Northern Transvaal at Loftus 17–15. In 1979, Eastern Province played Northern Transvaal in Port Elizabeth. Always a difficult side at home, EP lost the semi-final 16–6.

Northerns trounced South Eastern Transvaal 49–6 in a Loftus semi-final, and Western Province beat Eastern Province in Port Elizabeth (21–13) in 1980. The score was 36–12 to Northern Transvaal when they beat Northern Free State 36–12 in Pretoria in 1981. However, the Light Blues were run close by the Purple People Eaters, as Northern Free State took them to 24–21 in Welkom the next year, but they won convincingly enough in 1983 (32–15) at Loftus.

Eastern Transvaal lost 28–15 to the Free State in 1981, and the difference between the A Section and the B Section was shown up in Eastern Transvaal's 53–0 loss to Province at Newlands in 1984. However, on the same day, Natal showed the other side of the coin by beating the A Section's second best Free State 26–15 in Durban.

Western Province beat the Northern Free State 26–9 in 1988 and trounced Western Transvaal 71–9 the following year to secure the Currie Cup final berth against Northern Transvaal (on both occasions).

With the exception of the Boland semi-final against Province in 1979, the above play-offs were mostly not merit semis, but based on the contrived Currie Cup system in place for a particular year. This was an attempt to appease all unions, by pretending that they could all win the golden cup. Ironically, Natal, in the B Section and outplayed in the promotion-relegation match against Northern Free State, nearly did win the Cup in 1984! But that is another story.

It is interesting to note that Rhodesia, in a 'merit' semi-final in 1973, went down to Northern Transvaal at Loftus Versfeld. The year before, Rhodesia had been one of the four sides tied at the top of the Currie Cup A Section, but lost the play-off. Eastern Transvaal eventually went through to the final against Transvaal.

GILBERT
GWK

CHAPTER 6

Transvaal

Many people criticise Transvaal and the Golden Lions for being the underachievers of South African rugby, and the results over the years – only nine Currie Cup titles in their 122 years as a union – would seem to support this statement. Yet that is only a perception, not the whole truth.

Transvaal won their first Currie Cup final when they beat Western Province in 1939. That was their second title, and since then they have drunk from the golden cup on a further seven occasions.

These moments of glory, however, were few and far between, and the Currie Cup titles were mostly interspersed with barren years in between. So it was in 1922 when they won their first Currie Cup after 30 years of participation in the league format (but only 13 tournaments). It took them a further 17 years before that 1939 win (with only six further competitions in this period).

Then, in 1950, Transvaal beat Western Province in the final, and two years later accounted for Boland, thanks to a late drop goal. Another long wait of 19 years followed until they shared the Currie Cup with Northern Transvaal under bizarre circumstances in 1971. They were, however, not to be denied the following year against Eastern Transvaal. Almost predictably, the drought struck again, with the next title only coming in 1993. Transvaal repeated the feat the next year and also won the Currie Cup in 1999, in what was undoubtedly a golden era for Transvaal and the Lions.

However, only nine titles in 122 years do not tell full the story of a proud and nearly always strong side. There were also many close shaves in finals, a number of heartbreaking losses in semi-finals and a record score in a Currie Cup final. Furthermore Transvaal and the Lions have never been regarded as easy opponents

Two of the standout Lions players in recent years were loose forwards Cobus (Baywatch) Grobbelaar and Wikus van Heerden who is the ball carrier in the photo.

Former Transvaal and Junior Springbok captain Pa Pelser, one of many Transvaal and Lions coaches fired by Louis Luyt.

Luyt, right, is in discussion with coach Harry Viljoen who later became Springbok coach.

to milk for points on the Currie Cup log, not even in their lean years.

The Currie Cup win that president Louis Luyt so dearly wanted, materialised after a concerted effort which was well planned and well executed, namely to acquire top players from all over South Africa, and especially neighbours Northern Transvaal.

With the help of these players, the Currie Cup was won, even though a procession of coaches brought about a lack of stability.

It isn't far-fetched to say that in the years under Luyt a lack of forward planning displayed a short-sightedness that was largely responsible for the problems the Lions have experienced over the last years.

Although he didn't have the privilege of hoisting aloft the Currie Cup, Jannie Breedt is the man who set Transvaal and later the Lions on the march, winning the Lion Cup and leading the side in four Currie Cup finals.

However, Luyt and the Transvaal supporters had to wait for the new era after unification to see the Currie Cup drought of 22 years broken in 1993, after Breedt's leadership took Transvaal to finals in 1986, 1987, 1991 and 1992. The Currie Cup win in 1993 came nine years after Luyt had taken office and was achieved under the captaincy of François Pienaar.

In Luyt's 15 years at the helm, Pa Pelser, Apies du Toit, Derek Minnie, Ray Mordt, Kitch Christie, New Zealanders Alex Wylie and Laurie Mains, Dawie Snyman, Koos Ehlers, Hugo van As and Harry Viljoen, plus their many assistants, were among the coaches appointed and rejected by a man who wasn't prepared to give any of them a real chance to build a team.

The logical consequence was confusion among the players who constantly had to adapt to a new coach's methods and preferences in regard to players. It couldn't have benefited the coaches either!

Success eventually came after a near-super team was built, with Northern Transvaal's best as its nucleus. With them from across the Jukskei came coach Kitch Christie and his assistant Ray Mordt.

By then Breedt was no longer part of the Transvaal team – a travesty for this gentleman player who led by example and tried his best to lead his Transvaal teams to success in each of the 102 matches in which he

Coaches Ray Mordt, left, and Kitch Christie were lured over from Northern Transvaal and won the Currie Cup for Transvaal in 1993.

captained them over a period of seven years. However, he had laid the platform.

The 1993 Lions 21–15 win was achieved at Kings Park and it was Transvaal's third successive final. Natal dominated the first half despite playing against a strong wind, and Transvaal's fitness and the tactics they employed to neutralise the Natal strengths ultimately brought them victory in a match the home side could, and probably should, have won.

Wahl Bartmann, who was so influential for Natal in their first Currie Cup win in 1990 and again in 1992 when they repeated the feat, was given no opportunity to get his – and Natal's – drives going. With fine planning Christie and Mordt also neutralised the weight advantage of prop Guy Kebble by continually swapping the Transvaal props around.

Ultimately it was probably the greater fitness of Transvaal, who dominated only the lineouts up front, that kept them in the game. Transvaal nevertheless scored the only two tries in that final. The first came when Gavin Johnson picked up a loose ball, shrugged off Pieter Muller and went over with driving assistance from Rudolf Straeuli. Uli Schmidt, who was playing in his seventh Currie Cup final, scored his first try in a final after following up and exploiting a handling error from Natal wing Cabous van der Westhuizen. Transvaal's other points came from three penalties and a conversion by Johnson.

The Transvaal side to clinch this first win in 22 years included ten players who would help South Africa to win the World Cup at Ellis Park two years later. They were Gavin Johnson, Pieter Hendriks, Japie Mulder, Hennie le Roux, Johan Roux, Balie Swart, François Pienaar (capt.), Kobus Wiese, Hannes Strydom and Rudolf Straeuli.

The Transvaal team was unbeaten for a record run of 22 matches and became the first to provide a full pack of forwards for a Springbok touring team. With Theo van Rensburg and Hennie le Roux also in the team to Australia, Transvaal provided 12 Springboks in 1993 after Chris Dirks and Gavin Johnson (as Dirks' replacement) later went on the Argentinian tour.

It would be unfair to the players and to Breedt in particular – who had fought so valiantly in trying to break the lean years – to say that the Lions' golden era started

The Rev. Adrian Roberts' team in 1879 played a match against unknown opponents in Pretoria. The Pretoria Rugby Club took over the colours of blue and white hoops that have remained unchanged for more than 130 years.

in 1993, just as it would be unfair to say that Transvaal were a poor or average side between 1952 and 1971.

In fact, there were great achievements in the days gone by, and some unforgettable clashes that put Transvaal right at the top of the pile when provincial rugby in South Africa and possible Springboks for test teams were discussed.

Established after Western Province (1883), Griquas (1886), Eastern Province (1888) and in the same year as South Western Districts (1889), Transvaal is one of the oldest rugby unions in the country. The establishment of the Transvaal Rugby Football Union (TRFU) came about after the discovery of gold on the Witwatersrand, or The Reef as it was called. The mines provided employment and facilities, and in so doing played a major role in the

The 1922 Transvaal squad that broke the Currie Cup ice in the seven matches of the 14th Currie Cup competition was: JM Michau, DD Duncan, TL Kruger, LB de Villiers, H Butcher, N Bosman, SW Harris, ML Brink, JFS van Niekerk, N Hudson, AL Fielding, M Zeeman, N van Heerden, CH Kennedy, JE Simpson, CW van der Spuy, EC Boonzaaier, Dr NC Bodenstein, HJ Sanderson, HS van Wijk, EH Hudson, CJ Burger, JM Rentzke, M Ellis, Dr Coetzee, DE Joffe, C Louw, G Alberts, NJ Maree, P de Waal and J Berman.

Sanderson, a forward, later became president of the Transvaal Rugby Football Union.

The Transvaal team that made history in that very first Currie Cup final in 1939 was: H Hirst, O van Niekerk, J van der Spuy, CJ Roos, F Duvenage, T Harris, J Benade, F Louw (capt.), J Lotz, C Scrooby, J Smit, W Pretorius, L Badenhorst, J Kloppers, C Delaporte.

Flyhalf Tony Harris, who really made his mark as a top-class international on the 1937 Springbok tour to New Zealand, later also played cricket for South Africa.

The Transvaal side that won the Currie Cup for the first time in 1922.

development of all sports, and particularly rugby.

In the 1880s, men began converging on what was to become Johannesburg, and with them came the game of rugby from places like Kimberley, Cape Town and even the other coastal cities. Clubs sprang up, and were the forerunners of what became famous names like Pirates, Wanderers, Pretoria, Diggers and Potchefstroom.

As was the case in the south, the formation of a union to control the clubs and their competitions became necessary. In 1889 the TRFU was formed, with Bill Taylor as the first president of what is today the Rooibontes because of their red and white colours. (It wasn't so originally: dark-blue and white jerseys and blue shorts were Transvaal's first provincial colours.)

The TRFU's responsibility encompassed the whole of the former Transvaal province, including areas such as Limpopo, the Lowveld, the Western Transvaal (including Stellaland), and the Eastern Transvaal down to Volksrust. It covered the geographical area that was known as Transvaal, from the Natal and Free State borders up to what are today the Mozambican, Botswanan and Zimbabwean borders

One can hardly imagine the difficulty in selecting a team from such a vast area. That alone contributed to a slow start in the Currie Cup competition, especially if one considers the difficulty of travelling to play fixtures and watch matches for selection purposes and of the team coming together for provincial tournaments.

The first split came in 1920 when Western Transvaal decided to go it alone. Eighteen years later Northern Transvaal followed, and Eastern Transvaal became independent in 1948.

The early close ties between Transvaal and its offspring Northern Transvaal are illustrated in the election of Robert Loftus Owen Versfeld as a life member of the TRFU. He is the man after whom Loftus Versfeld in Pretoria is named, in honour of his efforts to obtain a permanent home for Northern Transvaal Union. Versfeld, who was so influential in setting up clubs in other unions and in his own right a player of no mean standard, died of a heart attack at Ellis Park in 1932 while attending a match between Transvaal and Free State.

The Second World War was also responsible for a fair measure of political difficulties and rather serious divisions between English- and Afrikaans-speaking administrators and players on the issue of whether to support

PIET MALAN – TRANSVAAL AND THE LIONS FOREVER!

Even at the age of 91, as he was during the 2010 rugby season, it would be a very rare exception if former Transvaal captain and Springbok flank Piet Malan missed a Lions match at Ellis Park.

In fact, after a Currie Cup or Super 14 match Oom Piet, as he has fondly been called and addressed by everybody for years, would also spend some time at the after-match function in the presidential suite, from where he watches the provincial matches as an honorary guest. Such is his love for his old province, now the Lions, that his son-in-law Piet Brummer and daughter Ettie tell the story of Oom Piet and his wife, Hansie, during a trip by road with them to Cape Town.

They stopped at their overnight accommodation in Beaufort West, and while Brummer was unpacking the car, Oom Piet stormed into the B&B where they were to stay the night. The Lions were due to kick off in a few minutes.

Moments later, at an even greater pace, he stormed past the car like a flanker on his way to the tryline, crossed the road, and with his wife in tow, found a vantage point in a franchise pub. The reason for this rush was that there was no television in their room! When the Brummers joined them ten or so minutes later, the elderly couple were calmly and very contentedly watching the match on television while sipping a drink.

Piet Malan became the oldest living Springbok at 86 years of age, after the death of **Howard Watt**, the longest-surviving member of the **1937 Springbok tour to Australasia**, in August 2005.

Oom Piet, who became a Springbok against the 1949 All Blacks at the age of 30, fondly remembers his 33 matches for Transvaal which included two finals and the Currie Cup title, which was won in 1950. He just shakes his head in exasperation about the laws that he feels spoil the game of today. 'Every referee can blow up any side at any ruck and be correct in his decision,' he says, 'but it still is a great game.'

Piet Malan

Ernst Joubert, a loose forward who captained the Lions in the 2007 Currie Cup final against the Free State, which the Lions lost 20–18 in Bloemfontein, is a grandson of the sprightly 91-year-old, and he is a source of great pride for Oom Piet.

'How was the game played in your time?' was a question asked of Oom Piet. And that really got him going.

'Those were wonderful times,' he reminisces. 'It was very different to what it is today.

'When we played in Cape Town, we left Johannesburg by train on a Wednesday evening and arrived in Cape Town on the Friday morning. The Sunday after the match we wandered about in Cape Town, and that evening we'd leave to arrive back on Tuesday morning – too late for work. That meant we were away for a week for a single match!

'The train trips were great fun,' he recalls. 'The new guys were initiated on those trips, and the belts holding up the train bunks in those days were used to give them the "bakoond" initiation on a bare bum. It certainly wasn't pleasant, but we all went through it, and it certainly helped to create a team spirit.'

The game in his time was as hard up front as it is today, says Malan, but much slower. 'We weren't as fit as today's guys. We couldn't train as hard, obviously, because we all had full-time jobs. When we got to the training field, we had an hour at most to train with a ball before it was dark, and then we did a little running. There weren't floodlights in those days.

'The result was that we battled hard in the rucks and scrums, but did a fair amount of walking on the field.'

Without touch judges (more often than not, the reserves of the two teams did that job) and television, there were also a little more "underground" activities going on, says Oom Piet. 'The odd fist would find its target, but you would know that the man on the receiving end would wait his turn and get you back, either in that match, or when you met again in a future match.

'When we played Western Province, someone would target Jan Pickard early on and give him a solid punch.

'Jan was a toughie, a man who liked to rough it up and keep the opposition busy with his unlawful deeds. A punch like that, early on, would upset him greatly. He would then wander around for the rest of the match trying to find the culprit, or take revenge if he knew who it was, and give us one opponent less to worry about.

'The fields on which we played often had no grass. Even Ellis Park, where the grass is now taken care of and watered daily, the ground was very hard to tackle and get tackled on.'

The 1950 final, which Transvaal won 22–11 against Western Province at Ellis Park, he remembers well: 'We strangled them with our forwards,' Oom Piet recalls. 'We scrummed them and beat them in the rucks, and thereby put pressure on their scrumhalf Ballie Wahl. He simply couldn't get the ball away and was trampled into the ground on a few occasions. The first time that happened, big Gert Dannhauser said to me: 'We've got them!' We knew then that the game was ours.'

'Were you paid?' Oom Piet was asked.

'Not a penny. All we got after a provincial match was a beer or two. Perhaps that was why the guys drank more beer in those days than the professionals of today.'

Piet Malan studied at Potchefstroom University until 1941, and then came to Johannesburg as a teacher. Those were war years, and no Currie Cup competitions took place between 1939 and 1946.

He joined Diggers, in those days – as indeed until the 1980s – a real powerhouse in Transvaal, as well as in South African rugby, with a tradition and pride that performed the feeder role to the provincial system extraordinarily well.

'Club rugby in those days was tough. We had strong sides to compete against: ERPM, Simmer and Jack, West Rand … it was good, hard rugby and the standard was exceptionally high.

'That helped to prepare us for the Currie Cup when the competition restarted in 1946.'

Transvaal, with Piet Malan in the side, lost the Currie Cup final to Western Province in 1947, and then won it in two back-to-back tournaments in 1950 and 1952.

Malan was still in the 1950 side, but had retired by 1952.

It is not generally known, but Oom Piet was instrumental in the establishment of the Craven Week as a provincial schools tournament. He suggested to Dr Danie Craven, then the president of the SA Rugby Board, that a provincial tournament for schoolboys be organised to coincide with the celebrations of the 75th anniversary of the **South African Rugby Board** in 1964.

That became a reality, and the first of the famous Craven week tournaments – unique in world rugby – took place, and have taken place annually since then.

Theuns Kruger, one of the three men who captained Transvaal in 1922 when they won the Currie Cup for the first time.

the war effort or refrain from fighting up north.

Although Transvaal played in the very first Currie Cup competition in 1892, they didn't complete their fixtures. They forfeited against Border in the five-team tournament, and won one match from three to end third on the log. (Border declined to take the two points for a win because of the scratching.)

Transvaal again forfeited a fixture in 1898 when their players attended the funeral of a teammate, Boy Tait. He and Davie Cope were on their way to represent Transvaal in the Currie Cup tournament in Cape Town when their train was involved in an accident at Mostertshoek. Tait was killed instantly. Cope died later from his injuries. Transvaal's match against Eastern Province was cancelled to enable the players to attend Tait's funeral.

Of the first 13 competitions between 1892 and 1922, Transvaal (like Western Province) missed only the 1899 tournament because of the impending South African War. Their best performances were five second places on the log.

When the great day came in 1922 and Transvaal were crowned Currie Cup champions for the first time, it came on the back of a very good 1920 competition, when they had finished a single point behind Western Province on the log. The 1920 tournament was the first after the First World War, and Western Province turned up as defending champions, having won the previous tournament in 1914. In 1920, the Currie Cup would be competed for in a tournament that was played in both Kimberley and Bloemfontein, thereby appeasing both these cities that wanted to host the event.

Transvaal were reluctant to participate. In the end, they played for fear of a backlash that could have included the withdrawal from friendly fixtures by Griqualand West and the Free State.

The 1920 Transvaal side, under CV Becker, drew with newly formed Western Transvaal in a scoreless match and lost to Western Province, who, in turn, were beaten by Griquas but were nevertheless crowned champions again because of the single point Transvaal conceded in the draw.

The good performance by Transvaal in the 1920 competition led to seven of their players being included in the 1921 Springbok tour to New Zealand, under the captaincy of Western Province's Theo Pienaar. The 1920 Currie Cup winners, Province, had 14 players in that touring side.

With no Currie Cup competition taking place in 1921, Transvaal had to wait two years to get another shot at being crowned South Africa's provincial champions, after coming so close in 1920.

They had also been close to the title in the past. Before the turn of the century, when Western Province dominated proceedings, Transvaal did well enough to be second in 1897, losing only to Province (3–0) in the Port Elizabeth tournament. They didn't take part in 1899, and when Currie Cup action was resumed in 1904, following the South African War, Transvaal finished third in East London, where Western Province (again!) beat them (13–5) and Border managed a 3-all draw.

The score was 5–0 to Western Province in Johannesburg in 1906, and Griquas further spoiled a good home tournament for Transvaal with a 3-all draw, but the home side had done enough to finish second.

In 1908 another 5–0 defeat to Western Province followed, this time at the Port Elizabeth tournament. Transvaal were second by a single point, after Western Province had been forced into a scoreless draw with Griquas.

Two losses (4–0 to Griquas and 14–8 to Province) gave Transvaal third place in 1911 at Newlands, but they returned to their now near permanent spot of second best team in the 1914 tournament in Durban, where losses to Western Province and Griquas (who else but those two?) with scores of 10–0 and 3–0 denied them the title.

Then came the First World War.

After their good performance in 1920, Transvaal were always going to be a factor in 1922, but the depth of Western Province stood between them and the title. In that year the Currie Cup competition was played under the new system of home and away matches for the first time. Transvaal were required to visit Western Province, Eastern Province, Border and Natal, and played Western Transvaal, Griquas and the Free State at home.

They won six of their seven matches; the other was a 3–all draw with Western Province in Cape Town – no mean feat! In their other tour matches, Transvaal beat Natal 7–0, while Border were trounced 24–3 and Eastern Province beaten by the comfortable margin of 15–0. At home, the former sub-union Western Transvaal made the Johannesburg team work hard for a 9–3 victory; Griquas were beaten quite comfortably (14–0); and Free State went down 12–0.

It was therefore an unbeaten Currie Cup season for Transvaal, under the shared captaincy of Springboks Theuns Krüger and Baby Michau and Denoon Duncan, ex-SACS, ex-Oxford and ex-Scotland forwards respectively.

In the following six Currie Cup tournaments, Transvaal were placed second three times, and third three times before their next win in 1939.

In 1925, as defending champions following the 1922 win, Transvaal could do no better than place third after their now virtually customary defeat against Western Province and also to Eastern Province (both played in Johannesburg) plus a draw against their old nemesis, Griquas. What made this a particularly disappointing

TOY'S PRAISE AS 'SYDDIE' SAVES THE DAY

Many Jewish players have, over the years, represented South Africa on the rugby field and virtually all of them were outstanding Springboks.

One just has to think of Louis Babrow, star of the famous 1937 Springbok team in New Zealand; Syd Nomis who, at one stage, held the South African record of 25 consecutive test matches as centre/wing; Okey Geffin, who kicked the Springboks to victory in the 1949 series against Fred Allen's All Blacks; and Joel Stransky who, of course, kicked that famous drop goal in the 1995 World Cup final.

One of the lovely stories about South African rugby is the one told of the legendary Toy Dannhauser. Toy captained Transvaal and also played for Natal.

In the late 60s, Gert Muller was making a name for himself in Western Province, where he studied, after establishing a huge reputation as a Durban schoolboy.

Province were playing Transvaal at Ellis Park, and Muller, big, immensely strong, and very quick, was on his way to the tryline and the winning score when Nomis hit him on the corner flag.

Jogging across the field to the ensuing lineout, Toy gave Nomis the thumbs-up sign and shouted from a distance: 'Syddie, you're the best Jew since Moses!'

Syd Nomis on the run.

Tony Harris, 1937 Springbok and instrumental in Transvaal winning the first Currie Cup final against Western Province.

season is that Transvaal were allotted six home games with only two matches on tour, according to the strange draw that was handed to the sides that year.

Two close defeats to Western Province (10-9) and Orange Free State (16–14) doomed Transvaal to second place behind Province in 1927. Transvaal were indeed a rugby powerhouse in that period, and their strong presence continued for the next four competitions before the Second World War.

In 1929 Western Province were beaten 11–9, but then Transvaal suffered a shock defeat at Ellis Park against Natal (17–11), and Griquas won in Kimberley (12–0), so Western Province were again crowned the champions.

As it was in those days, an arbitrary decision was taken that the next tournament would take place only three years later. Two losses against Western Province and Orange Free State gave Transvaal a third place in the 1932 season, when Border shared the trophy with Western Province on log points. No play-off or count-out on points differential, or any other method, was used to determine the winner, and the two unions shared the Currie Cup – a first in the Currie Cup competition. The same two sides also shared the trophy in 1934.

Transvaal's performances were rather disappointing. They had some of the greatest Springboks of all time in the side that lost to Border and Western Province and drew with Eastern Province. Ponie van der Westhuizen, Maurice Zimerman, Frank Waring, Fred Turner, Tony Harris, Charlie Newham, Ginger Dummet and Daunch Devine formed a backline that would've beaten most international sides, and up front they had big names in captain Fanie Louw, Harry Martin, Nic Bierman, Roger Sherriff, Ben du Toit, Lucas Strachan and Ferdie Bergh.

A large part of this group went to New Zealand in 1937, where they became the first Springboks to win a test rubber against the All Blacks. This side is still regarded as, arguably, South Africa's best of all time.

Then, in 1939, came Transvaal's second Currie Cup title. This was achieved without a number of their players who now played for Northern Transvaal, which had become an independent union the year before.

Transvaal nevertheless won their section despite a defeat against Natal in Durban, as they clinched victories over Griquas, Western Transvaal, Free State and Northern Transvaal. The match against Natal was one lost by Transvaal in the second half, after they led 8–6 at half-time. The home side came back strongly and eventually won rather convincingly 18–8.

The final against Western Province at Newlands was the first Currie Cup final in history. The Transvaal team was led by Fanie Louw, who was an experienced Springbok prop, while former Eastern Province player Fred Turner who had also represented Transvaal, captained Western Province.

The final was one of the events that earmarked the 50th anniversary of the South African Rugby Football Board, and the referee was Transvaal captain Fanie Louw's brother Boy, who had played test rugby against the British Lions the previous year.

Transvaal won 17–6 and the score flattered Province. Tony Harris, who was later taken prisoner during the Second World War but on his return also played test cricket for South Africa in 1947–1948, was the general of the Transvaal side. He dictated the match behind a strong scrum that had Western Province under pressure from the second quarter of the match. Fanie Louw, the legendary Jan Lotz and Chris Scrooby scrummed the home side into the ground and laid the foundation for victory. The home side, however, were in command in the lineouts.

Transvaal led 14–6 at the break, after a try in the first five minutes by Floors Duvenage. Fred Turner then scored a penalty for Province, and GJ Roos put the visitors up at 6–3. Matters were levelled when Piet de Wet scored for Western Province, but then the brilliance of Harris led to a try by great winger Otto van Niekerk, who never represented his country becasue of injury.

Van Niekerk repeated his effort (converted this time), and a try in the second half by Fatty Pretorius, a fitting reward for the hard-working forward who had played in all 11 matches that season including the friendlies, made it 17–6.

The Second World War then intervened and put an end to Currie Cup competitions for the duration. When war hostilities ceased and those in the Currie Cup had resumed in 1946, Transvaal were second in the north section, behind eventual Currie Cup champions Northern

Transvaal rugby icon Hennie Muller scores one of many tries for his province.

Transvaal who beat Western Province in the final at Loftus.

Transvaal had lost only one Currie Cup match when the Light Blues beat them 27–4, but it was also the season in which their captain, Hennie Muller, moved to Western Province, as did Otto van Niekerk. Muller scored a try against his former team in the friendly at Newlands.

Transvaal were in the next final, in 1947, after wins against Griquas, Western Transvaal, Natal, Northern Transvaal and Free State. Western Province were their opponents and this time made amends for the 17–6 loss in 1939 against Transvaal. The sides went into half-time tied at 9–all, but after a strong second half Province came out on top, 16–12. RG Bosch, the father of Transvaal kicking hero Gerald Bosch, who became a Springbok in 1974, played for Transvaal in that final at Newlands, as did Okey Geffin, the Transvaal prop who was later to kick the Springboks to victory against the 1949 All Blacks.

These two sides formed the nucleus of the 1949 Springbok side, and included Hennie Muller who was back in Johannesburg. Muller would become a playing captain on the 1951/1952 Springbok tour to the UK after the eye injury that put an end to tour captain Basil Kenyon's career. The side lost only a single match from 31 on a tour of four months and seven days, and won the Grand Slam against the home unions plus the test against France.

For the next two years, in 1948 and 1949 (when the All Blacks visited), there was no Currie Cup rugby. However, Transvaal were ready to show off the healthy state of their rugby at the next challenge, which came in 1950. Transvaal were now under the captaincy of Hennie Muller, as Jan Lotz had called it a day after playing in three full series against Australia and New Zealand (1937) and the British Lions in 1938.

Lotz was 37 years old when he led Transvaal to the 1947 Currie Cup final and was two months away from his 39th birthday when he captained Transvaal against the 1949 All Blacks. He retired after the 1949 season and, for years thereafter, played a major role as administrator, selector and coach.

Transvaal played 18 matches during the 1950 season, and fullback Johnny Buchler didn't miss a single game. Before reaching the final, Transvaal were involved in a play-off with Northern Transvaal, after the two sides were tied at the top of the north section log. The Johannesburg side won 17–9, which set up the final against Western Province, this time at Ellis Park.

The Western Province backline, with that fine flyhalf Dennis Fry partnering Ballie Wahl at halfback, Chum Osche at centre and Roy Dryburgh at fullback, were outstanding (especially in the first half) and had the crowd on their feet. Fry broke and after a brilliant run sent Jan Visser over for a converted try. Buchler replied with a drop kick from 45 metres out, but Western Province were next on the board as Osche beat the Simmer Express, Jimmy Kotze. With Okey Geffin kicking two penalties for the home side, Transvaal were 9–8 ahead at the break.

Then Hennie Muller put his side further ahead with a try, 12–8, before Osche scored his second to keep Province within a point at 12–11. Transvaal centre Des Sinclair showed the class that made him a Springbok for the 1951/1952 tour to the UK. He didn't play in any of the test matches on tour, but was selected for all four internationals against the 1955 British Lions. First, Sinclair scored a try himself, which was converted, and then picked up a lose ball to send HJ van Staden over. With Geffin again converting, Transvaal had won their first title in front of their home crowd with a 22–11 victory.

There were eight Transvaal players in the Springbok side to tour the UK, and Hennie Muller was the tour vice-captain. After the injury to team captain Basil Kenyon, Muller led the side in all five tests against the four home unions and France.

No Currie Cup competition took place in 1951 and in 1952 Transvaal had a topsy-turvy season, losing to Natal and sneaking a draw against Western Transvaal. They beat Griquas, Eastern Transvaal, Northern Transvaal and Free State. However, despite a rather lean season in which they also won only three of their eight friendlies, Transvaal made the 1952 Currie Cup final ahead of Eastern Transvaal, who were second on the northern log.

In the fourth final out of the five Transvaal had played to date, they had their fourth captain! This time the honour went to bald-headed flanker Basie van Wyk,

Springbok great Chris Koch, left, prepares to receive the ball from a Boland team mate in the 1952 final against Transvaal.

a Springbok in 1951/1952 who would, on that tour, against the visiting Wallabies in 1953 and the British Lions of 1955, play a total of 10 tests. Van Wyk was an automatic selection for the 1956 tour to New Zealand, but did not play a single match, owing to an early injury (a broken leg). By courtesy of the New Zealand Rugby Union, however, he remained a part of that tour to the very end.

Boland won the south section after a play-off win of 5–0 over Western Province, and Wellington became the 1952 Currie Cup final venue. This win was a surprise, as Province had won their league encounter 20–3. It was Boland's first chance in a final after 13 seasons since their establishment. That play-off win was their first against Western Province, and their success was largely built on a pack of forwards that didn't have their equal throughout the season. Chris Koch, Bertus van der Merwe and Piet Kriel were the front row, and Bubbles and Willem Koch the locks.

Boland fielded five players who were or would become Springboks: Buks Marais at centre, Steve Hoffman on the wing, Bertus van der Merwe at hooker and the Koch cousins, Chris and Bubbles. Chris' brother Willem – a Junior Springbok – was also in the big, abrasive pack.

The Transvaal team of Freddie Herbst, JC Visagie, Ashton Townsend, Flip Human, Frans Broderick, Natie Rens, Hansie Oelofse, Franz van der Ryst, Barry Schmidt, Koos Botha, Pieter (Pa) Pelser, Gert Kruger, Hoppy van Jaarsveld, Basie van Wyk and Jackie Rahn also included five future Springboks.

Boland missed at least two reasonably easy penalties and a conversion and they had a try disallowed. They were 0–3 down after only two minutes when Rens kicked an angled penalty. Boland's Buks Marais then scored a penalty goal with his right foot and a dropped goal with his left to take Boland into a 6–3 lead.

Pa Pelser, later a Transvaal and Junior Springbok captain and one of Transvaal's best coaches, scored a try which Rens converted to make it 8–6 at half-time. Boland regained the lead when Hoffman scored a fine try to put his team in the lead (9–8), but with time just about up, Rens landed the drop kick that would make him a Transvaal legend.

That drop took the score to 11–9 and gave Transvaal their first (and to date one of only two) back-to-back Currie Cup wins.

That drop kick earned Rens, according to one of the well-known stories, a special comment from one of the Boland supporters after the final whistle. Speaking in

The 1993 Transvaal team in the Currie Cup final included a number of players who represented South Africa in the 1995 World Cup.

Transvaal's team was: Gavin Johnson, Pieter Hendriks, Bernard Fourie, Japie Mulder, Chris Dirks, Hennie le Roux, Johan Roux, Balie Swart, Uli Schmidt, Heinrich Rogers, François Pienaar (capt.), Kobus Wiese, Hannes Strydom, Ian Macdonald and Rudolf Straeuli. Replacements: Porta Hoffman, Kobus van Deventer, Deon Lötter and Harry Roberts.

Pienaar, who had shown excellent leadership for Rand Afrikaans Universiteit and had previously been blooded as captain in the lesser first-class competitions, played in his first final as captain after playing under Jannie Breedt in Transvaal's final defeats against Northern Transvaal in 1991 and Natal in 1992.

Pienaar, of course, was to captain South Africa on debut in 1993 against the visiting French side and went on to lead South Africa to the emotional World Cup victory at Ellis Park in 1995.

In 1993 Transvaal also won the M-Net Trophy (shared with Northern Transvaal), the Super 10 series and the Lion Cup (beating Natal).

Hennie le Roux, influential whether he was at flyhalf or centre, helped the Lions to the Currie Cup and Lion Cup wins in 1993.

that broad Swartland accent of the rural area around Malmesbury and Moorreesburg, where the famous Kochs farmed, the man was alleged to have said, 'G-g-ens, jou moeg-g-g!'

It took Transvaal almost 20 years to win their next (shared) title. That was in 1971 and the draw with Northern Transvaal was achieved under extraordinary and controversial circumstances. In 1968 they lost the final to Northern Transvaal in Pretoria 16–3. That was the year when Wits flyhalf Alan Menter crossed the border to Pretoria to complete his medical studies at Tuks. Menter couldn't find a place in the Transvaal team, but

Natie Rens dropped the late winning goal for Transvaal in 1952.

was included in the Northerns team in place of Gerhard de Haas for the final, and was superb in controlling the game that no doubt played a major role in Menter becoming a Springbok.

In 1971 Transvaal had to beat Free State and Griquas in play-off matches. Then followed a semi-final against Natal. Meanwhile the Light Blues had been without match practice, except for a hastily arranged friendly against Rhodesia.

The final ended in controversy with a last-minute try that the Northern Transvaal players and supporters are still disputing.

A try by Northerns' lock Piet du Plessis, converted by Chris Luther, followed by a try by Tobias du Toit for the home team, took Northerns into a 5–3 half-time lead. Then a penalty and a drop by fullback Jannie van Deventer gave Transvaal a 9–5 lead.

However, two drop goals by Northern Transvaal flyhalf Dudley Gradwell steered the visitors to 11–9 up before Luther landed a mighty penalty on full-time that took the score to 14–9 in favour of Northern Transvaal.

It seemed all over, and the Pretoria supporters ran onto the field. According to referee Gert Bezuidenhout, however, time was not up. With spectators still on the field, Transvaal regained possession from the kick-off. Scrumhalf Gert Schutte, captain Piet Greyling and flank Simon Norwood launched an attack, and when they were stopped close to the line, Theo (Sakkie) Sauermann was there to drive it over. Van Deventer kicked the all-important conversion and it ended 14–14.

Kevin de Klerk, later to become a great and famous Springbok lock and president of the Golden Lions Rugby Union, played in that match. He partnered Jannie van Aswegen who had played such an important role in Griquas' win over the Light Blues the previous year.

The next year Transvaal first eliminated Free State in a play-off before beating Eastern Transvaal 25–19 in the only Currie Cup final ever played at Springs. It was Bosch's day, and the match seemed over at half-time, when Transvaal led 18–3 after a couple of early Gerald Bosch drop goals had put the home on their heels.

But Eastern Transvaal were not called the Red Devils for nothing. They were all fire and brimstone after the break and gave Transvaal a serious scrap in the second half. With captain Skip Henderson, Boesman Wilkinson, Ben Stander and Richard McKechnie in the pack, and Bennie Dercksen, Koos Mulder, Andries Strydom and Deon van Rensburg in the backline, Eastern Transvaal were difficult opponents. Each side scored two tries, with Bosch's boot making the difference. Mulder and Stander each scored a try for Eastern Transvaal, while Wilkinson added two penalty goals and a conversion and Dercksen contributed a penalty.

Tommy Symons and Johan Esterhuizen scored tries for Transvaal and Bosch kicked three drop goals, two penalties and a conversion.

As defending champions, Transvaal could not even reach the semi-finals of the 1973 Currie Cup competition, and a tour to France in the early part of the season was blamed. Despite some outstanding results on the tour and in friendlies, the rest of the season was an anti-climax. Touring sides San Isidro from Argentina and Newport were beaten 25–16 and 64–15 respectively and the match against London Counties was drawn 12-all.

At this time the Currie Cup competition was divided into four sections, and only four matches were played by each of the competing sides. The single 18–7 loss to

Kevin de Klerk on the charge against Free State. The former Transvaal captain and Springbok lock became president of the Lions Rugby Union in 2009.

Western Province at Newlands put paid to Transvaal's aspirations for that season.

With the strange three-section Currie Cup competition employed again in 1974, Transvaal beat all sides but Eastern Province in their cross-section league matches, and then trounced the men from the Eastern Cape in the semi-final (30–6). That set up the final against Northern Transvaal at Loftus, which the home side won 17–15.

Transvaal were not to contest another final before 1986 when they were beaten 22–9 by Province at Newlands under Jannie Breedt's captaincy. The next year Naas Botha's full house of 24 points accounted for the home side at Ellis Park when Northerns won 24–18. In 1991 Northerns beat Transvaal 27–15 at Loftus and in 1992 Natal sneaked in by 14–13 at Ellis Park.

After the 1993 win the Lions' fourth successive Currie Cup final in 1994 ended in a rout of the Free State in Bloemfontein, where the match had to be played at Springbok Park instead of the old Free State Stadium, which was being rebuilt. It was a strange season, with no team really dominant in the league phases. Only right at the end Transvaal and Free State earned the honour of contesting the final.

Transvaal were totally dominant up front and their backs cut the Free State line to shreds, as evidenced by the seven tries, one of which was a penalty try. Transvaal were ahead 31–16 at the break and were dominant enough to retain their composure to add a further 25 points in the second half to win by 56–33. Their winning score of 56 points was a record in a Currie Cup final. The combined 89 points by the two teams was another Currie Cup record, and it is a sobering thought that the Free State's 33 points had previously been bettered on only two occasions by a winning team in a final. Transvaal's seven tries set another record, and the total of ten tries in this feast of running rugby and poor defence was another final record.

Transvaal, holders of the Super 10 title, ended second

MORE THAN JUST A CAPTAIN

In the best years of Transvaal and Lions rugby, François Pienaar was a perfect foil for Jannie Breedt, as he followed up on the former Transvaal and Springbok skipper's spadework in getting Transvaal into four (unsuccessful) Currie Cup finals.

Of course, procuring the playing personnel was at the heart of it; and for that Louis Luyt, for everything else he might not have done right, deserves praise.

Pienaar was the man who led South Africa to the 1995 World Cup triumph at Ellis Park, and the picture of Pienaar accepting the Webb Ellis Cup from President Nelson Mandela was a symbol of togetherness of what was, at that stage, the 'new' South Africa.

Pienaar, who hails from Witbank and played his club rugby for the Rand Afrikaans University, made his debut for Transvaal in 1989. After the retirement of Springbok captain Naas Botha at the end of the 1992 tour to France and England – during which they lost two of their three matches following on two defeats against the All Blacks and Wallabies at home – a new national captain had to be found.

Under Pienaar Transvaal won the Currie Cup, the Lion Cup, the Super 10 and the Night Series in 1993, and repeated the feat in 1994 with the exception of the Super 10.

Pienaar made his debut for South Africa as captain of the Springboks against France in Durban in 1993. The Springboks drew 20–20 in this first Test, and lost by a single point in the second.

Francois Pienaar

It was a good enough start for Pienaar as captain, and over the next year South Africa beat Argentina, Scotland and Wales. Overall, the blonde flank played 29 test matches, and captained his country in all of them.

Shortly after the World Cup triumph, Pienaar organised a strike for improved remuneration with his Transvaal teammates. He was sacked; but the team's requests were eventually met and Pienaar was restored to the team.

last in their pool in this international provincial competition in 1994. The year 1995 will be remembered for the Springboks winning the World Cup. The huge contribution made by the 13 Transvaal players in the World Cup squad obviously affected the players' focus in the Currie Cup series, with Natal and Western Province contesting the final. But Transvaal were not finished yet. In 1996 they reached the final but were denied by Natal (15–33) at Ellis Park. They didn't slip up in 1999, however, when they totally outplayed Natal in Durban, winning 32–9.

Laurie Mains, replaced as All Blacks coach after the Springboks had beaten them in the 1995 World Cup final,

The man's character was severely tested in a stand-off with Luyt, in what threatened to become an unsavoury breakaway from South African rugby. But again, Pienaar played an integral role in taking South Africa's rugby into the professional arena.

Pienaar left the international game in 1996 after he was dropped by the then national coach, André Markgraaff. He moved to England and became player/coach for Saracens in London. Under his direction, the club finished the premiership season in second place, thereby qualifying for the Heineken Cup. With Pienaar at the helm, Saracens repeated the performance in the following two seasons, when they finished in third and fourth places.

He captained Saracens to the club's first win in 127 years in 1998, when they won the Tetley's Bitter Cup. He retired in 2000. Pienaar became CEO of Saracens in 2001, but left two years later after Saracens suffered a string of defeats.

Back in South Africa in 2002, he became CEO of the Rugby World Cup Bid Committee that tried to bring the 2011 World Cup tournament to South Africa for the first time since their 1995 victory.

His bestselling autobiography *Rainbow Warrior* was released in 1999.

Pienaar, with First National Bank, was behind setting up the famous Classic Clashes rugby matches between traditional rivals throughout the country, and FNB assisted in the sponsorship of universities. In 2008, Pienaar was one of the leading figures behind the FNB Varsity Cup competition that has taken the country by storm.

signed a three-year contract to coach the Lions, and in his very first year (1999) he struck pay dirt and also brought a new, refreshing approach to the Lions' playing style.

Andy Colquhoun, manager of strategic communications at SARU and also editor of the *SA Rugby Annual*, wrote in the publication of 2000, which was then still edited by the late Quintus van Rooyen: 'The Lions could only knock down what was put up before them – and knock them over they did emphatically as Laurie Mains' re-invented team romped to the last Currie Cup title of the century.' It was a match where the Sharks had to bid farewell to some stalwarts, namely André Joubert, Gary Teichmann, Henry Honiball (who was injured and didn't play) and coach Ian Macintosh. It was also the second biggest win in a final, with AJ Venter, Thinus Delport (2), Chester Williams and Leon Boshoff scoring five tries for the Lions in what proved to be a one-sided affair. Kobus Engelbrecht converted two and also kicked a penalty.

The golden years that Transvaal experienced on the field, and which saw their trophy cabinet bulging, coincided with Dr. Louis Luyt's term of office as president of the union. Their success was largely built on the controversial policy of buying players in what was still officially – until 1996 – an amateur era.

Luyt left just as controversially as he had first assumed the position of president of the TRFU. The writing was on the wall once Luyt resigned as president of SARFU in March 1998 after a vote of no confidence. This came in the wake of a court case that rocked South African rugby and politics, during which the presiding judge subpoenaed the President of South Africa, Nelson Mandela, to testify. Luyt lingered on at Ellis Park, but severed his ties with the union at the annual general meeting at the end of 1998 after serving as president for 14 years. He remained as chairman of both Ellis Park (Pty) Ltd and the Ellis Park Trust (which, according to Luyt, controlled the GLRU as it paid the players), relinquishing those positions only at the end of 2000. Since that win in 1999 the Lions have played in only two Currie Cup finals.

In 2002 they were well beaten by the Blue Bulls and a brilliant Derick Hougaard who scored a try and slotted five penalties and two drop goals to ensure a 31–7 win for the Blue Bulls at Ellis Park.

In 2007 the Xerox Lions made the final in Bloemfontein on the back of a 19–12 semi-final win over the Sharks in Durban after being routed there 19–3 just weeks before. They came very close, but lost 20–18 after being ahead 15–6 through tries by Willie Wepener (following some brilliance from flyhalf Earl Rose) and scrumhalf

Gerald Bosch – Transvaal's match-winning flyhalf.

The Lions – Currie Cup winners in 1999 under the coaching of former All Blacks coach Laurie Mains, on the right in the back row.

Jano Vermaak. A Rose penalty took it to 18–6 after 65 minutes, but then replacement flank Heinrich Brüssow scored a try, converted by kicking machine Willem de Waal. Tewis de Bruyn, the Cheetahs reserve scrumhalf, wriggled his way over near the corner to tie the scores with three minutes left, and De Waal did the rest to dash the hopes of the Lions players and supporters.

In 2008 the Lions blew hot and cold, and as in the Super 14, it was an inability to convert their chances more than anything else that cost them crucial matches (such as the semi-final, which they lost 14–29 to the Sharks) and another bite at the Currie Cup cherry. Their gradual downward curve has persisted, and in 2009 they missed out on a semi-final berth.

The Lions team that beat the Natal Sharks in 1999 was: Kobus Engelbrecht, Chester Williams, Jannie van der Walt, Wickus Venter, Thinus Delport, Hennie le Roux, Brett Johnstone, AJ Venter, Walter Minnaar, Jannes Labuschagne, Hannes Strydom (capt.), Bruce Thorne, Willie Meyer, Leon Boshoff, Marius Mostert.

AJ Venter and Thinus Delport later played for the Sharks and Venter moved to Western Province for his last playing years. Delport later played in the UK with Gloucester and Northampton and played in Japan in 2009–2010.

CHAPTER 7

Natal

For a long time Natal simply could not win the coveted Currie Cup trophy, despite the more-than-average boost given to them by players procured from elsewhere.

The Banana Boys, as they were called in the old days and in fact until the arrival of professionalism, arguably would have been Currie Cup champions in the 1960s, but when they were at their very best Currie Cup tournaments were few and far between. They had one or two near misses, but were regarded as 'the nice guys playing attractive rugby'.

The greatest moment in Natal's history was undoubtedly when they won the Currie Cup for the very first time by unexpectedly beating Northern Transvaal at their stronghold, Loftus Versfeld, in 1990. This win tasted even sweeter because it was achieved in Natal's centenary year.

It didn't just happen. It was a victory built on years of planning, and included the years 1982–1986 Natal spent in the B Section of the Currie Cup competition.

In this period there was only the near win in the 1983 Currie Cup semi-final, when Natal lost 7-3 to Western Province at Kings Park, the semi-final surprise win against the Free State in 1984, and the subsequent final against Western Province which gave Wynand Claassen's men a chance to compete against the top guns of the A Section.

In both those years Natal won the B section but were doomed to remain there. On each occasion they couldn't win their promotion play-offs against Northern Free State who were at the bottom of the A Section. Both times Natal had to regroup to try and make the final. (In those years, as an incentive and to let the B Section sides feel they were part of the Currie Cup competition, the system made

The centenary win. Natal captain, flanked by Wallaby hooker Tom Lawton and prop Guy Kebble, is chaired off the field after their surprise but deserved Currie Cup final win over Northern Transvaal at Loftus in 1990.

The man they called the Rolls Royce of fullbacks, Andre Joubert, cuts through the Lions defence with Springbok captain Gary Teichmann and scrumhalf Kevin Putt in support.

provision for the top side in the B Section to play a semi-final against the second side in the A Section.)

Gaining promotion to the A Section was part of the pain Natal had to go through in the 1980s as they built towards their Currie Cup dream. In fact, it was more than merely a dream. Former Springbok fullback Rodney Gould, then an administrator, had warned that Natal needed to win the Currie Cup to win the respect of the country's rugby fraternity. Finally the side of 1990, under the captaincy of Craig Jamieson, achieved this in the Currie Cup final. The road to the title, however, was a rocky one.

Although they won their opening Currie Cup match of a season for the first time since being promoted to the A Section in 1987, Natal were decidedly fortunate to take the log points against Free State. Free State fullback André Joubert's five missed goal attempts largely contributed to their win, and the 18–9 margin flattered Natal.

There followed a hard-fought 25–19 win against Transvaal, and then a fight-back draw of 18–all against Western Province at Newlands, with Natal coming back in the last ten minutes from 12 points down to salvage the draw.

A big win against Northern Free State, a 24–9 loss against a 14-man Northern Transvaal team at Kings Park, and a close win against Western Transvaal in Potchefstroom, were followed by a Lion Cup semi-final loss to Western Province. This was then followed by a one-point win against Eastern Province in Port Elizabeth.

It was obvious that the scrum needed to be strengthened and sharpened up. Scotland and later Springbok hooker John Allen returned for six matches, but wasn't available throughout because of club and international commitments overseas. Tom Lawton, a huge hooker from Australia, was procured to help Jamieson's side through the final phases in 1990, playing a role as big as his enormous frame in his eight matches for Natal.

Three Sharks coaches. Dick Muir, Ian McIntosh and John Plumtree enjoy a joke.

The bulk and expertise of the man who was regarded as the world's best hooker in those years did the trick. With big, abrasive Wahl Bartmann in his first season with Natal after moving from Transvaal, plus new acquisition Guy Kebble at loosehead, Natal cleaned up Western Province 21–12 at Kings Park in the return match.

It took a Joel Stransky drop goal to save them in the return match against Northern Free State in Welkom, which remained a venue of unhappy memories after the many promotion matches lost there. There followed a hiding of note when Northern Transvaal again overran Natal, this time in Pretoria (28–6). The dream was being threatened, and nearly became a nightmare as Transvaal came close (27–25) to winning at Kings Park. With three defeats and a draw, Natal finished second on the Currie Cup log. That set up the great day for Natal rugby at Loftus Versfeld, on 6 October 1990.

The Light Blues had come back magnificently in the second half, and Gerbrand Grobler used an overlap created by Naas Botha to put his team ahead. Botha had earlier also slotted his customary drop goal. The score was 12–9 to the home side when Natal right wing Tony Watson broke the hearts of Northern supporters with his try in front of the open eastern stand, thereby heralding the beginning of celebrations throughout the country. Over the years, Natal had always been popular and competitive, but as they hadn't won the Currie Cup, they were hardly regarded as a rugby power. This win changed that.

The team selection that largely neutralised Naas Botha; the lineout that worked for Natal; and a try that was, as Watson afterwards described it, 'well executed (by his fellow players) but somewhat lucky', helped Natal to the deserved win.

There was also the master plan of coach Ian McIntosh, who had brought in sports psychologist Ken Jennings. It was a new concept to the Natal players, and it brought calm to the team, took their attention away from the

WHEN A PLAN COMES TOGETHER

Although no less a rugby scribe than *The Sunday Tribune's* Darrell Thomson wrote in the *SA Rugby Annual* of 1991 that the 1990 Natal side would hardly go down as one of the great Currie Cup sides in history, the 18–12 victory in the 1990 Currie Cup against Northern Transvaal at Loftus Versfeld was enough for Craig Jamieson's team and their supporters.

Ian McIntosh, wily Natal coach, later admitted that the huge 28–6 win by the Light Blues two weeks before the final might have led to complacency at Loftus. It was also revealed that Natal, after that drubbing and while still in Pretoria, made a pact to win the Currie Cup.

These are just little asides. They may perhaps not be regarded as important to those who have not played rugby at a fairly high level, but they are crucial. The psychological aspect is so very, very important at the top level. Natal got that right in 1990; Northern Transvaal didn't.

Natal's success was also the result of proper planning and strategy. They selected a macro-pack (at that stage regarded as the biggest that the provincial side had yet fielded) with the object of putting pressure on Northerns' scrumhalf Robert du Preez, who played for Natal the very next year. Through pressure on Du Preez, they believed that the Light Blues' flyhalf, Naas Botha, wouldn't be able to dominate and control.

With Piet Strydom as convenor of selectors, the other two members of the selection committee, Dick Cocks and Poenie Holm, no doubt after long consultation with McIntosh, brought back stalwart lock André Botha after the injury to Steve Atherton. Botha had missed the early part of the season due to business commitments. Botha was not named in the starting side, however. Atherton, now fit again, was due to start, according to the announced team, with John Plumtree on the flank.

Shortly before the kick-off it was announced that Botha would play and that Atherton would be the flank. Plumtree replaced Atherton at the end of the third quarter, to provide a little more pace. The move was intended to control the lineouts and to add more weight to the pack to upset the halfbacks of the Light Blues.

It worked.

Too often for comfort, Northern Transvaal were forced to use no 8 Rudolf Straeuli (later a Sharks and Springbok coach) to pick up behind the scrum and feed Du Preez in an attempt to alleviate the pressure on the home side's halfbacks. Too often, the Light Blues played the blind, and not enough ball went to their backs, even though they looked dangerous when it did. Perhaps it was partly the result of the injury to centre Pieter Nel, who slipped in the tunnel as the team ran on and had to be replaced. That meant that fullback Theo van Rensburg had to move to centre at short notice, while Gerbrand Grobler was drafted in at fullback.

Grobler scored a try for Northern Transvaal and Van Rensburg did well enough on attack, but it was on defence that Van Rensburg, who became a Springbok in 1992, slipped up after 73 minutes and let Natal hero Tony Watson in. The Natal right-winger dropped his left shoulder, and Van Rensburg missed the chance.

This put Natal into a 15–12 lead. Jannie Claassens' late tackle in the in-goal area, after the try had been scored, was then penalised by referee Freek Burger on the halfway line. With the 50-metres penalty, Joel Stransky kicked his side into what moments before seemed an improbable 18–12 lead.

That was the final score after Natal had led 9–3 at half-time.

Currie Cup, and gave them the belief that they could win.

And although there were individual heroes, let one not forget the massive effort of the 16 players used in the match, and the other 19 who played for Natal in a season that had its ups and downs, injuries and disappointments. It would be unfair to single out men from this great team effort, but Wahl Bartmann's driving, bullocking play, the power and sheer weight of Tom Lawton and Guy Kebble, and the planning of Ian McIntosh, who loves to call everybody Master, probably deserve special mention as the 100-year dream came true.

Winning the Currie Cup title six years before the advent of professionalism, when players were paid and sponsors for teams became an everyday occurrence, also did Natal's income and balance sheets no harm. In 1991 the income from sponsors had risen more than fivefold to R1,5 million in the wake of the 1990 triumph.

Roy Dryburgh, Springbok captain whose versatility stood Natal in good stead in the late fifties and 1960.

Northern Transvaal prop Jaap Bekker after the second test against on the 1956 New Zealand tour. He deserved the rest and sat out the 1956 Currie Cup final against Natal.

Cas Labuschagne was a young flanker who played a huge role in Natal's semi-final win against Western Province in 1956 and also played in the losing final against Northern Transvaal.

After the win Northern Transvaal captain Naas Botha remarked that it had taken Natal a hundred years to win the Currie Cup, and it would be a hundred years before they did it again. Botha was wrong and the first signs that Natal would be a handful in the coming years were evident in May 1991, when Northerns were thrashed 54–15 at Kings Park. But that's another story …

The first Natal final was played on a blustery, cold day in Durban in 1956. The venue was Kingsmead Cricket Ground, which at that time was used for Natal's more important rugby matches. Natal included their only Springbok on the 1956 Australasian tour, Roy Dryburgh, in their team while Northern Transvaal's four Springbok players, namely Jaap Bekker, Salty du Randt, Tom van Vollenhoven and Daan Retief, were excluded. The Northern Transvaal executive had decided that the men who got them to the final should play in the final.

As it was 34 years later when Natal won the Currie Cup for the first time, it was good planning and tactics, and attention to the finest detail that stood them in good stead in the 1956 semi-final against Western Province. Izak van Heerden, one of the finest coaches produced in South Africa, and his captain Peter Taylor, colluded and devised and agreed that the best way to upset Western Province was to disrupt their halfbacks. It was a bold but well thought out decision, particularly against an experienced scrumhalf like Dick Lockyear (who would go on to play for South Africa against the All Blacks four years later) and Len Rodrigues at flyhalf.

It was a daunting task. Natal had never beaten Western Province since their first meeting in 1892. Like Northern Transvaal, Western Province had opted to overlook their Springboks returning from Australia and New Zealand for the semi-final at Newlands. Natal, on the other hand, selected the experienced and versatile Dryburgh. In collaboration with Van Heerden and Taylor the selectors decided he would be at flyhalf and would partner scrumhalf Titch Taylor.

It was a very light and inexperienced Natal side, and few gave them a chance of causing an upset. It was predicted that their only chance lay in winning the loose ball and using their pacy backs well. Both sides

The Natal side that lost their first final, against Northern Transvaal, in 1956.

preferred the running game but it was generally agreed that Province was the best-equipped team in the country to implement the expansive game.

Although the first Currie Cup title was only won 34 years later, Natal came of age in the rugby sense on that September day at Newlands. They outplayed Western Province for all but the last 15 minutes of the match and scored three tries (counting only three points at that stage) to two, and added a single conversion to Western Province's two.

Their plan to disrupt the halfbacks paid dividends, and the three loose forwards, Peter Taylor, Cas Labuschagne and Balfour Lang, played themselves to a standstill in putting pressure on the home halfbacks. Without any replacements allowed for injury, Natal centre Chris Young hobbled along with a strained hamstring that forced him to miss the final. Barry Simpson, too, limped for a great part of the game. Natal held out for the final 15 minutes, which included a missed penalty by Province captain Lockyear. But in the end they carried the day and carried it on merit.

In accordance with the rules of the competition, which was played in three sections, Northern Transvaal automatically progressed to the final, but had to play away from home. The final would therefore be played in Durban, a year before the Natal Rugby Union (NRU) moved their offices to their new headquarters at Kings Park.

The injury to Young created a problem, but it also opened the door for one of Natal's greatest rugby sons, Keith Oxlee, to show his promise and class. The selection committee decided that they would move Dryburgh

PUTTING NATAL ON THE MAP

Izak van Heerden was a rugby visionary. As a coach, he was arguably in the mould of the legendary Danie Craven and Oubaas Markötter. His methods are the forerunner of today's squad systems.

Like so many of the very best coaches, he was an above-average player. He represented Natal in 1934 as no 8, after playing centre, flyhalf and then scrumhalf at school and university. The Second Word War put an end to his playing career, however. As a prisoner of war in Italy, he escaped and took to the hills. There, for nine months, he lived off what he could forage, and remained active in the war effort by assisting the local partisans – at great peril to himself.

Once back, after the war, his coaching career started in earnest with Durban Collegians. He joined the club when he was appointed to the teaching staff of Durban High School in 1934. Collegians were to remain the only club of this loyal player and later coach. It was Van Heerden who took them to league honours in 1952 when they were threatened by relegation. His saving of the club, which ended up as Durban's top club in that very same year, saw him being called upon to look after the fortunes of the Natal provincial side in 1953.

Slowly but surely he turned the 'also-rans' into a side with a running game based on support, pace and skill.

Two of the architects of Natal's golden years between 1956 through to the 70s: flyhalf Keith Oxlee and coach Izak van Heerden.

This made Natal a force against even the best provincial sides in the country, and it helped them to reach most of their highest peaks until they eventually won the Currie Cup in 1990.

The first real sign of Van Heerden's success as a coach was in 1953 when the Wallabies capitulated in their tour match against Natal. With a former University of Natal teammate and friend, Basil Medway, as head of the Natal selectors from 1955, the 'new image' rugby, as Van Heerden called it, was well and truly on its way.

The new approach became almost immediately noticeable outside the borders of Natal. Supporters flocked to see Natal play their expansive game. This was also the case when Natal played away from home, despite the threat they posed to all the top provincial sides.

Those were the days in which the 'brotherhood', as Van Heerden called it, was forged. Blommie van Blommenstein, Dan Smillie and Medway were the three selectors; Van Heerden was coach, and that great leader of men and rugby sides, Peter Taylor, was captain.

The side that later held the famous 1955 British Lions to an 11–8 win, could call on only one forward (Taylor) and two backs from the 1953 team that had beaten the Wallabies.

The young Natalians were ready for the future and the new game that Van Heerden would base on a new approach.

It was Van Heerden who prepared the team for the 1956 Currie Cup final against Northern Transvaal at the Kingsmead Cricket Ground; a win which was only to be denied them in the last minutes.

The best players in Durban had by now moved their allegiance and membership to Durban Collegians. This was one of the reasons why this side quickly became the leading club in Durban and Natal. During and after Van Heerden's involvement, and with input from his disciples from the early years, Durban Collegians dominated the Moor Cup. They won the title 21 times and shared it twice in the 31 seasons between 1958 and 1987. They also won the Moor Cup five times in the eight years between 1958 and 1966.

Natal and Junior Springbok captain Brian Irvine.

The system whereby Van Heerden had the few players from Pietermaritzburg, who were needed for the provincial side, come down to Durban for two training sessions per week with his own club, was in fact nothing more than a very effective forerunner of today's squad training. However, it was not as intensive in hours and fitness training as today's squads are.

Durban Collegians, as core and base for the provincial side, played a major part in making Natal a team that was feared by opposition and loved by spectators. They were technically better equipped and were also much, much fitter for provincial games than most of the country's provincial sides, that only assembled for one afternoon or evening in the week before a provincial game.

It was, alas, not a period of much Currie Cup rugby. In the three years between 1957 and 1959 the Currie Cup was decided over the two seasons of 1957 and 1959, with 1958 declarted a 'rest' year because of France's first tour to South Africa.

In 1960, under Brian Irvine, Natal drew 6–all with the might of New Zealand rugby at Kings Park. In 1961 they were adjudged team of the year, going through unbeaten in their nine matches, with a draw of 9–all against Western Province being their only 'blemish'.

Natal lost 13–3 to the 1962 Lions but then, at last, Van Heerden was recognised as a coach at national level and put in charge of the Springboks. The three tests they won provided some of the best, most entertaining rugby seen from a Springbok side, without neglecting the basics.

In 1963, when Natal were unbeaten in ten matches, there was no Currie Cup; but the Wallabies were beaten again. In 1964, Western Province won the Currie Cup, which was decided on a league basis, and Van Heerden's side went down to the eventual winners at Newlands as well as to Northern Transvaal. The win against the Light Blues in the return match was not enough to end top of the log.

Then, in 1965, Van Heerden was sent to Argentina to assist their national team on the eve of their visit to South Africa. There had been previous contact between the two countries, with Junior Springbok sides visiting Argentina in 1932 and 1959. Initially he was to be on a month-long visit only, but his impact was such that he was requested to stay on longer. Van Heerden did just that. He accompanied the Pumas to and throughout South Africa and coached them to a victory over the Junior Springboks.

Van Heerden helped combine the best of the South African coaching techniques with the natural strengths and skills of the Argentinian players. He identified one of the greatest players of all time while in Argentina; the great Hugo Porta cut his teeth under the Natal mentor, whom they called 'Tito' in Argentina.

In 1965 Van Heerden went back to Argentina, with a double brief from the SA Rugby Board: to coach the Gazelle (SA under-23) side and proceed with coaching assistance to Argentina.

His philosophy of adaptability, whereby every player had to think for himself; his constant back-up and inter-linking

Both Natal captains and both no 8s. Tommy Bedford, above, also captained the Springboks and Peter Taylor skippered the Junior Boks.

between forwards and backs; his skills plus his knowledge of the game, brought an unprecedented number of Natal players to the national selectors' attention.

Van Heerden's era of coaching Natal produced two Springbok captains: Roy Dryburgh, who had come from Western Province, and Tommy Bedford. There were also two Junior Springbok captains, Peter Taylor and Brian Irvine, as well as a host of internationals.

Keith Oxlee, Mike Antelme, Trix Truter, Ormond Taylor, Snowy Suter, Hannes Viljoen, Rodney Gould, Martin van Rensburg, Don Walton, Klippies Kritzinger and Chris Denysschen had all come from the Van Heerden stable.

Add Junior Boks Lappies Labuschagne, Chris Holtshauzen, Gareth Williamson and Gazelle players Julian Bennett, Rex Greyling, Brian Borgen, Dok Louw, Malcom Swanby and Poenie Holm, and one has the picture of a man who could coach and mould players.

Van Heerden wrote a number of internationally famous coaching manuals, which are still being used today. He has indeed left a lasting rugby legacy, not only in Natal, but in South Africa as a whole, as well as in Argentina.

Peter Taylor

to centre in Young's place. Dryburgh's place at flyhalf, where he played against Western Province, would be taken by the young Oxlee.

It was a daunting task, taking on the Light Blues whose pack, even in those days, was the basis of their play and success. The Light Blues had a substantial weight advantage of more than six kilograms per man. Furthermore, they had an outstanding lineout duo in former Natal lock Hennie Nel and Frans de Jager, and a loose trio that was quick and, in close contests, also abrasive.

Natal, on the other hand, were probably a little more penetrative behind the scrum, and the thought was that Natal would use this avenue to try and secure their first cup win. It would be, as it was for many years to come, a matter of big forwards against quick, skilful backs.

It was a big game. Special trains and even special flights were used to bring in spectators from afar. Tickets were at a premium and the black market prospered. It was hoped that it would be Natal's biggest rugby day yet. But it wasn't.

Playing the territorial game at which they are still so very adept, Northern Transvaal took a stranglehold up front. They drove hard and aggressively and kept their grip on the tight phases, while the much lighter Natal forwards gave it all they had. They were well supported by their backs who created space from time to time, with Oxlee and Dryburgh at the heart of their attacks. Natal were 6–0 behind after a Northerns try made by wing Willa Esterhuizen following a break by scrumhalf Dennis Victor, who was probably the most influential player in the match. The Northerns' wing, Springbok Dolf Bekker, added three points when he marked, and then successfully dropped for goal.

Oxlee, who became the scourge of so many defenders over the years at all levels, then chipped ahead for Dryburgh to collect. At speed, the big Springbok back broke through the tackles, and sent Gavin Duffy over. Dryburgh converted, and added a long-range penalty to see Natal creep ahead 8–6 and lead at the break.

And so it stayed until about 15 minutes before the end. Northern Transvaal threw everything they had into their attack. Visions of Natal captain Peter Taylor remain: standing off the scrum and the breakdown to block any possible pathway to glory for Northerns around the scrum, where Victor and their loose trio had been so effective. Unfortunately, Natal could not hold out. It was Victor who put the visitors on close attack, and it was from there that Northern Transvaal drove effectively. There was confusion as to whether it was a try and about who had scored, but Natal referee Bawden Coombe had seen enough, and he awarded the try. Flanker Schalk van Dyk was credited with the points, and with five minutes left, it seemed all over for Natal.

Natal kicked off, and with less than two minutes remaining, Northern Transvaal transgressed under the pressure. The wind was a factor. Not only was it blowing in gusts, but also across the field, making it a difficult kick even though it was no more than about 35 metres out from the posts, and between the middle of the field and the touchline. Dryburgh struck it well, and the ball seemed on course, but at the very end, it veered to the outside of the upright, and Northern Transvaal had won their second title in their third final.

Natal had to wait for a further 28 years to play in their next final. That also came about after what had seemed a most unlikely semi-final win.

It was the era of the great Izak van Heerden, whose contribution to South African rugby was immense. Unfortunately for Van Heerden and the young players who were coming through the ranks in those years, and who were suited to the Van Heerden running style, there was little Currie Cup rugby in which to show their prowess. Between 1957 and 1959 one (very strange) Currie Cup title was decided over the two seasons of 1957 and 1959, with no Currie Cup rugby in 1958, as it was declared a 'rest' year because of the first tour by France to South Africa in that year.

Natal were unbeaten in 1961 and 1963, and were adjudged team of the year in 1961. But the next Currie Cup competition, again decided on a league basis, only came around in 1964. Natal lost twice: against eventual winners Western Province at Newlands and to Northern Transvaal in Durban. They beat Northerns in the return match at Loftus. Natal had arrived as a real factor.

However, when Currie Cup finals became an annual

THE COMRADES MARATHON IN RUGBY BOOTS

No history of Natal rugby would be complete without a reference to Bill Payn. In fact, he is probably worth an entire book on his own. The legendary Natal forward played for his province over a period of 18 seasons, and in that time represented Natal in 59 matches.

His love for the game and schoolboy rugby (he was a teacher at Durban High School) saw him move to the administration of schools rugby in Natal in 1933.

During the Second World War, as a prisoner of war, he helped to arrange 'test' matches between the POWs of South Africa and those of New Zealand. In fact, Payn served as a 'Springbok selector'. In one of these 'tests' in Poland, Payn related afterwards, a pit of green sand was discovered near the camp and that was used to mark the sandy field's lines. He was also involved in making green 'Springbok' jerseys. Red Cross vests were boiled together with olive green Russian battledresses to obtain the green colour, and the gold on the jerseys came from South African Medical staff who boiled up a solution of anti-malaria tablets.

Payn, who became a Springbok in 1924 when he played on the flank in two tests against the British Isles, was an extraordinary man. He represented Natal in five sports: cricket, boxing, baseball, athletics and rugby. He was an academic, and recognised as an outstanding English scholar; at the time, he was a leading South African expert in the science of etymology; a philosopher; a lover of rugby and the man who was the first to get official standing for the Natal schools side in 1933. He served on the schools' executive for 26 years, from 1933 until his death in 1956.

Payn was also known for his wit and humour and his sometimes strange exploits, of which running and finishing the Comrades Marathon in rugby boots and attaining eighth place in 1922 is probably the most famous. His one and only Comrades was the first 'up' run in the Comrades, from Durban to Pietermaritzburg. Finishing it was a feat in itself. Doing so in rugby boots was beyond belief, and what made it really incredible were Payn's stops for refreshments along the way.

He first had breakfast in a hotel near the roadside at Hillcrest, when he had stopped to put some ointment on the blisters that had already formed. At Botha's Hill he shared a curried chicken with a fellow-runner (an old friend) and at Drummond, the two of them went into a pub to quench what he described as a 'terrible thirst' with a few beers. Then Payn finished a tumbler of peach brandy offered to him by a little old lady next to the road near Pietermaritzburg, and as he entered the capital, he darted off to have tea and cake with his wife's family at the roadside.

With feet he described as 'pads of blisters', Payn had a good night's rest, and then ran out in a club match the next day. This time his sore feet forced him to play in takkies, which he should have used in the Comrades the day before!

The legendary Bill Payn.

occurrence in 1968, Natal were not represented in the play-offs then, or in the following year. In 1970 they played Northern Transvaal in the semi-final at Kings Park, but lost 24–8. In the following year Natal went down rather heavily again, when Transvaal beat them 23–10 at Ellis Park.

Then followed a period of quiet until 1982. By then Natal had been relegated to the B Section, and qualified for the semi-finals by virtue of the ruling that the top two sides in the B Section qualified for a play-off with the top A Section sides.

In 1982, under Wynand Claassen, Natal were trounced 47–18 by Western Province at Newlands. The following year the clash between these two sides saw Western Province sneak in at 7–3, this time at Kings Park.

Natal's first place in the B Section in 1984 saw them spring the surprise against the Free State in Durban mentioned above, and they qualified for the final against Western Province.

In 1986 Natal lost 18–4 to Transvaal and were, at last, promoted to the A Section by a boardroom decision. Four years later their first Currie Cup title was theirs.

Wynand Claassen, famous Springbok captain of the 1981 tour who did so much for Natal rugby and rugby in Natal, tells the story of that 1984 semi-final with the humour that is so typical of him, and also with a certain amount of glee.

'In the previous two years we had lost our semi-finals against Western Province. With the exception of our 1983 defeat to Province, all the defeats of the B Section teams in these play-offs were large margins.

'But we had worked very hard throughout the year. We were fit and we had, over time, given particular attention to our scrums.' This was something that started when Claassen came down from Northern Transvaal, and found that then coach Roger Gardner was also a believer in the scrum as a platform for success.

'The Free State captain, Gerrie Sonnekus, stated in television interviews that his team was "looking forward to the final against Western Province".

'From our side we played down our chances of winning the semi-final, but we had been planning for it,' tells Claassen.

He laughs when he tells of the decision to play Springbok Gawie Visagie, usually a scrumhalf, at flyhalf. 'When he walked into the change room after his selection he said: "Hi guys, meet Naas Visagie!"' In fact the freckled halfback did score a drop goal in the style of Naas Botha, South Africa's drop-kick king.

It was one of those hot, sultry days, Claassen relates, and he took the Natal side to the outside fields of Kings Park, adjacent to the changing rooms on the outfields, which had to be used as the stadium was under construction.

'We worked hard and got our rhythm right, to make sure that everything, including our technique, was a hundred percent. Meanwhile the backs ran their moves on the rest of the field.'

Later, huge Free State and Springbok lock Vleis Visagie, after he had joined Natal in 1987, admitted to how the Free Staters just sat in the changing room. 'They felt it was warm enough and that a warm-up was unnecessary.' Claassen laughs.

Free State went onto the field with a record as a great scrummaging side, and boasting the most exciting backs in the country.

'We knew we had to scrum well, that we had the technique and that we were fit. We got a great hit in that first scrum, and didn't let up.'

Natal were on top in the scrums; their backs rattled the free-running Free State runners, who showed up under pressure; and their loose forwards, with Claassen exemplary in this play and in his captaincy, won the day.

The result was that the home side scored four tries by wing Des Mclean (2), Claassen and his fellow loose forward Derek la Marque. Two of them were goaled by Hugh Reece-Edwards who also kicked a penalty, and Visagie scored that drop goal. The win by 26–15 set Natal up for their second Currie Cup final, against Western Province at Newlands.

Once again, Natal were given no chance. After all, they couldn't beat the bottom side of the A Section in the promotion game. They also had to lift themselves for a second week after their great heights of the semi-final. Added to that, Western Province were in the midst of a golden run after a last title in 1966 and a shared

THE SEMI-FINAL SHOCK

Tinkering with the Currie Cup system has over the years been a favourite pastime of the country's top administrators. Dr Danie Craven's principle of strength versus strength was at the bottom of the new merit-based division of teams in the early 80s, whereby the best were in the A Section of the Currie Cup competition, while the rest battled it out on their own in the B Section before small crowds and against opposition of lesser quality.

There was, however, a strange carrot of consolation for these second-class competitors, in that the two top sides in the A Section played on the fields of the two top sides of the B Section in so-called semi-finals.

The B Section sides were undoubtedly of lesser strength, as proved by the difficulty experienced by Natal to win their promotion-relegation matches in their effort to get back into the A Section.

This was also the case in 1984, when Northern Free State, last in the A Section, beat the B Section winner, Natal, 27–10 in Welkom to retain their place in the elite and financially more lucrative A Section.

That promotion-relegation match preceded what was probably the biggest semi-final shock in the Currie Cup, competition on 29 September 1984 in a hot and humid Durban.

Second-placed in the A Section, the confident Free State had to travel down to Durban while A Section log leaders, Western Province, faced second-placed Eastern Transvaal, a match they won 53–0.

Free State were overwhelming favourites, even away from home. They had just comprehensively beaten Northern Transvaal 29–7 in a play-off match to clinch second spot on the log and a virtually guaranteed Currie Cup final berth. This was a further boost to their confidence after they had trounced Transvaal 42–8 before seeing off Northern Transvaal.

Two old loose forward adversaries, Natal captain Wynand Claassen, on the ground, and Western Province's captain Boland Coetzee on the same side in a national trials match.

The Grand Stand was being rebuilt at Kings Park at the time, so the teams changed in changing rooms between Kings Park 2 and Kings Park 3. Wynand Claassen arranged for there to be a scrumming machine on Kings Park 4, and fifteen minutes before kick-off, Wynand had his team pushing against this heavy piece of equipment on a back field, while the backs ran around with enthusiasm in the heat. The scrumming session was especially vigorous.

By way of contrast, Free State did not bother to warm up. Onto the field the teams went, and Natal won the first scrum against the heavier pack and did not let up for the whole match. As a result their loose forwards prospered.

Within ten minutes Natal had scored three tries, two by Des McLean and one by Derek la Marque. Wynand Claassen scored the final try of the match. It was the great man's retirement year, a great way to finish, taking Natal from the B Section to the Currie Cup final.

The expected final between Western Province and the Free State was scheduled for Newlands, and complimentary tickets had been flown from Cape Town to Bloemfontein even before the Natal win. The tickets had the name of Free State as one of the finalists printed on them and had to be destroyed! Western Province won the final against Natal fairly convincingly (19–9), but a lesson had been learnt by the Free State: chickens should not be counted before they're hatched.

For Natal, in only their second Currie Cup final, there was the knowledge that anything was possible – except winning promotion back to the A Section of the competition, it seemed. On his return from the 1981 Springbok tour to New Zealand, Springbok captain Wynand Claassen found that his Natal side had been relegated to the B Section. When he retired at the end of 1984, Natal were still on the second tier of South African rugby, unable to win the annual promotion-relegation matches.

Promotion eventually came at the end of 1986 through an SA Rugby Board decision, and four seasons later Natal won their very first Currie Cup.

title in 1979. They had come back to win the Currie Cup in finals against Northern Transvaal in 1982 and 1983, and to add to all their advantages, the Newlands pitch underfoot was yielding.

'We got the fright of our lives,' Western Province captain Divan Serfontein admitted afterwards.

Two drop kicks by Gawie ('Naas') Visagie and a penalty by Hugh Reece-Edwards put Natal 9–3 up at half-time, after Province fullback Calla Scholtz had kicked a penalty. The home side's dangerous backs were put under pressure, as Natal had done with the Free State three-quarters, but two tries that went begging and one seemingly good try not awarded by Northern Transvaal referee Cassie Carstens ultimately made the difference.

As the heavy field began to work in favour of Western Province, they scored three tries through Rob Louw, Calla Scholtz and Neil Burger, with two conversions added to their first-half penalty, giving the Capetonians a third successive title at 19–9.

In 1986 Natal lost 18–4 to Transvaal and were, at last, promoted by a boardroom decision. Then Natal – without a semi-final – won their first Currie Cup final at Loftus in 1990.

By then, one of the most influential players and men in Natal's rugby history had called it a day. Wynand Claassen, who captained Northern Transvaal and played in three Currie Cup finals for what, at that time, had been the virtually perennial Currie Cup champions, had moved down to Natal in 1980.

He was made captain in that very same year. He took Natal to within six points of the visiting British Lions of 1980, who won 21–15. The margin was five points when Natal lost their last game of 1980 to Transvaal 27–22, to finish third on the Currie Cup log and miss out on a final.

Like Peter Taylor before him, who took Natal to the brink of the Currie Cup in 1956 and captained the Junior Springboks without ever donning the green and gold, Wynand Claassen seemed destined to miss out on test rugby, despite being in the frame for some years. In another parallel with Taylor, he led a good side, without many real stars, to a level of competitiveness by sheer example and motivation. And if it was a highlight when he was selected for the Springboks for his first test in

Tony Watson evades a Transvaal tackler.

1981, and was appointed the national captain to boot, the next best thing was the win over Northern Transvaal in Pretoria in 1980.

'It was my first visit back to Loftus since switching to Natal,' Claassen recalls. Northerns had to be beaten to keep up Natal's challenge for a place in the final or even the Currie Cup title itself.

'With Roger Gardner, we had worked hard. We stayed in the Palms Hotel in Pretoria. I read excerpts from Izak van Heerden's book *Target Tryline* to the guys; enforced the idea of continuous attack; told them to persevere if something didn't work and to come again and again, as Izak had written.

'We had talked about it. The team was motivated, and when we were up 16–3 at half-time, I knew we could make it.

'Roger came down to where we were drinking water at half-time, in front of the main stand where the players run on. In those days, no contact between coach and the team was allowed.

'He leaned over the fence and told me to talk to the players and tell them the win was on; that they now had to play for one another and for me, that it was important to me.'

That his men responded says much about the man who was leading them on his first return to Loftus.

Natal won 22–19, with Naas Botha lining up the equaliser but somehow missing it, to give Claassen a win he still cherishes.

Claassen captained South Africa in all seven of his tests, and emulated the previous Natal player to achieve the highest honour available to a South African player. Tommy Bedford captained the Boks in 1969. Like Claassen, he was also an architect.

Both of them were thinkers on the game and liberal thinkers in general; both were unwavering in their belief of what was right and outspoken about it; both were mobile and a touch light for their position as eighthman; they were both marvellous linking and cross-covering loose forwards; and both played for Durban University and Durban Collegians.

Whereas Bedford started with the university side and then moved to Collegians, Claassen moved from Collegians after his return from the 1981 Springbok tour. He believed that Natal needed a good university side to keep it strong, and his aim was to get the university side promoted back from the lower league. It took him two years to achieve that, as he played lower-league club rugby in that time. Claassen called it a day when he was months away from his 34th birthday, but he kept on giving unstintingly to the game he loved and the province he had made his own.

Although Naas Botha's remark after the 1990 final came back to bite him early in the 1992 season, 1991 was not an outstanding year for the new champions. Botha was to some extent vindicated when Northern Transvaal won the Currie Cup that year, after beating Transvaal 27–15 in the final.

But it wasn't altogether a bad year for Natal. As they had one or two results go their way the previous year, Natal missed out this time and lost a few close matches. Natal also found that the other sides were out to topple them, as is the wont of those slighted by the champions the previous year. And perhaps, just perhaps, there was a little complacency in the Natal camp. Added to a greater understanding, by opposing sides, of the new direct game McIntosh had implemented, better defence against the new game plan helped to keep Natal in their place.

It was also the end of the road for Craig Jamieson, after 10 seasons for Natal during which he captained them 77 times. The nuggetty little man had to make the choice between a career as rugby administrator and another year or two on the field of play.

In any case, Currie Cup losses to Transvaal (twice), Eastern Province, Western Province (twice) and Free State made it a rather average year, and with the friendlies and Yardley Cup fixtures added, Natal won only 11 of their 21 matches.

Gone was the inconsistency of the previous year when Natal won their first three matches (all friendlies) in 1992 by big margins, including a 46–12 win over Eastern Province who had beaten them in a Currie Cup fixture the previous year.

A record points tally of 31 points against Western Province in Natal's 31–19 win at Kings Park started off their Currie Cup campaign positively, but Naas Botha then scored all 27 points at Loftus as Northern Transvaal beat Natal 27–24. That was the last loss of the year for Natal in the Currie Cup.

One of the season's highlights was the 19–11 win over Western Province at Newlands and what made this special was that it was the first time since the semi-final in 1956, and only the second time ever, that Natal had won at South Africa's 'Seat of rugby'.

It was also the first time that Natal had finished top-of-the-log in the Currie Cup since the inception of the competition in 1892. However, that counted for naught, as the venue for the final was decreed to be Ellis Park by virtue of a ruling that two sides will change venue from the last time they met in a play-off, and that was in the 1986 semi-final in Durban.

Natal led 8–3 at half-time, after an early try by Gary Teichmann following a break by Pieter Müller. The first hour of the match belonged to Natal as they barged and hit the opposing backs in what had become known as 'McIntosh's direct rugby', and then took it wide with some good interplay.

Transvaal got their score 11 minutes after half-time, when Springbok centre Heinrich Fuhls scored. At 8–7 to the good, Natal had more pressure to contend with and in the end it was new Springbok Theo van Rensburg, now playing for Transvaal, who again let Natal through to drink from the golden cup with a 14–13 win.

But blaming Van Rensburg merely for the missed kick would be unfair. The better side had won because of great defence and control of the game for nearly 60 minutes, and their record throughout a season which showed only one Currie Cup defeat, to Northern Transvaal, and a draw against Transvaal in the league stages. They deserved the trophy.

Once again Bartmann was the scourge of his former side. He led well after the retirement of Jamieson, but it was the way in which he got his side across the advantage line with his powerful drives that made him the menace he was, in this and other matches.

It was Transvaal captain Jannie Breedt's fourth final loss as a Currie Cup captain, but he had put his side in the frame since the first lost outing in 1986. In 1993, François Pienaar had taken over the captaincy of what had now become the Gauteng Lions.

In fact, it was a season of change as Ian McIntosh became the Springbok coach; the Super 10 was played for the first time; Harry Viljoen had moved down from Johannesburg and filled the boots of McIntosh as Natal coach; and Natal blooded a host of new players because of call-ups to the Springbok side for the tour to Australia.

Under Viljoen, Natal stayed with McIntosh's direct rugby, but mixed it with an exuberance that was part of the young coach's lifestyle and his outlook on life. Records – tries, points and victory margins – fell by the wayside in their march to the final. Nine players from Natal toured Australia with the Boks, and Wahl Bartmann was injured for a large portion of the season. But they were back, and with brilliant performances behind them, Natal were ready to win their third title and their first at home when they faced the Lions on 16 October 1993.

Natal lost 21–16. Uli Schmidt pounced on a high ball that Johan Roux had launched after a lineout, Cabous van der Westhuizen couldn't field cleanly, and Schmidt broke Natal hearts just three minutes from time.

It was a game lost by Natal just as much as it was won by the Lions. However, the fact that Transvaal had won three of the four outings against Natal during the course of the season made the Currie Cup final result a just one, and that's without taking into account that the visitors had scored two tries to nil in the first Currie Cup final at Kings Park, with five Joel Stransky penalties accounting for all Natal's points.

The match brought an end to the wonderful career of Tony Watson, who was never capped for his country. Schmidt, jumping for a ball, smashed into the face of the man who had played more than 130 consecutive matches for his province out of a total of 144. Reconstructive surgery was needed, and Watson never played again.

It was the golden era of the Lions, as they won the 1994 Currie Cup competition as well. This meant that new Natal coach Harry Viljoen had lost his second Currie Cup final, the first for Transvaal against Natal and the second for Natal against Transvaal.

MAC AND THE WINNING GAME PLAN

The great Izak van Heerden first put Natal on the rugby map, but the input and influence of Natal, Springbok and Sharks coach Ian McIntosh can never be forgotten. Like a good many of South Africa's best players, McIntosh came from Zimbabwe. And it was an injury, as it so often is, that turned him to coaching.

Van Heerden assisted in coaching the Queens Sports Club from Bulawayo when they were on a tour to Durban, and made an immense impression on McIntosh.

Mac, the man with the big eyes and fixed stare when watching his team play, and who calls everyone Master, moved to Durban in the 1980s, and the day in 1986 when he first travelled as coach of Natal remains one of his proudest days.

Natal were still in the B Section then, but he slowly turned the team around, with a new approach and game plan that was not liked by all, especially in Natal! McIntosh, however, realised that the players were bigger, faster and quicker than when he started coaching, and the defence patterns were more sophisticated. Change had to come, and McIntosh was one of the first to effect it by implementing the 'direct rugby' game plan. Although still using the drills and skills that were Van Heerden's legacy, McIntosh had adapted the style of play. It wasn't as pretty as in the 1950s to the 1970s, but it was effective.

Australia coach Rod McQueen became a friend, and in 1992 McIntosh went to visit him in Australia. It was a period spent talking, and the Natal coach (soon to be the Springbok coach) watched the Wallaby coach training his squad, and came to understand and appreciate the coaching methods and game plan he used. A spell with Alec Evans, coach of the Souths club in Brisbane, also taught the Natal coach more about the new drills and angled running.

McIntosh could understand the criticism levelled at him, but he remained adamant: running the ball wide as they used to do was something of the past. He pointed out that Natal were still scoring the tries and winning matches with the new direct approach whereby possession and retention of the ball were what mattered.

His success is proof enough. Natal and the Sharks won the Currie Cup four times between 1990 (their first ever title) and 1999. McIntosh was the coach all four times. There was a break of two years when he coached the Springboks, and Harry Viljoen, Noel Olivier and Andy Keast took over the reins, but the man with the 'Mac Stare' was back in 1995.

McIntosh's interest in the game and his contribution to rugby after retiring as Natal and Sharks coach after 12 years (the longest reign after Van Heerden) continued, and among others he has been a national selector for four years, a position he still holds.

Ian McIntosh puts the scrum through their grunts

Sharks and Springbok captain Gary Teichmann.

If 1991 was a disappointment, 1994 was worse. Natal beat the touring England team 21–6, reached the final of the Super 10, but lost 21–10 to defending champions Queensland at Kings Park.

In the Currie Cup, Free State won both the Currie Cup fixtures. Natal were also beaten by Northern Transvaal. Eastern Province, Western Province and the Lions also beat Natal, who ended their Currie Cup campaign to finish with a record of only four wins from ten fixtures.

In 1995, Natal became the Natal Sharks and Ian McIntosh was fired as Springbok coach by Louis Luyt, shortly before the World Cup.

There were upheavals on the return of the now former Springbok coach to the Natal fold, with a number of players reluctant to have McIntosh back. In the end, after a management decision, some senior players' heads rolled and they didn't play for the Natal Sharks again that season.

Meanwhile, the Natal Sharks had secured the services of the outstanding French players Olivier Roumat (lock) and Thierry Lacroix (flyhalf), after a clandestine meeting between NRU president Keith Parkinson and the two stars who played against South Africa in the 1995 World Cup semi-final in Durban.

It was a season built on the kicking prowess of Luke Smith who had arrived from Northern Transvaal. He scored 158 points, some of them at crucial moments or at the end of a match when the kick would make the difference between winning and losing.

The Natal Sharks went into the 1995 final against Western Province with only two losses from ten matches (against Western Province and the Lions) and won back the Currie Cup. It was the first time the Sharks' supporters had seen them take the honours after Currie Cup final losses against Northern Transvaal (1956) and Transvaal (1993). The season also saw the appointment of Gary Teichmann as captain of the Sharks, in place of Bartmann who had called it a day because of injury and business commitments.

This time Cabous van der Westhuizen got the bounce from a kick by Thierry Lacroix, and made amends for his error in 1993 by stretching the Natal Sharks' lead to 10–3 when his try was converted by Lacroix. With Lacroix and Western Province's Joel Stransky trading penalties, the score stood at 16–12 when Province's Tiaan Strauss scored. Stransky missed the conversion and two late Sharks penalties gave the home side a 25–17 win.

In 1996, the Sharks reached the final of the first Super 12 competition but went down to the Auckland Blues at Eden Park (45–21). They piled up the records again with the most tries in a Currie Cup season and the most points. Henry Honiball equalled the Natal record with four tries against Boland, and also set a record of 38 points in a single match in that encounter.

The new Currie Cup system, in which all 14 unions (reduced from 22) took part in two sections, saw huge scores and little of the strength-versus-strength concept that had marked the Currie Cup competition in previous years.

The Sharks won the quarter-final against Griquas 51–3 and the semi-final against Free State by 35–20. And once again the Lions awaited them.

The 1996 final had a special edge. François Pienaar, the man who had taken the Springboks to the World Cup title and had overseen the resurgence of the Lions with two Currie Cup titles in 1993 and 1994, had been dropped by Springbok coach André Markgraaff. Markgraaff had replaced Pienaar as Springbok captain with Gary Teichmann, and the rugby fraternity was upset, especially at Ellis Park where the final was played.

The game turned on a moment just into the second

Sharks flyhalf and playmaker Henry Honiball.

quarter when Sharks centre Jeremy Thomson ran the perfect line to score from a ruck. Gavin Lawless, son of Springbok Mike, who played in the late 1950s and 1960s, kept the home side in the picture at 10–9 when half-time came. Lawless won the lead back for Transvaal with his fourth penalty (12–10), only for Henry Honiball to slot one. With Lawless responding, the score stood at 15–13 to the Lions when, with only 15 minutes to go, André Joubert cut in to receive on the inside from ball carrier, Jeremy Thomson. The gap was there and his acceleration carried him through. Five minutes later it was again the Rolls Royce of fullbacks, as they called Joubert in Durban. He chipped ahead, got the bounce, and the Natal Sharks had, at last, made it with back-to-back Currie Cup titles.

It was also their fourth Currie Cup title in the 1990s.

In 1997, the Sharks again reached the Super 12 final against the same opponents and at the same venue. This time they lost 55–36.

With their Springboks overseas, the Sharks went on to record 29 successive wins since the previous year. They were on course for a hat-trick of Currie Cup wins, but then, in their last league match, they went down 33-28 to Northern Transvaal, who were now the Bulls. Natal Sharks lost the semi-final against Free State 40–22, and they were out of it.

Current Springbok Ryan Kankowski is a devastating runner.

And so it was again in 1998. The Sharks lost two successive matches without their seven Springboks who were on tour. This was how the Currie Cup competition was now being played, and in future years it would become even worse, with returning Springboks grounded to get some decent rest in between the Super series, test matches and the Currie Cup. First Griquas beat the Sharks 23–17, then the Lions won 11–10 at Ellis Park. A draw against Free State and a loss against Western Province saw the Sharks contesting the semi-final with the Blue Bulls, who won rather comfortably, 31–17.

The Blue Bulls won the 1998 final against Western Province 24–20.

After two Super 12 finals and a semi-final in the first three years of this international competition, the Sharks didn't qualify for a play-off in 1999.

But they did so in the Currie Cup competition. With the World Cup taking place, the Sharks had nine players unavailable for large portions of the competition.

They duly reached the semi-final and won against the Free State Cheetahs (Free State's new name) 45–8 after suffering defeats against Griquas (29–23), SWD Eagles (28–14) and Eastern Province (22–16).

However, with the Lions waiting again, the Natal Sharks were simply not up to it, and lost 32–9 at Kings Park.

There was probably a reason for the big defeat that had nothing to do with the ability of the two teams. Beforehand, much was made of the retirement of four

Sharks captain Johann Muller, right, shares the joy of the 2008 Currie Cup after this side had beaten the Blue Bulls.

Natal and Natal Sharks heroes: coach Ian McIntosh, captain Gary Teichmann, flyhalf Henry Honiball and full-back André Joubert.

McIntosh said afterwards that he had expected problems in the match, as all the players were too keyed up beforehand in order to give the departing four a good send-off. He was proven right, as the Lions ran in five tries to nil, with Thinus Delport, later to play for the Sharks, scoring two of them.

It was the end of the 1990s and the end of an era, but the Sharks were not done with play-offs or titles quite yet.

There was another lost final in 2000. Rudolf Straeuli had taken over the coaching and had a young but exciting and promising side, interspersed with some experience, to tackle the season. They qualified for the final, but went down 25–15 to Western Province in Durban, at what was now called the ABSA Stadium.

Western Province were on somewhat of a roll, and retained the Currie Cup the next year, this time beating the Sharks at Newlands 29–24.

A 40–19 defeat to the Blue Bulls in the 2003 final followed before the Sharks took revenge five years later when they beat the Blue Bulls in Durban 14–9.

'The significance for us was that this Sharks team needed to realise that they could win a final; that a final was not something that was going to always prove a bridge too far for them,' Sharks coach John Plumtree

Currie Cup celebrations at Absa Stadium after the 2008 win.

said afterwards to Ken Borland of MWP, writing for the *SA Rugby Annual, 2009*.

The Sharks won 12 of their 14 matches to end top of the 2008 Currie Cup log. They went on to beat the Golden Lions 29–14 in the semi-final in Durban. That set them up for a final against the second-placed team on the log, the Blue Bulls, who had beaten the Free State Cheetahs 31–19 in Pretoria in the other semi-final.

Two tries, both converted, to nil tell the story of the Sharks' dominance in their 14–9 win over the Blue Bulls that broke the run of four Currie Cup final losses and a 12-year drought since their last Currie Cup title.

In 2009, the Sharks again topped the log and again won 12 of their 14 league encounters. This time they faced the Free State Cheetahs in the semi-final and were shaded 23–21 in Durban, while the Blue Bulls beat Province 21–19 in Cape Town. The Bulls won the final against the Cheetahs 36–24.

Sharks coach John Plumtree and his happy team after they had beaten the Blue Bulls in the 2008 Currie Cup final.

dacom
VALKE

CHAPTER 8

Free State

Breakthrough after 82 years

Why is it that a province, after years of being competitive but not quite good enough to make the finals or even semi-finals, suddenly develops into a side that dominates an era? Is it the coach? Or is it the result of a strong management structure that ensures good planning and retention of players after completing school, university, or army call-ups? Perhaps it is merely a case of success breeding success, with more good players flocking to where things are happening.

Natal took the lead in the late 1950s and early 1960s, with a hitherto unknown fitness level that was only paralleled by Northern Transvaal in the last years of that decade. In those years it was probably one of the main factors that saw Natal and Northerns surge ahead of the chasing pack, and also improve on their own fortunes of the past. Of course, like all schools and clubs, there were also the outstanding players to help the various unions in their golden eras.

Whatever the reason, Free State – always very competitive but seldom good enough to really challenge for honours – suddenly blossomed from also-rans to bridesmaids and then champions in the 1970s.

Rugby in the Free State, before the division into many sub-unions and smaller unions like the Northern and Eastern Free State, has always been a serious matter. Big, hard men cried when they lost the 1975 Currie Cup final to Northern Transvaal after that famous Pierre Spies try, and did so again when Free State won the Currie Cup in 1976.

Yes, the Currie Cup was a serious matter …

Heinrich Brussow was a match-winner for the Springboks in the 2009 series against the British and Irish Lions and a scourge for the other teams in the Currie Cup.

THE 1976 FREE STATE TEAM THAT WON THE UNION'S FIRST CURRIE CUP IN 1976 WAS:

Gysie Pienaar, Edrich Krantz, Dirk Froneman, Joggie Jansen, Gerrie Germishuys, De Wet Ras, Barry Wolmarans, Tiny du Plessis, Eben Jansen, Theuns Stofberg, Klippies Kritzinger, Ross van Reenen, Rampie Stander, Wouter Hugo (capt.), Martiens le Roux. Gerrie Sonnekus replaced Eben Jansen in the second half.

The whole backline of the 1976 team played test rugby for South Africa, as did forwards Eben Jansen, Theuns Stofberg, Klippies Kritzinger, Rampie Stander, Martiens le Roux and replacement Gerrie Sonnekus.

Doyen of rugby writers in Bloemfontein, Herman le Roux, tells of how, after the All Blacks' defeat in the second test in 1981 against the Springboks, he witnessed how a very upset Frank Oliver kicked a wooden pillar in a hotel with his big boots. Oliver's language was also fairly crude!

'Calm down,' someone called in an attempt to save the situation, 'it's only a game.'

That really upset the big man, according to Le Roux. 'It's murder, it's a disaster ...' was Oliver's reply.

Just as a rugby test was a matter of life and death for the All Blacks lock, the Currie Cup competition is a serious matter for South Africa's leading players, and their teams' supporters.

The Free State had to wait 82 years before they won the Currie Cup for the first time. That was in 1976, and Bloemfontein became a place of unparalleled joy and festivities that night after the 33–16 win over Western Province. Free State had come a long way in those 82 years before drinking from the golden cup. In fact, it really was more than 82 years, as rugby in the Free State (or the Orange Free State and Basutoland Rugby Union as it was known in the early days) was first played in the 1870s.

The influence of the opening of the diamond field at nearby Kimberley was of course important to the development of the game in the Free State. Kroonstad and Bloemfontein were the mainstays of the Rugby code in the Free State with Association Football having a stronghold in areas such as Harrismith, Jagersfontein and Heilbron.

By 1893 Bloemfontein had four club sides that not only competed among one another, but also frequently played against sides from Kimberley, which had become part of the Cape Colony as the result of some political skulduggery to gain control of the diamond fields there. The opening of the railway line between Kimberley and Bloemfontein did much for this cross-border rugby and the development of the game in both towns – or were they cities?

The four club sides that had carried the Orange Free State in the years prior to the official creation of a union were Pirates, Bloemfontein, Grey College and Railway. Grey College, of course, continued as a school, from which the University of the Free State evolved and, as both school and university, continued to provide the 'old' and 'new' Free State with magnificent rugby talent. Not being a formal union did not deter the Orange Free State from sending a side to take part in the 1894 Currie Cup competition at Newlands in Cape Town.

The Orange Free State only officially became a rugby union in 1895 – six years after the formation of the SA Rugby Football Union in 1889. The Phoenix Hotel was the venue of the meeting where the Orange Free State Rugby Union became an official body on 27 March 1895, and within weeks the show grounds had been procured as a venue. On May Day, 1895, the first match for the brand new Challenge Cup was played between Bloemfontein and Grey, with the former winning by 7–3.

The forerunner of the Blue Bulls, against whom Free State – over the years, but especially in the 1970s and the 2000s – have had so many memorable battles, paid a visit to Bloemfontein. First blood went to the combined Bloemfontein team that beat the Pretoria side 8–5.

Another visit in their first year of existence was by

Western Province. They had won the 1895 Currie Cup tournament held in Johannesburg and stopped over in Bloemfontein. Free State had not sent a team to Johannesburg for the Currie Cup tournament. The Currie Cup champions' win by a 15-point margin was a severe drubbing in those days. Yet there was generally a great improvement in the standard of rugby in Bloemfontein, and in 1896 they led a strong Diggers side from Johannesburg until late in the game, before going down 13–8 to the visitors. That was also the year that Grey College won the Challenge Cup for the first time, after Bloemfontein had won the inaugural competition in 1895.

In 1897 the Pretoria Cavalry, selected from Transvaal President Paul Kruger's bodyguard, visited Bloemfontein, but lost their tour match.

In another noteworthy happening for Free State rugby, the Collegians club was formed in 1902 by a number of ex-public school boys. The club was to exert a great influence on rugby in the Orange Free State in the years to come.

It was followed by the Old Greys Club which was established in 1905.

Meanwhile, the team known as the Orange River Colony gave the 1903 British team of Mark Morrison a fright in going down only 17–16 in Bloemfontein, with the local side packed with players from the Collegians club.

Orange Free State languished at or near the bottom of the log in its first five Currie Cup outings in 1894, 1897, 1898 and after the South African War in 1904 and 1906. In 1908 Orange Free State were third from the bottom, and then had their best year yet in 1911. They finished fourth in the eight-team tournament, and the Free State's winger Boetie McHardy had done enough in that competition to warrant his place in the 1912–1913 Springbok team.

He remained the only Free State Springbok until 1928, despite the Free State sides' (Orange River Colony, Free State and Free State Country Districts) good performances against touring sides. After the above-mentioned 17–16 loss to the 1903 British side, a 12–9 loss to the 1910 British tourists, and wins of 6–0 and 6–3, by the Free State Country Districts and the Free State respectively, against the 1924 touring British team, showed what talent there was in the province.

In 1928, Hennie Potgieter (Old Greys) played in two of the three tests in the drawn series against Maurice Brownlee's All Blacks. In 1914, the Free State side improved even further and finished third on the Currie Cup log in the Durban tournament, and then dropped back somewhat in the next two tournaments.

Then, in 1925 when the Currie Cup was again being contested, Free State showed that they had become a power, and finished second behind Western Province. They followed it up with a third place in 1927 and a fourth position in 1929.

The promise deceived, however, and Free State, despite always being competitive throughout and playing an entertaining brand of rugby, didn't really count among the serious contenders when the Currie Cup spoils were contested until the late 1970s. They did, however, feature in a semi-final in the strange three-section competitions that cropped up from time to time as a Currie Cup system. In 1954, they bowed out to Northern Transvaal, in a close match won 9–8 by the visitors at the Free State Stadium.

It was a case of third time lucky for Free State when they eventually won that first Currie Cup title in 1976. Before that, Northern Transvaal won 30–22 in Free State's first Currie Cup final which was played at Loftus Versfeld in 1973. Then, in 1975, the Free State had the

STOFBERG WINS WITH THREE PROVINCES

Only one player has won the Currie Cup with three different unions. Former Springbok captain Theuns Stofberg won Currie Cup titles with Free State (1976), Northern Transvaal (1979 and 1980) and Western Province (1982 and 1983).

Nelie Smit: captain and coach.

De Wet Ras – a prolific points scorer who kicked the ball the proverbial mile.

Currie Cup in the palm of their collective hand until Pierre Spies scored a spectacular try just before the final whistle. With Keith Thorreson converting, Northerns won 12–6. The Free State players and their supporters were shocked and shaken. It was so near, yet so far.

That Monday morning after Spies' try, Free State's Kleintjie Grobler entered Herman le Roux's office at *Die Volksblad* with a letter in his hand. The Springbok no 8 was extremely upset that the referee, Dr. Justus Moolman, had not awarded what he regarded as a certain try. Grobler had no doubt that he had scored the try that would have assured victory, and the Currie Cup, for Free State. And so Kleintjie had decided to write the letter to Moolman to tell him a few truths.

A referee must realise that rugby players are only human, he wrote, and that it was a traumatic experience for a player when he believed he had scored, only for the try to be denied, especially when it was in a Currie Cup final and could have been the possible winning score. Grobler had, however, written it in his own words and had held nothing back in what was a rather crude letter.

It cost a great deal of persuasion by Le Roux to convince Kleintjie that a letter in that vein would reach the waste paper basket before Moolman had finished reading it! They discussed the letter and then rewrote it, with a rather less aggressive tone. What was obvious from that letter was that the Currie Cup meant a tremendous lot to a rugby player.

For Kleintjie Grobler, as for players like Frans de Jager, Sakkie van Zyl, Johan de Bruyn, Chum van Staden and many other great characters in Free State rugby, a Currie Cup match wasn't just another provincial game.

Sakkie van Zyl (121 matches for Free State) and his great friend Nelie Smith (60 matches) never had the honour of playing in a Currie Cup final. They did, however, coach the Free State sides for their first three Currie Cup finals in 1973, 1975 and in 1976, when Free State's Currie Cup drought was at last broken.

They also come very close to a first final in 1954, but Free State were beaten 9–8 by Northern Transvaal in the semi-final. They were denied when what would have been the winning try was not awarded after a light knock, although the ball was not dropped as in the case of Pierre Spies' winner in 1975. Still, it was a knock-on, according to the laws of the game in 1954.

The win in the 1976 final was only the third by the Free State in any Currie Cup match against Western Province, and came after they had lost the previous two league encounters against the Cape team that year. Despite these defeats, Free State made it to the final thanks to Natal's 7–6 win over Transvaal and the latter's defeat against Northern Transvaal.

It was indeed a final to remember and it was a team effort of the highest order by Wouter Hugo's team that secured the win. This time there was no try shortly before the end to clinch the title, but the first try, by new Springbok Edrich Krantz, was memorable. The right wing scored after 30 players had handled the ball in the 94 seconds that the ball was in play.

There is also the memory of the Western Province pack being marched back metres near to the end of the match, and De Wet Ras punishing them with a 55-yard penalty, as well as of scrumhalf Barry Wolmarans who defied the pain of an injured ankle to become one of his side's heroes. He scored a try and dropped a goal from a mark from 40 metres out.

Free State and Cheetahs Springbok Meyer Bosman.

FEEDER SCHOOL FOR MORE THAN JUST THE CHEETAHS

The former Free State, and now the Cheetahs, have over the years been the feeder union for many other rugby teams in the country, and have in turn relied largely on the rugby production line that is Grey College, the oldest school north of the Orange River, which opened on 17 January 1859.

Football was first played against another school in June 1881. The opponents were the Anglican school in Bloemfontein, St Andrew's. The game they first played was a version of the Winchester Game, as brought to South Africa from England and played by Diocesan College in Cape Town in the 1870s.

In the 1890s Grey College regularly played against men's teams in the Orange Free State. They became the second winners of the OFS Grand Challenge Cup in 1896.

Grey, almost always a very strong rugby (and cricket) school, really became a rugby powerhouse in the latter half of the 20th century. They probably reached their peak between 1986 and 1990 when Grey College were unbeaten in 80 successive matches.

Grey have produced more players for the Craven Week than any other school, and has also produced more players for the national schools side than any other school in the country. They also hold the record of six players from Grey College in the 1981 SA Schools side.

Herman van Broekhuisen, who was a Western Province player, represented South Africa in 1896 and was the first Grey College old boy to do so. Among the Grey College old boys who have played for South Africa are the following: Herman van Broekhuisen, Boet McHardy, Sarel Strauss, Henry Martin, Louis Babrow, Piet de Wet, Popeye Strydom, Gert Cilliers, John Wessels, Johan Spies, Morné du Plessis (captain), Dawie Snyman and his brother Jackie, Theuns Stofberg (captain), Robbie Blair, Jaco Reinach, Helgard Müller and his brother Pieter, Andries Truscott, Johan Steyger, Heinrich Fuls, Ruben Kruger, Ollie le Roux, Naka Drotské, Werner Swanepoel, CJ van der Linde, Ruan Pienaar, Jannie and his brother Bismarck du Plessis, Frans Steyn, Heinrich Brüssow, Adriaan Strauss, Wian du Preez and Flip van der Merwe.

The school has also produced five test match referees, namely Reg Stanton, Att Horak, Steve Strydom, Justus Moolman and Gerrit Coetzer.

Doc Craven said afterwards that the 1976 final was one of the best, if not the very best, of the 16 finals played to that date. Free State won 33–16, which was the highest score in a final, and also provided a new record margin for a win. There was a third record. The 18 points scored by De Wet Ras beat the 17 of Gerald Bosch for Transvaal in their 25–19 win over Eastern Transvaal in 1972.

After their first win in 1976, Free State went on to clinch three more Currie Cup titles, in 2005, 2006 (shared with the Blue Bulls) and in 2007. By then, they were the Free State Cheetahs. All three of these finals were titanic struggles. The Currie Cup title in 2006 was shared after the two sides were still level after extra time, and in 2005 and 2007 the winning scores came just before the final whistle. In 2005 Meyer Bosman, then only 20 years old, scored the winning try against the Blue Bulls at Loftus Versfeld, six minutes before the end. The score was 29–25, and it was the only time that the Free State had beaten the Blue Bulls in their nine Currie Cup final encounters.

In 2005 all 14 Currie Cup teams kicked off in a first round split into two sections, with the top four of each section going through to the Premier Division, and each section's bottom three playing in the First Division. Free State finished second to Western Province in their section, but the latter came unstuck to the Free State Cheetahs for the second time in two seasons when they went down 16–11 in Cape Town. Free State's Newlands bogey had clearly been overcome, and the home side's 10–3 deficit at half-time simply couldn't be made up in the last 40 minutes.

The Blue Bulls were the top side in the competition, and went through the Premier Division's eight matches unbeaten. They accounted for the Lions at Loftus (31–23) to set up a home final.

The Free State Cheetahs' defence in the competition had been outstanding. In 16 matches they conceded only 28 tries, including one each in the semi-final at Newlands and the final at Loftus. This defence, added to the superlative kicking of flyhalf Willem de Waal, who scored 195 points in the competition, won the season for

Jubilant Currie Cup winners after beating the Blue Bulls at Loftus Versfeld.

the Free State. The Free State backline lacked real penetration, but Bevin Fortuin and Meyer Bosman rounded off a thoroughly satisfying season for Free State when they scored second-half tries to see their side home, after trailing 12–9 at half-time.

In the 2006 Currie Cup final, which showed up the very best of the competition, Free State scrambled and drew in Bloemfontein as the Bulls twice came back when it seemed that they were beaten.

This time the competition was decided between the top eight sides in a double round, with the top four battling it out in the semi-finals.

The Free State Cheetahs beat the Natal Sharks 30–14 in Bloemfontein, and the Blue Bulls set up a repeat of the 2005 final when they beat Western Province 45-30 at Loftus Versfeld.

With the lead changing hands four times in ten minutes in the second half, Kabamba Floors' try and Willem de Waal's penalty shortly thereafter seemed to have sealed the match for the Free State. The passionate final was far from over, however. After a sustained attack on the Free State Cheetahs' line, Blue Bulls centre JP Nel burst through. Morné Steyn, who replaced Derick Hougaard, converted from wide out with three minutes remaining. Into extra time they went. Steyn kicked a penalty, and Meyer Bosman's penalty hit the crossbar. The Blue Bulls were still ahead, 28–25.

Then, six minutes before time, just as in the previous year's Currie Cup final, Bosman struck a long, angled kick to make it 28–all. That was the final score.

The match ended in controversy when the Blue Bulls were awarded a penalty near the halfway line. Bulls captain, Gary Botha, fearing that Free State could run from their own line and perhaps take the spoils, ordered that the ball be kicked into touch. This decision brought about a change in the Currie Cup regulations to ensure that no final will ever be drawn again.

The Free State Cheetahs' display over those two seasons was credited to a new approach by young coach Rassie Erasmus. He decided on less running rugby and an approach where mistakes were minimised, and reaped the spoils of two Currie Cup titles in two years.

However, the Free State and the Cheetahs' heroes are not only players who scored the vital points in Currie Cup finals, but also those (and there are hundreds of them) who were stalwarts throughout the years that

The Free State Cheetahs after their last-gasp 2007 Currie Cup title win against the Lions in Bloemfontein.

they vied for the Currie Cup title. High on this list of players is Sakkie van Zyl, who deservedly and belatedly became a Springbok when he was 32 years old. In the days when provincial matches were infrequent, he played 121 matches at prop in a career spanning 16 years, from 1956 to 1971. It was a record that stood for years. The record now belongs to Helgard Müller, who played 245 matches for Free State, of which 142 appearances were in Currie Cup matches.

Sakkie van Zyl set another record after his retirement when he coached Free State for a further 14 seasons. Over a period of 30 years he was therefore involved in 343 matches as player, coach and selector. Van Zyl made his debut in 1956, together with Nelie Smith, and both of them toured with Dawie de Villiers' Springbok side to Australia and New Zealand.

Smith, who captained the Springboks in four tests, coached the Springboks in 1980 and 1981, losing only three of his 15 tests as Bok coach. Smith also played in the match against Western Province in 1964 when Free State drew at Newlands – the first time they had not lost to Western Province at Newlands in 70 years.

The final of 2007 was another close squeak. The Lions, under Ernst Joubert, had against all expectations qualified for the final after finishing third on the log and then beating the Sharks 19–12 in the semi-final in Durban. Both sides scored two tries, but the fairytale for the Free State Cheetahs is that their second came three minutes from the end, with Lions wing Ryno Benjamin in the sin bin. His team was behind by 18–13 when Cheetahs scrumhalf Tewis de Bruyn squirmed through in the left-hand corner. Willem de Waal, who for the fourth consecutive season was the top scorer in the Currie Cup, kicked the conversion from the touchline for a 20–18 win, a day before Lions coach Eugene Eloff's birthday.

There was another near win in 1997, when a pass from Helgard Müller to speedster Jan-Harm van Wyk was adjudged forward by referee André Watson, who was in a perfect position to make the call. Again, it was so close for the Free State side, as they lost 14–12 at Newlands. Van Wyk was the season's top scorer with 16 Currie Cup tries and, in a career of 77 matches, he scored 63 tries as one of the country's most lethal attackers. Although he never played for the Springboks in the 15-man code, he represented the Boks sevens the next year.

The man who was responsible for that final pass that

Big Springbok and Free State centre Joggie Jansen in action for his club side, the Shimlas.

was adjudged forward, Helgard Müller, is one of the legends of the Currie Cup competition. He was 34 when they lost that match at Newlands. Capped only twice for the Springboks, he played in 245 matches for Free State – a record. He captained the Free State 89 times, and at one stage played 65 consecutive matches, all of them as captain.

A Currie Cup title was not destined for him though, and in his other final in 1994 he was captain when Free State lost 56–33 to Transvaal at Springbok Park – a Currie Cup record of the wrong kind if you're a Free Stater.

Helgard has since ploughed his considerable experience back into the game, and has been the Free State Cheetahs' manager for some years.

His younger brother Pieter played 33 tests for South Africa.

Springbok wing Gerrie Germishuys represented Free State over seven seasons, from 1971 to 1977. He played in 72 matches, and his record of 51 tries stood for years. Later he also played for Transvaal, scoring 42 tries in his 50 matches, and became an outstanding Springbok wing.

Martiens le Roux, a prop, was one of the greats in Free State's Currie Cup history. Like Sakkie van Zyl, he had to wait longer than most for his international colours. Le Roux's 162 matches for Free State in all matches was a record at the time. He also captained Free State 25 times and was captain of the side beaten 23–6 by Northern

THE BEST FROM BLOEMFONTEIN

As with most of the other South African rugby unions, Free State and the Free State Cheetahs over the years produced some outstanding provincial and international players, many of whom count among the best South Africa has produced.

However, unlike the other provinces, there can be no dispute about the very best who has played in the white and orange of the Free State Cheetahs.

Os du Randt made his debut at loosehead prop for South Africa as a 21-year-old in 1994 against the visiting Argentina. Thirteen years and three World Cup tournaments later, he called it a day after collecting his second gold medal in three World Cup tournaments in France in 2007.

It could so easily have been four World Cup tournaments. Os did not make the 2003 tournament in Australia because of injury that saw him miss four international seasons and 46 test matches, which limited his appearances to 80 tests and 85 matches in the Springbok jersey.

A scourge in the scrums and lively in the loose, and blessed with excellent handling skills, his play around the fringes of the rucks and mauls was also outstanding. More often than not he counted among the players on both sides with the highest tackle count in a match.

His work ethic as a tight forward was exemplary, and one would never find him among the backline speedsters as is the wont of so many of today's forwards who use the new laws to motivate their shirking of hard work.

Du Randt scored five tries in his 80 tests. He also played in 105 matches for the Free State Cheetahs despite the injury lay-off, and spent a season with the Bulls. His initial Super Rugby was played as a member of the Cats team and in 2005 he helped the Cheetahs to their first Currie Cup title in 29 years after he was coaxed back to the game by Rassie Erasmus, who was then the Cheetahs coach.

Not giving a return to international rugby any thought, he was brought back into the Springbok fold by then Bok coach Jake White and played test rugby for the next three seasons.

The great man was there as a Free State Cheetahs supporter in 2007, after the World Cup glory, to see his team win the Currie Cup again with a 20–18 squeaker against the Golden Lions.

Du Randt is now the official scrummaging coach of the Springboks after taking up that role for the Cheetahs in 2009.

Gerrie Sonnekus, Springbok scrumhalf and No 8.

Transvaal in the 1981 Currie Cup final in Pretoria.

Joggie Jansen played in that first final win and represented his side in 61 matches. One of his best matches for Free State was in 1971 at the Free State Stadium. He scored two tries to help beat Transvaal 26–12 in a Currie Cup match, and also held the two Springbok centres from Transvaal at bay with his fearsome and fearless tackling.

Barry Wolmarans played 116 matches for Free State. The little Springbok scrumhalf was one of the real heroes of the 1976 Currie Cup final win with a try and a drop kick from a fair catch (mark). His 72 successive matches for Free State are a record, as is his halfback combination of 89 matches with De Wet Ras. Wolmarans, who played for Boland from 1972 to 1974, captained Free State in 1979, 1980 and 1981.

Theuns Stofberg captained the Springboks, and won the Currie Cup five times with three different provincial sides. He played in seven Currie Cup finals for Free State, Northern Transvaal and Western Province.

Gerrie Sonnekus played for the Springboks as a back (scrumhalf) and a forward (no 8) and played in 104 Currie Cup matches in his total of 160 games for the Free State.

Gavin Passens, Springbok wing of the Blue Bulls and Free State, won five Currie Cups.

One of the all-time greats of Free State and South African rugby was Gysie Pienaar. Father of Springbok and Sharks halfback Ruan, he played 165 matches for the Free State, and scored 906 points. In his 101 Currie Cup matches the mercurial runner scored 448 points, in a time when the great De Wet Ras did most of the kicking.

Gysie Pienaar on the run. He became one of South Africa's very best attacking fullbacks.

Rassie Erasmus – youngest Currie Cup winning coach and a former captain of the Free State Cheetahs who also captained the Springboks.

Basie Viviers, Free State and Springbok captain.

He was renowned for his attacks from fullback and his outstanding tries on his home field, the Free State Stadium, and he was in the 1976 side when Free State won the Currie Cup for the first time.

With him in that 1976 final victory was De Wet Ras, a prodigious kicker who would have played more tests for the Springboks than his eventual two, had not been for the great Naas Botha. A match-winner of note, he could slot kicks from his own half, and was a very important cog in the Free State machine of his years. Between 1974 and 1986 Ras scored 1 707 points – a Free State record, just like his 1 101 Currie Cup points. Ras scored 30 points in a Currie Cup match against Eastern Transvaal in 1978, and played 141 times for the Free State and 13 matches for Natal.

Willem de Waal is a great kicker and has improved on the one Currie Cup title win of De Wet Ras. Now with Western Province and Stormers, flyhalf De Waal played in three successful Currie Cup finals for the Free State Cheetahs. He boasts a total of 1 213 Currie Cup points – third only to Naas Botha (1 699) and Eric Herbert (1 402). De Waal's points at the end of 2009 were just three more than those of Ras, who played in 106 Currie Cup matches for Free State and 13 for Natal.

Rassie Erasmus became the youngest coach to win the Currie Cup when the Free State Cheetahs won the title in 2005 two weeks before his 33rd birthday. Now with the Stormers and Western Province as director of coaching, Erasmus played 119 matches for the Free State Cheetahs, 33 times as captain. He also captained South Africa in the first test against Australia in 1999.

The present Free State Cheetahs coach, Naka Drotské, captained the side in the 2005 Currie Cup final. He played 123 matches for the provincial side, captaining them in 41. The World Cup-winning hooker of 1995 also played five times on the flank during his career with Free State, and is the present coach of the side.

Drotské's front rank mate in the Free State side on many occasions was Os du Randt. One of South Africa's all-time great props and players, Du Randt won the Currie Cup twice with the Free State Cheetahs (in 2005 and 2007). He also played in three World Cup tournaments, collecting gold medals in 1995 and 2007, and played 105 matches for Free State and the Cheetahs. Du Randt was appointed the Springboks' scrummaging coach in 2010 after his success with the Cheetahs scrum in 2009.

Over the years, all the heroes of the Free State were not necessarily Currie Cup heroes, and most of them didn't have the honour of playing in a Currie Cup final. But they, as much as those that did, helped to keep the province competitive over its first 82 years without a Currie Cup title.

Some of these many stalwarts and stars over the years include Popeye Strydom, former Springbok captain Basie Vivier, Gert Cilliers, Jannie de Beer, Japie Wessels, Dougie Heymans, André Joubert, Chris Badenhorst, Andre Venter, Piet Goosen and Steve Strydom. But there are literally hundreds.

Before the Second World War the Free State also produced a number of players who represented South Africa with distinction.

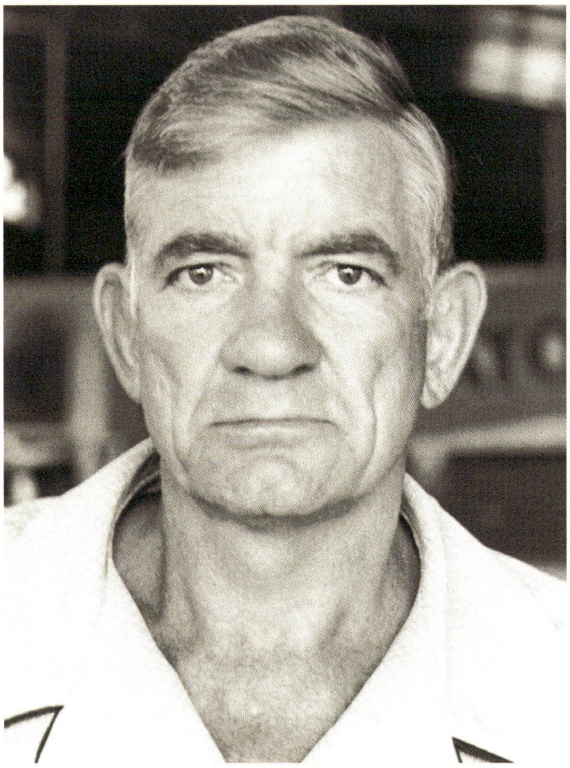

Springbok lock Piet Goosen.

Gerrie Germishuys, speedy wing of the Free State, Transvaal and the Springboks.

Flank Andre Venter, one of the very best produced by the Free State and Cheetahs.

Juan Smith in full cry for the Cheetahs.
He is the current Free State captain.

PIET STRYDOM, A STALWART FOR TWO PROVINCES

Piet Strydom, who has left an indelible mark on rugby in this country, made his debut for Free State against Northern Transvaal at Loftus Versfeld in 1968. 'We lost 28–11, but it was a great experience playing against some of the world's best players like Frik du Preez, Mof Myburgh and Piet Uys. Mixing with opposition after matches was always a highlight and an occasion where so many lasting friendships were made.'

He vividly recalls that Currie Cup final in 1975, when Pierre Spies scored the winner for Northern Transvaal in the very last move of the match.

'What a day it was,' he recalls. 'We stayed in the President Hotel on the Friday night.

'Our plan was to run the ball as much as we can against the heavy Northern Transvaal forwards, but then it started raining on the Saturday morning. With the three curtain raisers going ahead, the field was a mud bath by the time we ran on.

'I'm still amazed at the way the ball bounced from that kick of Northern Transvaal centre Christo Wagenaar, and when Pierre Spies tapped and then controlled the ball, there were anguished shouts from the Free State players.

'I'll never forget those few seconds that broke our hearts. We so wanted to win, to hold the Currie Cup aloft and get our winners' medals.

'But it was not to be.'

Piet's outstanding memories are of the times he was involved in the six Currie Cup wins.

The first one came in 1976, when Free State beat Western Province 33–16 in Bloemfontein. It was a record score and record-winning margin at the time.

Strydom had by then been replaced as provincial fullback by the great Gysie Pienaar. As an official replacement, Strydom did, however, receive the coveted gold medal for the 1976 win, which to some extent compensated for the previous year's loss.

As a wicketkeeper and batsman, Strydom also represented Free State in 51 cricket matches between 1965 and 1976. His highest score was 92.

Into his 30s, his rugby career ended when he broke his cheekbone in a club match for Durban Collegians and decided to call it a day.

Strydom was one of four brothers, three of whom (himself, Steve and Willie) played rugby and cricket for Free State while their other brother, Corrie, represented the province in cricket.

Steve was later a president of the Orange Free State Rugby Union and a test referee. He officiated in seven tests and six Currie Cup finals, making him second to only André Watson. Steve was also desperately unlucky not to be included as a fullback in the 1965 Springbok side to Australia and New Zealand.

Piet was appointed as Natal's team manager in 1980, and occupied this position in 286 Currie Cup matches over a period spanning 25 years before resigning in 2005. With his duties in the Super Rugby competitions, Strydom managed Natal and Natal Sharks sides in over 400 matches in the period 1980–2005.

In this period, the Natal side and Sharks franchise had eight coaches. Strydom and Ian McIntosh worked together as manager and coach in 154 Currie Cup matches.

Strydom was also the youngest chairman of a Natal selection panel and held the position from 1983 until 1995.

Other rugby positions Strydom held are those of administrative manager of the Sharks (1994 to present) and assistant manager of the SA 'A' side to the UK and Ireland. He was a freelance rugby and cricket commentator between 1977 and 1996 and was adjudged the SAB Commentator of the Year in 1992.

vodacom
CHEETAHS
vodacom

The Free State/Free State Cheetahs and Northern Transvaal/Blue Bulls have met in nine Currie Cup finals.

Free State and Springbok wing Boet McHardy's four tries in a match against Border in 1914 is still a record, equalled by Kleintjie Grobler, Gerrie Germishuys, Theuns Stofberg, Edrich Krantz, Jan-Harm van Wyk and Richard Strauss.

Like McHardy, Springbok wing Jan Stegmann also scored a hat-trick in a test in 1912.

Charles Kohler played for Free State over a period of 19 years (1914–1932) and captained the side in ten of his 44 matches.

Players like Arthur Barlow, Gubby Barlow, Eric Hill, Att Horak, Mike Rest, Springbok flyhalf Tiny Francis, the Springbok forwards Hennie Potgieter and Lappies Hattingh, Hans Hefer, Jack King and Wa Lamprecht are other players who kept the Free State a factor in the 30s and during the war years.

And now there are the players of the present era like Heinrich Brüssow, Juan Smith, Meyer Bosman and Adriaan Strauss, who carry the proud legacy into the future.

While these players and others helped to make and keep the Free State a strong provincial union, the coming of the professional era in particular robbed the Free State Cheetahs of some of their best players. The loss of players isn't a new occurrence, and it's not limited to the advent of professionalism. Players like Nic Bojé (father of national cricketer Nicky) moved from Bloemfontein to Northern Transvaal in the 1960s, followed by high-profile Springboks like Edrich Krantz, Ruben Kruger and Theuns Stofberg.

De Wet Ras, Vleis Visagie, Tjokkie van der Merwe, John Knox, Ollie le Roux, Pieter Müller, Henry Honiball, Gawie Visagie and André Joubert are among the big names that went to Natal (the latter two had attended Northern Natal schools) in the days when moving between provinces was more infrequent than now; and Free State props Henning van Aswegen and Toks van der Linde moved to Western Province. Add to that the schoolboys from the Free State schools like Bok greats Morné du Plessis and Dawie Snyman, and the loss of a basis to build on is clear.

It became more accentuated as the grip of professionalism tightened. Later, players such as Frans Steyn (who went to the Sharks) and Deon Stegmann (who went to the Bulls) moved from school to provincial rugby for other unions or franchises. In Bloemfontein, the Natal Sharks in particular were blamed for pilfering established players as well as future young stars. The joke: 'Where do the Sharks stay when playing in Bloemfontein?' followed by the answer: 'With their parents', is well known. Bismarck and Jannie du Plessis, Ruan Pienaar, Ollie le Roux and Andries Strauss moved to Durban, some of them established in the Free State/Cheetahs side, others on the brink of senior provincial honours. More overtures to Free State Cheetahs players were made in 2010.

The Free State also lost players of the quality of Rassie Erasmus (for a year) to the Lions, Gurthrö Steenkamp to Northern Transvaal, Bevin Fortuin to SWD, and Willem de Waal to Western Province. AJ Venter moved on to the Lions then from there to the Sharks and lastly Western Province.

The Free State Cheetahs simply have not had the finances to retain many of their brightest young stars. Of course, it was to some extent also a case of win some lose some, as money starting determining the allegiance and loyalty of players. However, there is a perception in Bloemfontein that they have lost more players than they have gained over the years, and they question why other unions are not producing the youngsters, as they have been churning them out for years.

dacom
vodacom
PVM

ABSA
CURRIE CUP
MORNÉ
GILBERT
5de
FINAAL
LOFTUS
31-10-2009
BLOU BULLE VS CHEETAHS
vodacom
ABSA

CHAPTER 9

Northern Transvaal

The R20-million kick, they called it, when Morné Steyn broke Western Province's hearts with a last gasp 52-metre penalty in the Currie Cup semi-final at Newlands in 2009 to make the score 21–19 to the Bulls. Had Steyn missed the pressure kick, the Western Province Rugby Union stood to make an estimated R10 million from hosting the final. As it was, the Blue Bulls Rugby Union had a sell-out for their final against Free State the following weekend and they pocketed the spoils.

This was in stark contrast to the 1980s, when the top side in the competition didn't necessarily have the right to host the final. In those days, when two sides who had previously met in a final qualified to do so again, the venue would be different from the previous one. The profits then were also divided on a different basis from the present system.

Anyway, the heartbreak for the WP fans was doubled in the game's aftermath at Newlands, when quick calculations confirmed the small fortune that the union had lost because of that kick.

Close it was, but ultimately the Blue Bulls not only cashed in on their income statement, but also in the Currie Cup competition when they won their 23rd title (four of them shared) by beating Free State 36–24 at Loftus in what was yet another exciting Currie Cup final. The Blue Bulls had threatened to run away with the Bloemfontein side who were surprise finalists, having resurrected themselves from a disastrous Super 14 tour to Australasia. Yet the visitors were down 24–0 after 25 minutes, thanks to some outstanding work from the Blue Bulls scrumhalf Fourie du Preez. He played a major part in all three early tries, with two sublimely accurate kicks that set up tries for wingers François Hougaard and Bryan Habana.

Blue Bulls flyhalf Morné Steyn sunk Western Province in the 2009 semi-final with a killer-kick that also had an effect on their finances.

Northern Transvaal's side that played the British Lions in 1938 – their first season when the Currie Cup was not contested.

He also gave Habana a pass that saw the speedster finish off his second try.

Then Free State fought back, at one time trailing by only nine points at 30–21. There were anxious faces around Loftus Versfeld, traditional fortress of the Bulls and Blue Bulls which had seen 17 Currie Cup finals, including 14 wins and three defeats by the end of 2009.

The field had also seen many, many close shaves in finals. However, it was at Newlands, the Free State Stadium and Ellis Park where Northern Transvaal were more often than not involved in the real chillers, with matches going down to the wire. And let's not forget the Kingsmead Cricket Ground in Durban and the hard surface of the De Beers Stadium in Kimberley.

The Northern Transvaal challenge for the Currie Cup only started in 1939. Up until 1938, the area that now constitutes the Blue Bulls Rugby Union was part of the Transvaal Rugby Football Union and players from Pretoria played for Transvaal.

In 1938 Northern Transvaal became an autonomous union, and rightly so, after Pretoria teams had won the Pirates Grand Challenge for 14 of the 18 years between 1919 and 1936. It was felt that there was enough talent and clubs in Pretoria to go it alone.

It was normal practice, in those years, to see club supporters cycle to Johannesburg to watch their teams play. The players travelled by horse-drawn cart and later by train to play their fixtures.

Springbok forward Ferdie Bergh was the first Northern Transvaal captain. Under the captaincy of mainly Lucas Strachan, Northern Transvaal played in their first Currie Cup campaign in 1939.

The Light Blues, as they were fondly referred to by their fans, were not an instant success despite including big names from 1938's victorious Springbok side against the British Lions. Even seven Springboks couldn't help Northerns beat the touring Lions or win the Currie Cup in 1939. They did, however, win the next Currie Cup competition in 1946, after a lengthy break in the competition because of the Second World War.

After that, it became almost habitual for Northern Transvaal and later the Blue Bulls to play in Currie Cup finals. By the end of 2009 they had won 23 of the 52 titles on offer since they started playing Currie Cup rugby in 1939. They were involved as finalists in 31 of the 49

Lucas Strachan was involved as Northern Transvaal captain, player and coach over a period of more than 40 years.

Danie Craven had a profound influence in the early years of Northern Transvaal rugby.

finals, winning 19 times and sharing the Currie Cup on four occasions.

Renowned for their powerful forwards and a simple yet effective, game plan, which they stuck to through the years, the great Northern Transvaal teams of the early years were partly the result of the police and the defence headquarters being in Pretoria. Northern Transvaal abused this by having players transferred to these headquarters through some of their management and friends in these institutions. It was alleged that they also had players called up for military service when they were short of quality in certain positions. There might have been truth in some of these allegations. However, it doesn't explain why the former Pretoria Combined and their clubs were so strong up to when Northern Transvaal became an independent union in 1938. It also doesn't explain the successes of the provincial side in their golden period between 1968 and the late 1980s, when Tukkies players dominated the Carlton Cup competition and representation in the provincial side.

However, shortly before the Second World War and after Garrison and Police were the leaders in the uncompromising Carlton Cup league. It is to this league – and the importance that the players, administrators and supporters attached to it – that the Northern Transvaal success in the Currie Cup can largely be attributed.

In 1938 a 'political war' between supporters (Garrison) and opponents (Police) of the Second World War nearly prevented the first Carlton Cup final since Northern Transvaal had become an independent union from being played. (The Carlton Cup had been played for since 1904.)

According to Danie Craven, Springbok captain in 1938, Garrison and Police were supposed to play the final on Saturday. However, as he and opposing captain Lucas Strachan also had to play the third test against the British Lions that weekend, the Carlton Cup final was brought forward to the Tuesday.

'Our preparations were as though we were preparing for a test,' Craven recalled in the book Northern Transvaal Rugby 50. 'It was one of the toughest matches I ever played in, far tougher than the test.'

It was from that strong club basis that the selectors worked in selecting the Northern Transvaal team for the friendlies of 1938, as well as for the first Currie Cup challenge in 1939. It remained thus until the professional era dawned in 1996.

The first Northern Transvaal team to win the Currie Cup just before the kick-off in the 1946 final against Western Province.

The great Danie Craven was included in the first Northern Transvaal side, a mere two weeks after he arrived in Pretoria as an officer at Garrison. The Light Blues lost that friendly to Transvaal.

Craven captained the Light Blues in two matches, one of them against the 1938 British Lions of Sam Walker. He was also the Bok captain in the three-match test series.

But of course, there were many Springboks from Pretoria before the breakaway from Transvaal in 1938. JEC Partridge, a Welshman, and Hilton H Ferris were the first, and represented the 1903 South African side (the first to win a series) against Mark Morrison's British Lions. A further 19 players from Pretoria donned the national colours of South Africa as Transvaal players.

A rugby basis was, therefore, well and truly established when Northern Transvaal (unsuccessfully) played in their first Currie Cup tournament in 1939 and won their first title in 1946. That final, in 1946, was played in the amateur days. The teams played in two leagues: North and South; and Western Province had qualified to host the match.

As a gesture, probably because it was Northern Transvaal's first final, Western Province offered to play the match at Loftus. That those were indeed amateur days was emphasised by the fact that both teams attended the same function the night before the match!

The match was a sell-out; so much so that the press were requested not to give it any more publicity. However, on the match day it was suddenly realised that some 3 000 tickets on the south stand were still available. This was broadcast and the tickets were snapped up.

It turned out to be one of the most dramatic Currie Cup finals played to this day. It also confirmed the game plan of the Light Blues had stood the test of time, according to the match report in *Die Burger* of 30 September of that year. The reporter felt that Hansie Brewis, who kicked two drop goals, one with either foot, kicked too much. He also bemoaned the fact that the ball did not once reach the Northern Transvaal wings, and reached the outside centre only once.

Brewis killed the game as a spectacle, *Die Burger* wrote, but his forwards ground out a win that had looked unlikely 45 seconds before the final whistle. Then Brewis kicked and the ball rolled and rolled and rolled. Wing Johnny Lourens chased it for all of 75 yards with Western Province players in pursuit.

Hannes Brewis, a flyhalf who kicked and ran.

LEADING THE WAY

One of the reasons for the success enjoyed by the Blue Bulls is the outstanding leadership they have had through the years. Some of South Africa's greatest captains have led the Blue Bulls on the field in their 72 years as an independent union.

It started in 1938, the year in which the Northern Transvaal Rugby Union was established and had to go it alone. The Springbok captain of that year, Danie Craven, captained Northerns against the visiting British Lions. The appointed captain for the year, Ferdie Bergh, was also in Pretoria at that time and led the Light Blues into Currie Cup fray. He was the new union's first captain, before Craven took over for the match against the British Lions.

The first captain that led the side for an extended period was Lucas Strachan. He was captain in 11 matches and became one of the cornerstones of Northern Transvaal's success as player, coach and mentor. Springbok Flip Geel was captain in 1946 when Northern Transvaal won the Currie Cup for the first time, and captained the side 31 times, an outstanding achievement in the days when there were relatively few matches in a season.

Hennie Nel was captain when Natal were beaten 9-8, with a try in the last few minutes, in the 1956 Currie Cup final at the Kingsmead Cricket Ground. Players like Louis Muller, Hannes Brewis, Fiks van der Merwe, Christo Wagenaar and Willie Matthyser are other long-standing captains who did the province proud. Louis Schmidt, another Springbok from the 1930s, Roger Sheriff, Daantjie van den Heever, Albie Bates and one of the very best, Oupa du Piesanie also led the side to glory in the Currie

Salty du Randt was the first player to become Springbok captain while playing for Northern Transvaal when he led the Boks in the first test of the 1956 tour.

With the ball close to the tryline, Western Province fullback Con de Kock tapped it over the sideline, which was just a foot or two away, or so he thought. Instead, the ball bobbled over his foot; Lourens picked it up and scored, and Northern Transvaal had their first title, winning 11–9.

Brewis was feared for his boot and especially for his drop kicks. Before the arrival of Naas Botha and later Jannie de Beer, he held the South African test record of five drop goals, which he scored in his ten internationals. Brewis also scored 22 drop goals for Northern Transvaal, half of those with his left foot.

Northern Transvaal missed the two finals in 1950 and 1952, the first of which was Transvaal's second final win over Western Province, having won the inaugural final in 1939. The 1952 final was also won by Transvaal – their third win in the four finals played to that date.

Western Province were later to be known as Northern Transvaal's 'auld foe from the South', and it probably started in 1954 when they denied Northern Transvaal by winning the final at Newlands 11–8. This meant that at that stage Northern Transvaal could lay claim to only the one Currie Cup title (in 1946) from six campaigns.

Then it changed. Northern Transvaal beat Natal in Durban in 1956 and missed out on only two of the next 16 finals between 1968 and 1983. They won the Currie Cup on nine occasions and shared it twice. The period from 1968, when Buurman van Zyl was appointed coach, signalled the real arrival of the Currie Cup final giants.

His sides won nine titles, shared two and lost only one final in his 13 seasons at the helm. In 1976 Northern

Cup and other matches, as did Piet Uys and Burger Geldenhuys in later generations.

The great Frik du Preez, of course, captained the side in that controversial draw of 14–all with Transvaal in 1971. He was captain on 16 occasions in his 109 matches for Northern Transvaal, and on his retirement held the record of 38 test matches with Jan Ellis.

Then there was Thys Lourens. In his 168 provincial matches he captained Northern Transvaal no fewer than 84 times, second only to Naas Botha. Lourens was the oldest captain to lead a side to victory in a Currie Cup final: he was 35 years and 138 days old when he held the trophy aloft after the 13–9 victory over Free State in Bloemfontein in 1978. Of the eight finals Lourens played in – four as captain – the Light Blues won seven and drew one.

Two years later it was Botha who became the youngest Northern Transvaal captain to win the Currie Cup. That was in their 39–9 win over Western Province at Loftus in 1980, when Botha was only 22 years and 217 days old.

Of the more recent players, Victor Matfield, Anton Leonard, Gary Botha and Joost van der Westhuizen all made their mark and had the honour of lifting the most coveted trophy in South African rugby (and arguably South African sport).

Salty du Randt was the first player to become Springbok captain while playing for the union, although Danie Craven played for Northern Transvaal when he captained them against the 1938 British Lions team of Sam Walker. Craven captained South Africa in the first test against New Zealand in 1937, while at Western Province.

Others who became Springbok captains while playing for Northern Transvaal are Theuns Stofberg, Naas Botha, Adriaan Richter, Joost van der Westhuizen and Victor Matfield.

Happiness is....Blue Bulls captain Victor Matfield and his deputy Fourie du Preez - a fine captain in own right - are obviously elated after winning the 2009 Currie Cup against the Free State at Loftus.

Wynand Claassen played for Northern Transvaal in 1973–1979 and was captain of the Light Blues in a single match before leaving for Natal and captaining the Springboks during the 1981 demo tour of New Zealand. Piet Greyling and Jannie Breedt became Bok captains when they were Transvaal players, after they had represented Northern Transvaal. Felix du Plessis, who played for Northern Transvaal from 1941 to 1944, led the Springboks in the first three tests against the visiting All Blacks of 1949. Basie Viviers, who led the Springboks on their 1956 tour of Australia and New Zealand, played for Northerns between 1947 and 1950 and Basil Kenyon, captain in the fourth test of 1949 and to Britain in 1951–1952, represented Northern Transvaal in 1942.

Transvaal lost out on playing in the final and in 1972 Van Zyl didn't coach for health reasons.

Van Zyl's first Cup victory as a coach came in 1968, when Northern Transvaal beat Transvaal 16–3 at Loftus. But before that, Northern Transvaal had lost the 1954 final at Newlands, mainly owing to good Western Province tactics that partially neutralised Northern Transvaal's captain and ace flyhalf, Hansie Brewis. There were also two strange decisions by referee Ralph Burmeister, which he couldn't explain satisfactorily afterwards.

In 1956 the Springboks returned from the tour of New Zealand where they were beaten by the All Blacks for the first time in a series. Although many of the internationals were tired after a tour lasting 15 weeks and during which 29 matches were played, Northern Transvaal's four Springboks, namely Salty du Randt, Jaap Bekker, Daan Retief and Tom van Vollenhoven, were adamant that they wanted to play Currie Cup rugby.

The Northern Transvaal Rugby Union, however, decided that the players who had carried them through during the season would play in the final. Consequently, Northerns travelled to Durban without their Boks. Natal,

BUURMAN VAN ZYL – CURRIE CUP COLOSSUS

As a coach, Buurman van Zyl was a colossus, the most successful at Currie Cup level to this day, and the man who guided the former Northern Transvaal to their first golden era. Nine Currie Cup titles plus two shared and only two unsuccessful campaigns in his 13 years of coaching Northern Transvaal are testimony to his success. His only loss in a final came when Griquas beat Northern Transvaal 11-9 in Kimberley in 1970. In 1976 Northern Transvaal didn't qualify for the final. Van Zyl missed coaching the side in 1972 because of illness.

As well as these finals, Buurman van Zyl's Northern Transvaal sides between 1968 and 1981 played in 116 Currie Cup matches, winning 99, drawing four and losing only 13. And 35 players coached by Buurman van Zyl became Springboks.

It was a travesty that he never coached the Springboks. Buurman van Zyl, or Brigadier Jacobus Gerhardus Marthinus van Zyl, to give him his full title and names, had been earmarked to coach the Springboks in 1982, but died in January that year.

While he was a policeman in Port Elizabeth, 'Oom' Buurman, as he was known by all his players and the press, played 79 matches for Eastern Province over a provincial career spanning 15 years, from 1937 to 1951. This included the match against Fred Allen's 1949 All Blacks. The former Upington schoolboy also represented Eastern Province as a javelin thrower and took part in South Africa's 1936 Olympic trials.

'Oom' Buurman became Northern Transvaal's coach in 1968 at the insistence of Prof. Daan Swiegers, chairman of Northern Transvaal's selectors, who later became the convener of the national selection committee. Before Van Zyl's appointment the provincial selectors took turns to coach the side.

In Pretoria the rugby faithful from those years still speak in awe of what was known as the 'triumvirate': Buurman, Thys Lourens and Naas Botha were the pillars on which the success of that golden era was built. In Lourens, who at that time still played for Defence, Van Zyl found the perfect ally to take the team to great heights.

'He taught us three things without which a sportsman cannot perform,' said Lourens, a legendary captain of Northern Transvaal who deserved to play in more tests than the three against the 1968 British Lions.

'Oom Buurman called it BDF: basics, discipline and fitness. The basics had to be right, you have to exercise discipline in everything you do, and you have to be fit to perform at your maximum. These are things that also prepared us for life outside of rugby.'

That was also the feature of Van Zyl that stood out for Naas Botha, who was plucked from the Tukkies under-19s by the coach, and went on to become the biggest match winner in South African history and a man who captained Northern Transvaal in 63 matches under Buurman van Zyl.

'He taught us life lessons that we could apply years after retiring,' said Botha, and added that Van Zyl's philosophy was that his players must be happy off the field to perform on it.

Burger Geldenhuys, the Springbok flank who holds, with Botha, the record of playing in 11 Currie Cup finals during his 13 years with Northern Transvaal, says Van Zyl's people skills were remarkable. 'He knew exactly how to work with a player,' said Geldenhuys, who was on the winning side in finals six times, with the trophy shared on two occasions.

Geldenhuys, who played under Van Zyl for the first five of his 13 years as a provincial player, and eventually played in 184 matches for Northern Transvaal, captaining them 54 times, made this observation on the Blue Bulls' website: 'Oom Buurman had the ability to spot a talented rugby player, and once he selected you, he remained loyal to you.

'He did not only teach us a lot about rugby, but he worked with us and we played for him. He selected me and I wanted to perform for him.'

The Light Blues, as they were generally known, played to a simple, basic pattern, and to this day the Blue Bulls stick to a structure that is difficult to break or subdue. It was not well liked outside of Pretoria, but was always effective. The BDF philosophy was at the heart of the success as much as Buurman van Zyl's vision in selecting youngsters like Naas Botha.

The finals involving Northern Transvaal with Buurman as coach between 1968 and 1981 are shown on the following page (year, home team and score, visiting team and score, venue, referee).

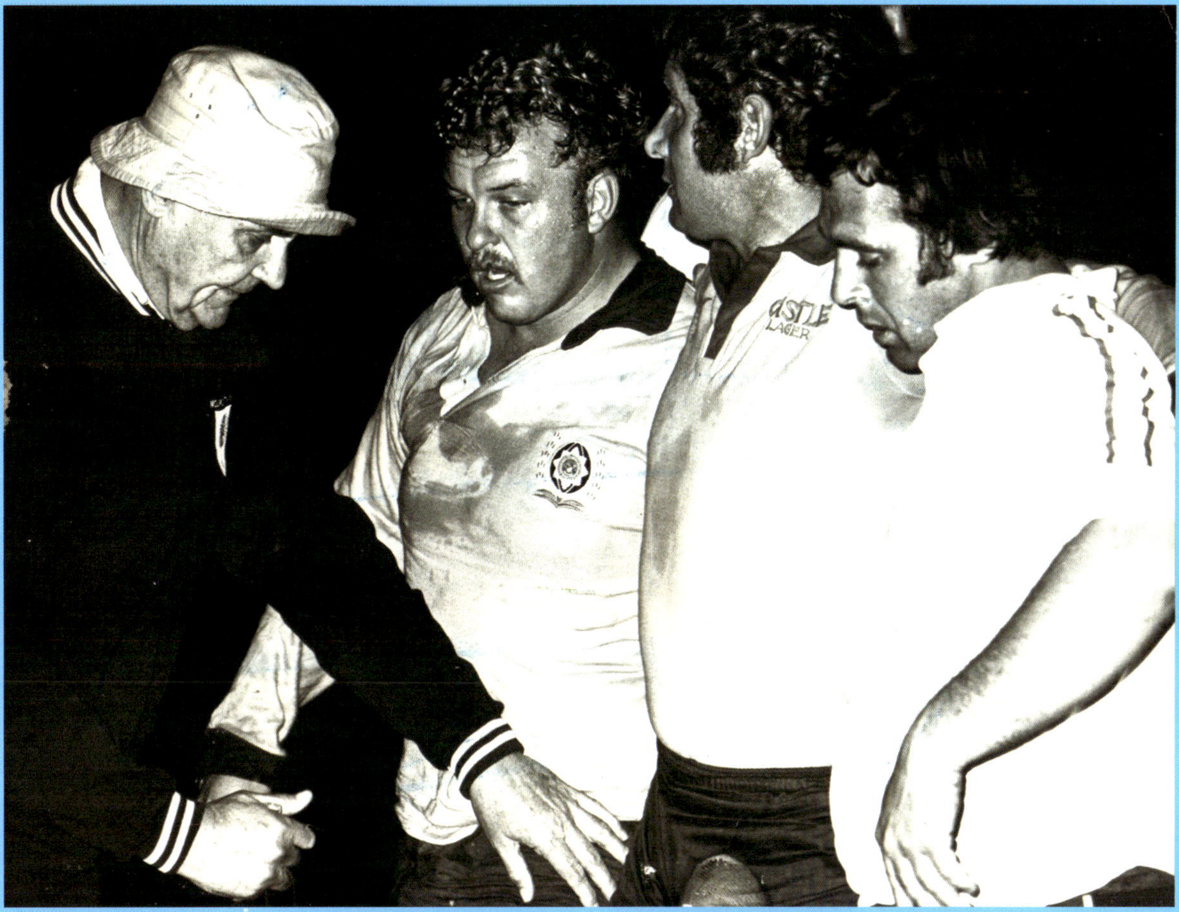

Buurman van Zyl showing front-rowers Tuffy Reyneke, Willie Kahts and Jan Oberholzer the ropes.

1968	N-Tvl	16	Transvaal	3	Loftus Versfeld	Bertie Strasheim, N-Tvl
1969	N-Tvl	28	WP	13	Loftus Versfeld	Fonnie van der Vyver, N-Tvl
1970	Griquas	11	N-Tvl	9	Kimberley	Ben Calitz, Griquas
1971	Transvaal	14	N-Tvl	14	Johannesburg	Gert Bezuidenhout, Transvaal
In 1972 Buurman van Zyl handed over the coaching to Salty du Randt because of illness.						
1973	N-Tvl	30	Free State	22	Loftus Versfeld	Piet Robbertse, E-Tvl
1974	N-Tvl	17	Transvaal	15	Loftus Versfeld	Steve Strydom, Free State
1975	N-Tvl	12	Free State	6	Bloemfontein	Justus Moolman, EP
In 1976 Free State and Western Province contested the final in Bloemfontein, WP won 33-16. Transvaal's Gert Bezuidenhout was the referee.						
1977	N-Tvl	27	Free State	12	Loftus Versfeld	Jimmy Smith-Belton, EP
1978	N-Tvl	13	Free State	9	Bloemfontein	Gert Bezuidenhout, Transvaal
1979	WP	15	N-Tvl	15	Cape Town	Steve Strydom, Free State
1980	N-Tvl	39	WP	9	Loftus Versfeld	Steve Strydom, Free State
1981	N-Tvl	23	Free State	6	Loftus Versfeld	Johan Gouws, E-Tvl

KEEP IT DOWN, SONNY!

Frik du Preez was South Africa's Player of the Millennium. Known for his sayings on and off the field, he was a great in the full sense of the word, and, with Jan Ellis, held the South African record of 38 test matches for many years, until the professional era made a mockery of that total.

He played for Northern Transvaal from 1958 to 1971, a period of 14 years, and did many great things on the field, and said many off the field! Some would say he wasn't the fittest player, and that he did not try very hard in matches where it didn't matter. There was some justification for this view, and it's exemplified in an anecdote about the great man, in a club match for Defence. In the days when wings were still the guys throwing the ball into the lineout, the youngster who had to perform this duty threw it way over the head of the world's greatest lineout men. Frik didn't even try to jump for the ball, simply admonishing the wing: 'Hell, no man, that was an international throw and this is only a club match!'

Another famous story told about Frik was the way he was literally brought to earth in 1968, in a provincial match against North Western Cape, for whom the old warhorse Herklaas Engelbrecht played for so many years. Earlier in the season Frik had scored that wonderful try (his only in a test match) against Tom Kiernan's 1968 British Lions side. It was the result of perfect execution, with Frik peeling from the back of the lineout to receive from Mof Myburgh, and then bursting through the front of the lineout. It worked against the Lions, but Frik admitted to it later on: it never worked again!

The two teammates were confident of success on the hard field of the North Western Cape, however, and up to the point where Frik came around the front, it looked like a perfect move. Then the Springbok was dumped hard and unceremoniously into the dust that passed for a rugby field. As a shaken Frik got off the ground, Herklaas Engelbrecht helped him up with the words: 'We've been waiting for you for two weeks now, Frik!'

in the strange three-section competition format, had won the only 'semi-final' of the 1956 Currie Cup competition against Western Province at Newlands 11–10, recording their first ever win in Cape Town in the process. They took to the field at the Kingsmead cricket ground with their only Springbok of 1956, Roy Dryburgh.

It is ironic that Dryburgh was the man who missed the kick that could have won the final and the Currie Cup for Natal against Northern Transvaal. Gusty wind took the kick to the left of the posts, however, and instead it was Northern Transvaal's flank Schalk van Dyk who scored the winner four minutes from time. Natal won 9–8.

In the period 1957–1959 South Africa held the strangest of all Currie Cup tournaments, played over two seasons and a period of three years before the next Currie Cup title was decided in 1964. Both these tournaments were decided by league format and Western Province, happy to not play the format that necessitated play-offs, won two more titles.

Then Oom Buurman came along.

In his very first season as coach, the SA police officer took Northern Transvaal to the final and a Currie Cup title. What's more, the 1968 final was the first to be played in Pretoria since their win in 1946, when they reached – and won – their first Currie Cup final, which was also only the second final played.

Eastern Province and Transvaal (11–all) had to meet in a play-off to determine which side would advance to the 1968 final. Transvaal, under the captaincy of lock Toy Dannhauser, won the encounter 25–3. Transvaal came off a very good season. They had beaten the British Lions 14–6 and trounced Western Province 35–6, in the days when a try was worth only three points.

Their journalists, among them Gert Kotze and John du Toit (the latter had played at no 8 for both Northern Transvaal and Transvaal) were convinced that the Pretoria side had little chance even though the match was to be decided at Loftus and was expected to be tough.

Northern Transvaal had, meanwhile, quietly marched to the final with an unbeaten record. Free State, Eastern Transvaal and Griquas all succumbed to the force of the Light Blues. There was only one narrow squeak. Against what was then South West Africa, fullback Chris Luther had to kick a last-minute conversion of a penalty try to keep Northerns on track.

In Johannesburg there was a perception that the Northern Transvaal's forwards did not have the staying power to keep Transvaal at bay. The match they lost against the touring British Lions, when Northern Transvaal squandered a 13–5 lead to eventually lose 22–19, was at the crux of that argument.

When the sides for the final were announced, the Light Blues' selectors caused a stir when the name of Alan Menter was read out. The Wits medical student was now in Pretoria to finish his studies and could not find a place in the Transvaal side earlier in the season. As a tactical kicker he was probably the best in the country, and his selection showed that the Northern Transvaal selectors presumed that the game would be decided up front.

Word on the street was that if the referee didn't keep an eye on the illegal tactics Transvaal employed to counter Eastern Province in the lineouts in the play-off match, Northern Transvaal would see to this themselves. It was a ploy often used in Pretoria: draw the attention of a match-day referee to some transgression expected to occur on the field during the match.

It was a forwards clash of the very highest order. Northern Transvaal won the tight phases and the loose, and, as Barry Glasspool wrote in the *Sunday Times* of 25 September 1968: '... it was not only their domination of the exchanges that was so significant, but the way so much clean possession gave Alan Menter – and his scrumhalf Piet Uys – so much time and room in which to indelibly stamp their mark on the game.'

Northern Transvaal won 16–3, but, as Glasspool went on: '... for gallantly as Transvaal battled against the blue tidal wave that swarmed all over them, Northerns were always winning this game – and winning it well.'

It was Northern Transvaal's third Currie Cup title. The era of Buurman van Zyl was underway.

In the unbeaten 1969 season there was the fine performance in a friendly against Western Province, who were 21–0 ahead at the break. With 15 minutes remaining they led only 21–19, and then Northern Transvaal took the lead after a brilliant run by Frik du Preez, rounded off by Piet Uys and converted by Chris Luther.

LAYING THE PLATFORM

Just as Naas Botha was the points machine and Buurman van Zyl and Heyneke Meyer the coaches that brought out the best from a bunch of very good players, Thys Lourens will be remembered as the captain of Northern Transvaal who laid the platform for their string of Currie Cup successes.

The flank – 'I played no 8 when there was nobody else available!' – formed a partnership with Buurman van Zyl that was expanded to a near unbeatable triumvirate when young Naas Botha came onto the scene.

Eight Currie Cup finals, with a draw against Transvaal in 1971, the only blemish on an otherwise flawless record, is a tribute to a man who was consistency itself. Four of those Currie Cup wins came when he was captain of the Light Blues.

A motivator par excellence who inspired with his general play, and also a shrewd tactician, Lourens rates his first match for Northern Transvaal – against Western Transvaal in Potchefstroom in 1965 – as a stand-out memory. His first Currie Cup final and his selection for South Africa were also highlights.

Lourens played in only three test matches, running on in the last three tests against the 1968 British Lions. He deserved more at the highest level.

He was also a member of the unbeaten 1971 side to Australia where he played in eight tour matches for the Springboks under Hannes Marais when the side was known as the Invincibles.

Lourens represented Northern Transvaal in 168 matches and captained the team on 84 occasions. Only fellow Springboks Louis Moolman (171), Naas Botha (179) and Burger Geldenhuys (184) have played in more matches than Lourens.

Buurman van Zyl and Thys Lourens.

The score was 24–21 to the home team and a frenzied crowd was jubilant. HO de Villiers spoiled some of their fun with a late drop goal to tie the scores and the match, but they knew a great season was ahead.

But just more than a month later, the unthinkable happened: Frik du Preez was dropped from the Springbok side for the first test against the touring Wallabies. He was replaced by pharmacy student André de Wet, from Stellenbosch and Western Province.

Frik is finished, they said, except in Pretoria, of course, where they warned: 'Wait until Frik gets hold of De Wet.' That didn't happen. De Wet withdrew from the Province side and was replaced by Teddy Hoffman, a medical student from Stellenbosch.

That was Frik du Preez's day. His exploits in scoring a try, dropping a 70-metre penalty, and succeeding with a place kick from his own side of the halfway line (to give the guys a break, he explained afterwards) have been well documented. That was the day that Ou Frik, familiarly called by only his first name after more than a decade at the highest level, reached what was a pinnacle, even for the man considered South Africa's Player of the Millennium. It was the date that he 'dropped, placed, and scored,' as his great old pal Mof Myburgh said afterwards.

Suffice it to say that Du Preez's nine points in 11 minutes turned things around, after Western Province had gone into the break only three points behind at 16–13. The final score was 28–13 to Northern Transvaal. Revenge was sweet after the Currie Cup loss of five years before that had put Western Province on their way to a Currie Cup title that was decided on league matches and had also signalled the end of the legendary Louis Schmidt as a Northern Transvaal player.

Just as Northern Transvaal had scaled the heights of excellence in 1969, so they faltered in 1970. Many call it the greatest shock in Currie Cup history, but that would be taking away from the performance of Griquas, who, on the day, deservedly beat the Light Blues 11–9 in Kimberley.

It was not a once-off and should definitely not be placed in the 'shock' category. No side with a coach of the calibre of the great Ian Kirkpatrick, a captain and player like Mannetjies Roux, and stars like Piet Visagie, Joggie Viljoen, Jannie van Aswegen, Piet van Deventer and the Smith brothers Peet and Tos, to name only a few of the heroes in the final, could fall into that category.

It is true that Northern Transvaal were too casual in their approach. The discipline, then and now the basis of Northern Transvaal and the Bulls' rugby, was absent. Captain Piet Uys struggled to get his team together for the traditional team talk during tea on the morning of an away match. As was the habit, the players would go to their rooms after lunch to relax. That wasn't possible. Some of the players had brought their wives along for the match – the first time in the history of Northerns' away matches. Room-mates had to move out to other rooms to accommodate the wives.

Frik du Preez, according to Johan Volschenk's book *Die Ligbloues*, said to Mof Myburgh while they were relaxing in their room: 'Strange things are going to happen today. This is not how one prepares for a final.'

In his after match speech Piet Uys, *Die Transvaler* writing on the Monday, thanked the wives who had stayed at home.

As is the case in rugby, it is more often than not impossible to change a team's mindset once they've run on. It is always impossible when that is the case against a team of quality that is motivated and determined to win. So it was that day. Griquas were 8–0 ahead after 30 minutes, after two tries by wing Buddy Schwarz, following two breaks by centre Koos Waldeck who transferred to Mannetjies Roux, and by scrumhalf Joggie Viljoen. A Chris Luther penalty gave the home side an 8–3 lead at half-time.

Playing with the wind in the second half, Northern Transvaal threatened to take control. Luther added a penalty and Du Preez scored a try, and the defending champions were 9–8 up with only four minutes to play.

Roux called up flank Peet Smith. From 53 metres out, and against a strong breeze, even though the wind had subsided somewhat, he struck it true and straight. Northerns tried in the little time left, but it was too late and the jubilation belonged to Griquas.

It was only their third Currie Cup title after the two won in 1899 and 1911, on both occasions breaking what

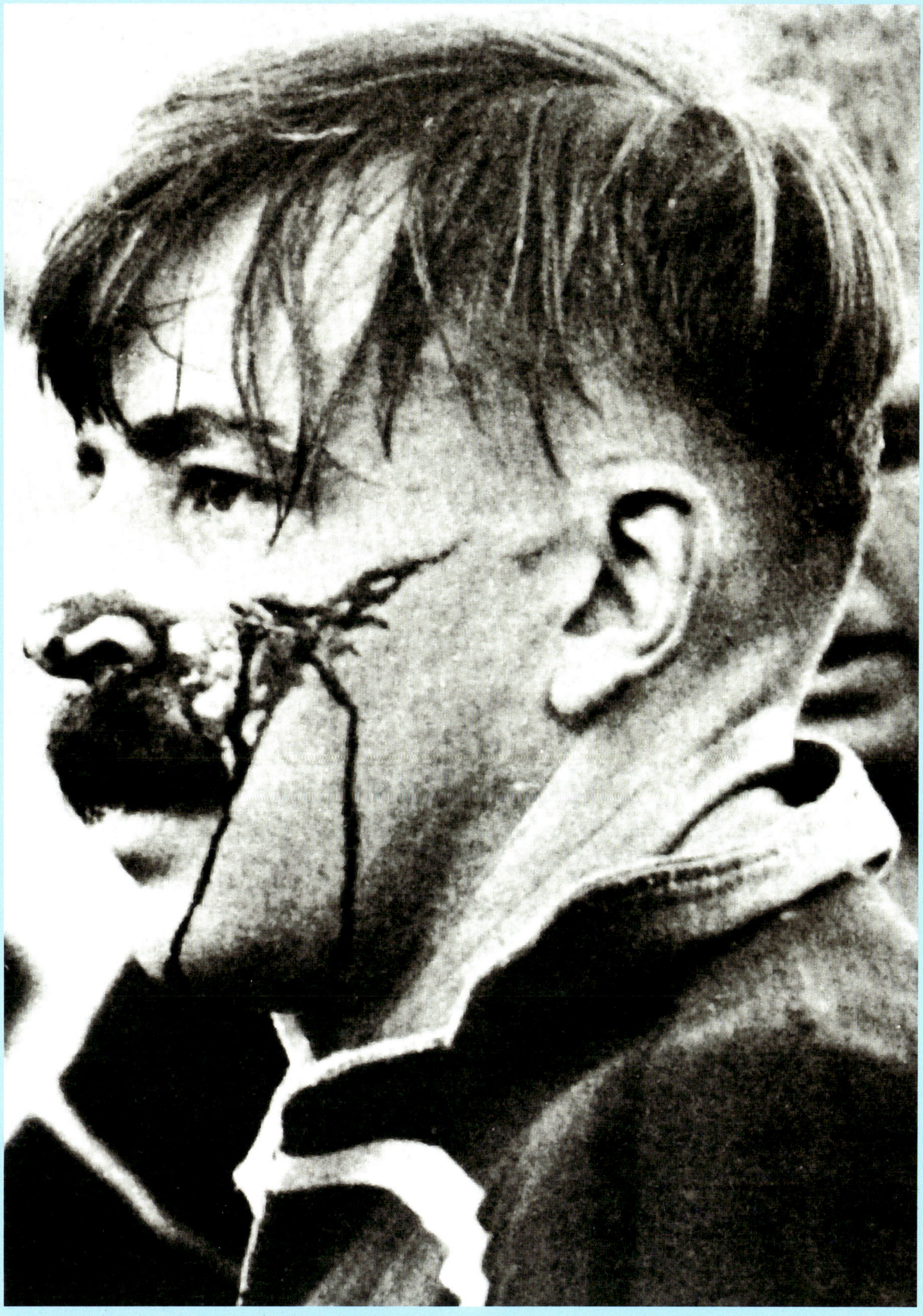

Louis Schmidt, a legend as Northern Transvaal player and captain.

NAAS – GENIUS AND MATCH-WINNER

Naas. Simply Naas.

That's how they referred to Hendrik Egnatius Botha, as the Pretoria faithful had done in the case of heroes like Hannes Brewis, who was simply Hansie or Kiewiet (plover) because of his thin legs, Frik (du Preez) and Joost (Van der Westhuizen).

It started in 1977, when the skinny, long-haired 19-year-old made his debut for the former Northern Transvaal against South-Eastern Transvaal.

The youngster was plucked from the obscurity of the Tukkies under-20 side by Northerns coach Buurman van Zyl. At 19, Botha was 15 years younger than his provincial captain Thys Lourens. He continued playing first-class rugby in South Africa until 1995, when he was 37.

He was adored by Northern Transvaal fans but disliked or even hated by opposition supporters. He was also, arguably, the greatest match-winner the world has seen, but was denied the opportunity he should have enjoyed to impress at international level.

'He couldn't pass,' said his detractors from outside the borders of the Northern Transvaal Rugby Union. It was also said that he kicked too much. 'That's all Naas can do,' these detractors said. 'He was so intent on the kicking game that he had to be introduced to his inside centre,' mocked those who were hurt by his demolition of their favourite sides.

They opted to forget Botha's brilliant display of running rugby for a World XV at Twickenham in 1986, during the International Rugby Board's Centenary celebrations. This was the Naas Botha whom those who had watched club rugby in Pretoria over the years had come to know.

Botha's defence, in particular, was regarded as a weakness his critics loved to target. They conveniently overlooked the great try-saving tackle in the north-east corner of the Free State Stadium against the British Lions in 1980 in his first year of test rugby. There were many more telling tackles in his career.

Coach Buurman van Zyl was the man who ordered Naas: 'Stay on your feet, you don't help us by being on the ground or in a maul.' Van Zyl maintained that others could do the defensive work. He was so serious about this that a special defensive strategy was devised to keep match-winner Botha on his feet to ensure a win for his team by means of tactical or drop kicks.

The proof is in the pudding, they say, and in Botha's era Northern Transvaal dominated the Currie Cup scene, and South Africa's backline was feared throughout the rugby world. This was arguably the best backline the Springboks have fielded, and included great players like Divan Serfontein, Danie Gerber, Willie du Plessis, Gerrie Germishuys, Ray Mordt and Carel du Plessis.

There can be no doubt that Naas Botha was a rugby genius. 'He will be our greatest ever,' Doctor Danie Craven told me, after the 1980 test against South America in Durban. That was only Botha's second test. Three drop goals, a penalty and the conversion of captain Morné du Plessis' lone Springbok try in that test, saw Botha accumulate 26 points out of the 44 that the Boks scored in the two-test series.

Botha was a brilliant kicker, either out of hand or at the posts. He was a distributor of the highest order and a tactician par excellence.

He was also an outstanding captain.

In the period 1977–1995, spanning 18 years of top-class rugby, Botha played in only 28 international matches for South Africa. He did, however, do enough to set a string of records at international and provincial level: most points, most drops, most Currie Cup titles and most Currie Cup finals played (shared with Northern Transvaal teammate, Burger Geldenhuys).

Botha's greatest matches, from many outstanding performances, were arguably the 1985 mud bath against Western Province at Newlands and the Currie Cup final in 1987.

The match at Newlands was a Lion Cup (knock-out) match. Everything favoured the home side that had won the Currie Cup for the three preceding years and had repeated it in 1985 as well as in 1986. The field was wet and the mud was thick. The boys from Pretoria were not familiar with playing in wet conditions, let alone mud that made constructive rugby almost impossible. Barely recognisable in the mud that was Newlands, Botha covered, and even tackled, but above all, he turned Western Province around endlessly with his great tactical kicking. The only try in the 12-3 win came from his cousin Hendrik Kruger.

But was that mud show his best performance?

Naas Botha's victory salute after the 1989 Currie Cup final win at Loftus Versfeld.

'No,' Botha says, 'the win in 1987 against Transvaal must take pride of place. Don't forget, that was a Currie Cup final.'

The 1987 Currie Cup final win was particularly satisfying, as the Transvaal press had made it clear that it was their team's turn for honours. Transvaal had lost the 1986 final to Western Province at Newlands the previous year, but were looking to capture the trophy in 1987.

Botha warned that 'the Currie Cup isn't won in May'. Indignation and derision followed this statement. But Botha had the last laugh. He kicked four penalties and four drop goals in the 1987 final at the cold, rainy Ellis Park, where hail also pelted down during the match. Transvaal were ahead 15–9 at the break and it looked as if their cup dreams of earlier in the season would come true. Botha, however, had other ideas. His team talk at the break was short, sweet and very clear: 'Just give me the ball,' he instructed in a simple summary of Northern Transvaal's second-half game plan.

In that second half, 15 of Northern Transvaal's 24 points came from Botha's boot. Their forwards, with Adolf Malan imperious in the lineouts, took control courtesy of Botha's long field kicks that kept them on the attack and Botha within drop-kick distance. They won 24–18.

It is interesting to note that Botha was absent from the Light Blue side from June in 1983 until March 1985. He tried out with the Dallas Cowboys gridiron team as a kicker, but didn't make the grade. He became a professional for half of each year as he played for Rovigo in Italy from 1987 to 1993 and then returned to help the Bulls in their Currie Cup campaigns.

Botha's stint at Rovigo and his deeds for the Italian club saw the title of honorary citizen bestowed upon him.

With Naas back, the Pretoria team won the Currie Cup in 1987 and again in 1988 when they beat Western Province. They shared the trophy with Province at Newlands in 1989. They then lost it to Natal in 1990 but regained it in 1991, with Transvaal the losers once more.

Botha's last Currie Cup season saw Transvaal and Natal fight it out for the coveted Currie Cup, with Transvaal again denied in 1992.

Botha, King of the Currie Cup, bowed out in 1992. It is sad that the Currie Cup eluded him in a last year of disappointment, with his Springbok side also losing to the All Blacks and Australia (at home) before drawing their two-test series against France on tour and being thumped by England at Twickenham.

It wasn't quite the end of the road, however. Springbok World Cup-winning coach Kitch Christie needed an icon and experience in his 1995 World Cup team. After two seasons of retirement, Naas, who had a run in club rugby for Adelaar, was given a match at Ellis Park where it was hoped that he could show his skills in an invitation XV.

But time had caught up with the great player at 37, and Christie had to shelve his plan.

Here is a summary of Botha's amazing career:

In 1977, when he was only 19, Botha made his debut for Northern Transvaal.

He captained Northern Transvaal in 1980 when he was 22.

He made his test debut against the South American Jaguars in 1980 and also played against the British Lions.

He became the youngest captain to win the Currie Cup at 22 years and 217 days.

He secured a win in the third test against the Lions in Port Elizabeth in 1980 when he converted a try from touch in a near gale-force wind and driving rain. He was then dubbed the 'Nasty Booter' by the British press.

In 1981 he scored 20 of the Springboks' 24 points in the second test against the All Blacks in Wellington.

Botha still holds the Currie Cup record of 1 699 points. He kicked five drop goals against Natal in 1992 and a total of 20 drop goals in the Currie Cup in 1985.

His total of 179 matches for Northern Transvaal included 123 Currie Cup matches.

Botha played in 11 Currie Cup finals, a record he shares with Springbok flanker Burger Geldenhuys, who also captained Northern Transvaal.

With Thys Lourens and coach Buurman van Zyl, Botha formed the triumvirate that was nucleus of the Light Blues' success. Botha and Lourens hold two contrasting records: Botha was the youngest ever Currie Cup winning captain, and Lourens the oldest at 35 years and 138 days.

Botha's SA record of 138 points in Currie Cup finals is well ahead of the second-placed 54 by Morné Steyn, incumbent flyhalf of the Blue Bulls.

Botha captained South Africa to a series win over the New Zealand Cavaliers in 1980 and was captain when South Africa were readmitted to international rugby in 1992. In all, he played in 28 tests and was captain in nine.

In 1979, 1981, 1985 and 1987 Botha was voted South Africa's Player of the Year – a record. In 2006 he was also admitted to the IRB's Hall of Fame to underline his standing in international rugby.

The State President's award in 1992 is another accolade Botha cherishes.

threatened to become a Western Province monopoly.

The defeat was the only one in a final that Buurman van Zyl would suffer in the 13 seasons he coached Northern Transvaal, although they also didn't make the final in 1972 when Transvaal and Eastern Transvaal did battle for the honours.

Before that, however, there was the great confrontation in 1971 of neighbours Transvaal and Northern Transvaal. It ended in a 14-all draw, and that was the day that big, jovial, laughing Frik said of the disappointment of a draw: 'It's just like kissing your sister!'

It was hard, uncompromising, exciting, and ultimately also filled with confusion and controversy.

The season was out of the ordinary, much different from the stoic, predictable way that things are done in Pretoria. There was an upheaval at executive level, and the selectors picked 41 players during the course of the season. Although their performances did not show it, and their ultimate successes underlined the depth at Northerns despite the inconsistency in selection, the question was asked: how can a club like Tukkies start off with a single player in the provincial side, and by season's end have nine representatives?

The feeling between Transvaal and Northern Transvaal (at the level of the supporters, it must be pointed out) could be gauged by the cheers that went up at Loftus during a Carlton Cup match, as Transvaal were cleaned up 26–12 by Free State in Bloemfontein. That meant the Johannesburg side had to play two further matches against Free State and Griquas, and this was received with glee in Pretoria. After all, with Transvaal having to play two eliminators as well as a semi-final before they met Northern Transvaal, they would be fatigued.

But Transvaal president Jannie le Roux used the SA Rugby Board to switch the dates for the semi-finals, and Transvaal had a week's rest between their remaining matches. Five weeks of tough competition sharpened the Rooibontes, while the Light Blues had to kick their heels at training in what was, by then, a very warm Pretoria spring. A single friendly against Rhodesia had to suffice as preparation. Transvaal duly won through in the play-offs and beat Natal 23–10 in the semi-final.

It was an outstanding Currie Cup final by two of the strongest sides that had done battle up to then – hard, exciting and brutal in the positive sense. There was excitement throughout, especially with the dramatic finish of Sakkie Sauerman's converted try, which was scored as spectators poured onto the field. The reality, however, is that Northern Transvaal had relaxed their focus when the home side kicked off, with just more than a minute remaining. Chris Luther had, moments before, increased Northerns' 11–9 lead to 14–9.

Transvaal scrumhalf Gert Schutte – there must be a number of selectors having sleepless nights about how they, over years, denied him a test cap – started the try. Piet Greyling and Simon Norwood were involved, and then Sauermann and the try converter Jannie van Deventer wrote their names into the history books in the fifth minute of injury time.

It was the great Frik du Preez's final match, and like his good friend Piet Uys the previous year, he went out on the crest of a Currie Cup season that should have been won but wasn't. At least, in Du Preez's case, Northern Transvaal had a share of the trophy.

The giant prop Mof Myburgh, together with Du Preez and Uys the other member of Northerns and the Springboks' 'three musketeers', also called it a day.

In 1972, Northern Transvaal failed to make the final. Buurman van Zyl didn't coach that year due to illness, and Transvaal and Eastern Transvaal contested the final in Springs. Transvaal won 25–19.

In 1973, Northern Transvaal qualified to play Free State in the Currie Cup semi-final at Loftus. The previous years' cry that Northern Transvaal's rugby was dour and not in the interest of the game, had by now swelled to a choir.

Free State were the sentimental favourites because they were prepared to run with the ball and provide thrills for spectators. The whole of the Transvaal province, where teams such as Western, Eastern and South Eastern Transvaal competed with Transvaal and Northern Transvaal, were playing an outdated game with their big, hard, grinding forwards.

And so it happened that Northern Transvaal played not only Free State in that semi-final, but were also up against the collective hopes of the whole of South

Moaner van Heerden, epitomising the uncompromising, abrasive type of forward on which Northern Transvaal and the Blue Bulls built their success over the years.

Africa. The home side won 15–9 and a single act will remain with those who were fortunate to see the final.

Northern Transvaal's Chris Luther placed the ball six metres outside his own 22-metre line and close to the touchline. It was unbelievable. To add to the tension felt by the entire stadium as the ball carried towards the posts, it bounced on the cross bar, then went over, in what must surely be the longest kick in South Africa's first-class rugby history. Tremendous tackling by the Northern Transvaal backs clinched it, and Northern Transvaal were in yet another final.

In 1974, the shortcomings of the three-section Currie Cup system became clear. If Transvaal were to lose against Eastern Province in Port Elizabeth, it would mean a semi-final against the same side, a week later, at Ellis Park. Nobody will ever know or admit whether they did so on purpose, but lose they did, in rainy, windy conditions that suited Eastern Province. In so doing, Transvaal averted a semi-final at Newlands against Western Province. A week later, however, Transvaal beat Eastern Province 30–6. For the second time in three years, it would be neighbours Northern Transvaal and Transvaal in the final, this time at Loftus.

It was, if possible, harder than the final in 1971. Thys Lourens suffered broken teeth, Transvaal hooker Dave Frederickson ended up in hospital with internal injuries after a legitimate tackle by Moaner van Heerden, and the tough man Van Heerden himself barely got up after a tackle from the kick-off. That tells the story of the relentless forward struggle.

Three tries by Northerns' backs, to a single try by Transvaal, underlined that the Light Blues had the backs. They just didn't run with every ball – only when it counted. What was interesting in this match was that not a single penalty was awarded to Northern Transvaal close enough for a shot at the posts. It was close, and even the Loftus crowd admitted that the bounce of the ball denied Transvaal on two occasions in the home side's in-goal area. And then there was one of the most famous tight heels, in the days when scrumhalves still put the ball in straight at scrum time. With four minutes to go, with Northerns 17–15 ahead and Transvaal's flyhalf Gerald Bosch ready to drop the winner, Willie Kahts

Pierre Spies evades Kleintjie Grobler's despairing tackle while Gerrie Germishuys is left helpless moments before the clincher try in the 1975 Currie Cup final in Bloemfontein.

struck with the assistance of big, amiable Hans Weber on his tighthead side, as Transvaal's Paul Bayvel fed the scrum.

And that was that!

The 1975 final was won 12–6 by Northern Transvaal, after that famous try by Pierre Spies. The win came on a wet, muddy field, and the scores were tied when the last movement and kick forward by Christo Wagenaar set up the try for Spies.

In 1976 there was a rare absence of a Northern Transvaal side. For the first and only time while Buurman van Zyl was at the helm, they failed to contest the Currie Cup in a final. That was Free State's year.

In 1977, however, it wasn't, and Northern Transvaal were back at the top of the pile as they won 27–12 at Loftus. The season will be remembered for Naas Botha's arrival on the scene, and the inauguration of the new main stand.

It was a rather one-sided match, probably sealed in the first two scrums when Northern Transvaal simply went on the run with the Free State pack. It was also a surprise, as the Free State were once again regarded as the favourites by the press and the experts around the country.

In those days, however, it was folly to bet or predict against Northern Transvaal for any match at Loftus Versfeld. Three tries, by Christo Wagenaar, Daan du Plessis and Pierre Spies, again underlined the worth of the underrated Northerns backs, with the Free State stars again not convincing when it counted. The 19-year-old Naas Botha contributed 15 points in his first final, including his first drop goal in a Currie Cup final.

The 1978 final was closer. Again Northerns played Free State, this time in Bloemfontein, and Northern Transvaal won only 13–9, although the scoreboard flattered Free State somewhat. Once again two tries by Northern Transvaal's backs and none by Free State was food for thought for those who had criticised the Light Blues' backs and lauded those of Free State.

The worth of Buurman van Zyl as coach was never illustrated more clearly than in this year. He lost captain

Two outstanding captains. Transvaal's Corrie Pypers is held without the ball by Northerns skipper Thys Lourens.

Thys Lourens, match-winning speedster Pierre Spies and strongman Nic Bezuidenhout, one of the best looseheads produced by South Africa, to injury. Lourens returned when the newly appointed captain Wynand Claassen was seriously injured. However, a super-fit pack; Naas Botha who had matured into a match-winner of the very highest order; a will to win; and some youngsters such as Tommy du Plessis, Burger Geldenhuys and Pierre Edwards who had started making their mark, took them to another final. It was Lourens' eighth final and his fourth as captain. In those eight matches he was never on the losing side.

In 1979, it was the final of the Du Plessis. Morné captained Western Province, and Daan was appointed captain when Thys Lourens was injured. The Newlands clash was a disappointing encounter, and the draw of 15–all was probably a fair reflection of a match neither side deserved to win. Naas Botha took the decision at the end to drop when a try was a possibility, and that tied the scores. He scored all 15 of Northerns' points, which included two drops.

Earlier that year, NTRU president Fritz Eloff had warned that other sides were catching up, and that Northern Transvaal would have to work harder to retain their supremacy. He was right, although it took a year or two before his prediction came true. His team beat

WYNIE STRYDOM – REFLECTING THE BULLS' FORTUNES

It's a serious matter... two Northern Transvaal and Bulls stalwarts, Naas Botha and Wynie Strydom, in discussion during a Bulls match.

The Springbok blazer in his cupboard was more than deserved, but the Blue Bulls and Bulls manager Wynie Strydom will not necessarily describe his stint as assistant team manager of the Springboks in 2009 as the highlight of his career in team management.

The man whose tense face when the Bulls are in trouble, and his elation when they win, is well known to all rugby lovers in South Africa. He has been involved with the Bulls as team manager for close to 400 matches over 14 years, and his most treasured memories centre on the many friends he has made since he first took up this job in 1997.

Oom Wynie, as the players call him, has been on duty in Super 12 matches since the days when the Bulls were still Northern Transvaal; in the Super 14 campaign where the Bulls were three times crowned as the champions; in the Currie Cup competition, through the years when the Blue Bulls were at their very lowest ebb since the union became independent as the Northern Transvaal Rugby Union in 1938; and also during the good years of 1998, 2002, 2003, 2004 and 2009, when they won the Currie Cup outright.

Strydom was also the Bulls manager when they played against the British and Irish Lions of 1997 at Loftus, and when the team played in Scotland and Zimbabwe, as well as during tours to Fiji, Argentina and Georgia. What's more, he hasn't missed a single Bulls or Blue Bulls match in this span of 14 years between 1997 and 2010.

'My job entails everything that happens off the field,' Strydom says. 'That includes kitting out the players, ensuring that passports and visas are in order, arranging accommodation, transport, meals, even the change rooms at training venues.'

Highlights in his time with the Bulls, whom he represented as a scrumhalf in 1979, are obviously the 92-3 win over the Reds in 2007, when the Bulls were chasing a semi-final berth in the Super 14; the win in that year's final over the Sharks in Durban; the 43-10 win over the Stormers at Newlands in 2006, when the Bulls needed a win by 33 points to advance to the semi-finals; and of course the two Super 14 wins in 2009 and 2010.

Not to mention those Currie Cup wins …

Western Province 39–9 in a tremendous performance at Loftus in 1980, scoring five tries to none, and being denied three more by refereeing decisions. Edrich Krantz (2), Thys Burger, Willie Kahts and Moaner van Heerden scored tries, and Botha's customary two drop goals plus three penalties and two conversions, added 19 points to his Currie Cup tally.

Northern Transvaal also beat Free State 23–6 in 1981, when they included their Springboks from the tour to New Zealand and the United States. Free State, on the other hand, used the players who had taken them to the Currie Cup final, and the two divergent decisions caused quite a stir in South African rugby, with the two camps arguing the merits thereof. In the end it was very much a no-contest as Northerns' eight fit Boks (Willie Kahts and Theuns Stofberg were injured) showed their experience and class. Three tries were scored in the 23–6 win, including a by now customary Naas Botha drop goal!

The barren years did come. Early in 1982 Buurman van Zyl passed away, and Western Province's golden era had dawned. Province won the finals from 1982 to 1986, beating Northern Transvaal in 1982 (24–7) at Newlands and then 9–3 in Pretoria. The score was 22–15 in 1984, in Cape Town.

Northern Transvaal came back in 1987, however. They

Northern Transvaal's Burger Geldenhuys and Western Province captain Carel du Plessis with the shared Currie Cup after the drawn final in 1989. The two unions' presidents Fritz Eloff and Jan Pickard are behind their captains in a picture that tells of the frustration after a drawn match.

played Transvaal, in rain and hail, at Ellis Park. It was Naas's game, as he scored all 24 points in the 24–18 win. There was also the great second-half performance of the Northern Transvaal forwards on the wet, slippery field, but ultimately it was probably Botha's very, very best in a long career of outstanding performances. In fact, he himself thinks it was.

The following year, Northern Transvaal beat Western Province in Pretoria, 19–18. This was the year when the unthinkable happened: Naas Botha was dropped from the side which was to play Transvaal in the second round at Ellis Park.

Botha was outstanding in the final, his last match before leaving for Dallas to play gridiron. Three penalties and two drop goals, added to Christo Spangenberg's solitary try, showed his class. The role played by the winners' lineout forwards was also immense, and 12 of Northern Transvaal's 26 lineouts were stolen from Western Province throw-ins.

Botha, in this season, improved the record for drop goals in the Currie Cup competition to 108, and the South African record for drop goals in all first-class matches to 163. He increased his tallies after his return from the United States.

In 1989, Western Province were again the opponents. It was a game, as the *SA Rugby Annual* of 1990 describes it, that Northern Transvaal should have won and Western Province could have won. The great Carel du Plessis scored the equaliser after his brother Michael switched and put him over, but newcomer Riaan Gous couldn't convert from touch. It left Northerns with a deserved share of the trophy.

It was hard and uncompromising, but Northern Transvaal had the major share of the territory and dominated the lineouts, winning a number of balls from their opposition. Western Province, however, succeeded in keeping the driving play of the defending champions to a minimum, and thereby neutralised their most lethal weapon. With 80 percent of the possession, the Light Blues were in control for all but the first five minutes and the last five minutes of the match, but that cost them sole possession of the title.

Then came the 90s. Northern Transvaal won in 1991, but then experienced a Currie Cup drought. As their meagre crop of Currie Cups in the 1990s continued, and the Blue Bulls had to fight for survival in the top tier of the competition in 1999, it was obvious that the professional era had caught the union unprepared.

The first shock came in the early 90s. Not only did Naas Botha retire from provincial rugby at the end of 1992, but Louis Luyt, then president of Transvaal, pulled the rug from under the NTRU's feet by poaching a considerable number of the top Northern Transvaal players. They included Uli Schmidt, Theo van Rensburg, Gavin Johnson, Heinrich Rogers, Rudolf Straeuli, Johan Roux, Hannes Strydom and Gerband Grobler. Only Grobler was not a Springbok.

Furthermore, the Union's financial problems were exacerbated by the advent of professionalism in 1996. Northern Transvaal didn't have the financial muscle to respond to the contracting requirements of the time, and they were without their best players. Their frustrating Currie Cup decade started in 1990 when the Sharks won the title for the first time. And to rub it in, they did it at Fortress Loftus.

Naas Botha, with an ill timed and ultimately unprophetic remark, upset Natal supporters and many others when he said that it had taken Natal a hundred years to win the Currie Cup and that they wouldn't do it for another hundred! He was wrong. Natal won the cup again in 1992, repeated the feat in 1995 and again in 1996.

Robert Denton – paving the way for professionalism.

Northern Transvaal won the Currie Cup in 1991, and Botha held the revered trophy aloft for the last time. Then there was a gap until 1998, when Eugene van Wyk as head coach and Chris Buitendach as his assistant brought the Currie Cup back to where Northerns' supporters believe it belongs: Loftus Versfeld.

These supporters are the people who have made Loftus and Northern Transvaal what they are, a fact realised by the first full-time secretary of Northern Transvaal Rugby Union, Robert Denton. A marketer par excellence, Denton realised that amateur rugby was on its way out. It was his innovative thinking that brought spectator suites to Loftus in a groundbreaking move in the 1970s. He was also the man who helped to make Northern

HEYNEKE MEYER – A COACH WITH VISION

Heyneke Meyer is a perfect example of the expression 'from zero to hero'. Despite the personal humiliations the man who led the Bulls and Blue Bulls into their second golden era had to endure, such as when Bulls' supporters cursed and spat at him at Loftus in the less successful days, Meyer planned his strategy and proceeded on the road he believed to be the right one.

Meyer was at the helm when the Bulls ended last in the then Super 12 competition of 2000 and again two years later after he was recalled and they lost all 11 of their matches. The Bulls conceded 500 points (a record) and had 76 tries scored against them.

Yet in that same black rugby year for the Bulls, they came back to win the 2002 Currie Cup. That heralded the second golden era of the Blue Bulls/Bulls, and two more Currie Cup titles followed in 2003 and 2004 before Free State put a stop to the monopoly. The Bloemfontein side won 29–25 in 2005. In 2006 a share of the Currie Cup title belonged to the Blue Bulls when they drew with Free State.

Meyer was also the coach in charge in 2007 when the Bulls won the Super 14 title following a 92–3 trouncing of the Reds at Loftus in their last league match. That set up a home semi-final win against Crusaders, and the controversial last-gasp try by Bryan Habana in the final against the Sharks.

The appointment of Meyer in 2002 came as a surprise after the 2000 last-place fiasco. He was surely on his way out, one would have expected, after 11 losses from 11 Super 14 outings.

It was Meyer's vision of building up the province's junior teams as a first step that ultimately led to their success. To this day, the overall strength and depth of the Blue Bulls and Bulls in all the national leagues they compete in, lies at the heart of their success.

One can safely say that it was the visionary thinking of Heyneke Meyer that gave the union unparalleled depth as they started to dominate. In fact, as early as 2003, each of the Blue Bulls sides playing in national leagues reached at least the final of their competitions.

So great was Meyer's influence, not only in Pretoria but also at national level, that when he decided to terminate his involvement as coach with the Bulls in 2007, it was the end of an important era in coaching in SA rugby.

When the team won the Super 14, Bulls' 2007 captain, Victor Matfield, said that any player who missed being coached by Meyer was the poorer for it. Former Bulls' captain, Anton Leonard, said Meyer has the gift of inspiring players to believe unconditionally in his plans.

There can be no greater proof than that 92–3 win over Queensland in 2007 that set the Bulls up for Super 14 glory. Before the last of the Bulls' 13 league games, they were only sixth on the log. The Bulls needed a bonus point win against the Reds to climb to fourth spot, which would have given them an away semi-final against the Sharks in Durban.

There was an alternative, though, whereby they could finish third or even second on the log. The permutations were easy: victory by 45 points or more would put the Bulls third, which meant travelling to Christchurch for a semi-final against the Crusaders. If the Bulls could beat the Reds by 72 points or more they would be certain of a home semi-final.

According to Wynie Strydom, long-standing team

Transvaal the pace-setter of the era, with his proposal that a statue be erected behind Loftus. It is the statue of the Unknown Rugby Player, a piece of sculpture that does not honour any particular player or group of players but is also a tribute to all who contributed to the success of the former Northern Transvaal Rugby Union and now the Blue Bulls Rugby Union. This includes the club players who have made Northern Transvaal the Currie Cup force it has been throughout the years.

It is one of the sad realities of the wonderful game of rugby that Denton, who gave so much to the union as its first full-time secretary, played Carlton Cup rugby for so many years and accompanied Northern Transvaal on many trips as a travelling Currie Cup reserve, never got the Northern Transvaal cap he so coveted. He did, however, represent Combined Northern Universities, SA Universities and Combined Pretoria.

The 1991 Currie Cup final win was against Transvaal again, and again it was Jannie Breedt, the Transvaal captain in four losing finals, who was at the helm.

manager of the Bulls and Blue Bulls in nearly 400 matches, Meyer never, at any stage, doubted which option he would follow.

'If Heyneke Meyer is your coach, he aims for one thing only – the best. Which is why the day before the match he told us he had made every player a shareholder in his belief that the team would beat the Reds by at least 72 points,' said Strydom in the book *Blue Bulls: 70 Years of Glory*.

The Bulls went much better than Meyer had demanded. They won by 92-3 (and lost against the Reds the next year!).

Meyer represented Lowveld at the Craven Week at junior and high school level. As a resident, Meyer began to coach the Mopanie hostel at the University of Pretoria because 'there was no-one else to do so'. Injuries had also played a role in forcing him into coaching. At the age of 23 he had completed every coaching course available and at 29 he was an assistant coach to the Springboks.

Meyer's success could be put down to planning. The structures he put in place after his return in 2002 are proof of that. Yet, while planning was one reason for the success, Heyneke Meyer also had his minimum requirements that he believed were needed to win the Super 14 competition. They were:

Experienced leaders of whom at least five had captained a team at that level;

Eight players who had played in at least 50 Super 12/14 and 50 Currie Cup matches;

Eight players who had played in at least 20 tests;

Consistency in selection;

At least 10 players with international experience;

A substitute in every position – as good as the first choice – as back-up, or to be used as an impact player.

Coach Heyneke Meyer turned things around after a barren period in the Blue Bulls and Bulls' proud history.

The Bulls had all of the above and proved Meyer right in 2007. His motivation and philosophy rubbed off on the players. He was prepared to work hard and expected the same from them. They responded ... and the rest, as they say, is a pleasant history.

It was a strange season for Northern Transvaal, who had to work hard to get back to the top after the unlikely defeat by Natal in the 1990 Currie Cup final. Two big hidings, 54–15 against Natal in Durban and 24–9 against Transvaal, led to a jittery and unconvincing start to the season of revenge. The strangeness of the season was underlined by the almost unbelievable turnaround and the 62–6 win against Natal, this time at Loftus, in the Lion Cup final.

Perhaps the first two defeats showed just how much Naas Botha was worth to his team. After his return from Rovigo, the Lion Cup title followed, and Nortnern Transvaal then beat Transvaal 35–12, while Western Province succumbed 28–9. Yes, Northern Transvaal were on the march and nearly back to their very best.

However, it was too little, too late, or so it seemed. To have any chance, Northern Transvaal had to rely on Free State to beat Western Province. They did so. A spectator ran onto the field as Western Province's Springbok FC Smit surged towards the tryline, and

Joost van der Westhuizen was one of South Africa's very best scrumhalves and led the Blue Bulls to the 1998 Currie Cup titel.

tackled him. It happened well inside Free State's 22-metre area, and a try was not a certainty, but a definite possibility, and would have sealed the match for Province. Instead, Izak Beneke scored a surprise try right at the end for Free State, and suddenly there was a three-way tie for second place, with Transvaal sitting pretty at the top of the log.

'To all intents and purposes we were out of the Currie Cup,' recalls the Northern Transvaal coach, Eugene van Wyk. 'We were spending the weekend at Sun City, as a thank you gesture to the players, their wives and girlfriends. But with Free State winning, we realised we had better get home and prepare for the play-off match against Province on the Wednesday.'

Within four days, Northern Transvaal beat Western Province at Loftus (34–21) and then went to Bloemfontein where they accounted for Free State 27–23.

Northern Transvaal now had a week to prepare for the final in which they beat log-leaders Transvaal convincingly, 27–15. It wasn't a good final. The heat obviously got to the players, and handling and other errors abounded. In the end, the greater fitness of Northerns, and their better composure under pressure saw them through.

Three missed penalties in the first half, and two possible tries that the Light Blues left on the table, made matters more difficult as they went into half-time tied at 6–6. In the last quarter, however, there was no denying Northern Transvaal as they had the territorial advantage and pressured the visitors with better possession from the scrums and the lineouts. Four tries to nil tell the story of their domination, and in the end, the three-week break forced on Transvaal, and their gamble in fielding players just back from injury, helped to make this an unlikely fairytale year for the Light Blues.

Van Wyk had sipped from the Currie Cup before when Northern Transvaal shared the spoils with Western Province. At that time he was assistant coach under head coach John Williams. In fact Van Wyk, who played 30 matches for Western Transvaal, and a few for Northerns' B side when he moved to Pretoria and played club rugby for Oostelikes, was probably involved with Northern Transvaal teams as coach and assistant coach for longer than anyone else except Bierman van Zyl. He became head coach in 1990, with the 1995 Springbok World Cup coach Kitch Christie as his assistant. After the Currie Cup win against Transvaal in 1992, Van Wyk took Northern Transvaal into the years without Naas Botha. After being replaced by Williams from 1994 to 1997, he was once more appointed head coach in 1998. His assistant was Chris Buitendach, a greatly underrated coach, who was never given the decent opportunity he deserved at a higher level.

The return of the Currie Cup to Loftus, in 1998, came in the year when Northern Transvaal had become the Blue Bulls. Their Super 14 team was called the Bulls because it was, in theory if not in practice, a different team selected from a number of unions united in one rugby franchise.

Northerns regained the Currie Cup in 1998 after a 24–20 victory against Western Province after what would have been the match-winning try by Chester Williams was disallowed because the final pass to him was adjudged forward.

Joost van der Westhuizen had taken over the captaincy, as Ruben Kruger was not available because of injury. The Blue Bulls had reached the final for the 24th time, after coming back from 17–3 down against the Sharks in the semi-final. At that stage it looked as if the Blue Bulls were out of it, and Van Wyk admits he didn't believe his team could make up the leeway.

However, Van der Westhuizen, leading by example, kept the Blue Bulls going. Two penalties by Franco Smit reduced the deficit, and then Piet Boer dived over for a try. The spectre of time loomed large (a result was obligatory), but stand-in captain Van der Westhuizen made the difference by showing the qualities that would make him captain of South Africa the year after. With a sniping break Van der Westhuizen set off and stocky flanker Nicky van der Walt, who had worked his heart out, dived over for the try. That put the result beyond doubt at 31–17.

For the Loftus final Van Wyk and Buitendach decided to gamble and play the experienced and underrated

BULLS

Francois Hougaard scores an early try against the free State Cheetahs in the 2009 final at Loftus Versfeld with Jacques-Louis Potgieter too late to prevent the try.

scrumhalf Conrad Breytenbach on the wing, following Grant Esterhuizen's injury against Western Province in a league match. At half-time, with the Blue Bulls 14–6 to the good, it looked to be a stroll home. Western Province had other ideas, however, and converted tries by Chester Williams and Charl Marais reduced the deficit. Then, with time on the clock almost gone and the score at 24–20 in the Blue Bulls' favour, Springbok centre Robbie Fleck sent Williams over for his second try. However, referee André Watson, who was on the spot to adjudge the legitimacy of the pass, ruled it forward, and the Blue Bulls could add another Currie Cup to their trophy collection.

Rugby is a team sport, and it was a poignant moment when Van der Westhuizen called the captain for that season, the injured Ruben Kruger, to the podium to join him in accepting the Currie Cup. Grant Esterhuizen (injured as well) was also there to share in the victory celebrations.

The year 1999 was unsuccessful, and Van Wyk's stint as coach at the Blue Bulls came to an end after they finished only fifth in the 2000 Currie Cup campaign. Heyneke Meyer was put in charge of the Northern Bulls as they were then known, but after a disastrous season in which the Bulls lost nine of their eleven Super 14 matches, he was replaced for 2001 before being reinstated in 2002.

The Blue Bulls simply had to perform to retain their Currie Cup status. Only the top six sides would go through to the Currie Cup competition in 2003, and those six would be decided on the combined performances in

We are the champions... The Bulls celebrate their 23rd Currie Cup title (four of them shared) after the win over the Free State Cheetahs in 2009.

2000, 2001 and 2002. Meyer's success story, discussed earlier in this chapter, began in 2002. The Blue Bulls won the Currie Cup in 2002, repeated it in 2003 and again in 2004.

They beat the Sharks in Durban in the 2002 semi-final, and in the final at Ellis Park young Derick Hougaard 'did a Naas Botha' on the Lions when he kicked two drop goals, five penalties and scored a try in his team's 31–7 win. Hougaard's 26 points established a new individual record in a final.

After two early losses in 2003 against Griquas (19–15) and Western Province (63–26), the Blue Bulls won their next seven matches and thrashed the Sharks 40–19 in the final, running in five tries.

In 2004 the Lions beat the Blue Bulls outfit, inflicting their only loss as Meyer's side marched on and into the final in which they beat the Free State Cheetahs 42–33 at Loftus.

The Bulls played in their fourth successive final in 2005, but Free State beat them 29–25 in a very rare final loss for the Bulls at Fortress Loftus. In 2006 they were held to a 28-all draw in Bloemfontein – again against Free State.

Their sequence of finals appearences ended in 2007, however, when Free State and the Lions played in the final. The Bulls were back the next year, marching to Durban after their 2008 semi-final win over Free State, but the Sharks won their first final since 1996 14–9.

Then came the Bulls' best year ever when they won both the Super 14 title and the Currie Cup in 2009, bringing the Golden Cup back to Loftus after a 36–24 victory over the Cheetahs.

CHAPTER 10

Final Records

Scores of more than 30 points

56 Transvaal v Free State, 1994 final score 56–33*

42 Blue Bulls v FS Cheetahs, 2004 final score 42–33

40 Blue Bulls v Sharks, 2003 final score 40–19

39 Northern Transvaal v Western Province, 1980 final score 39–9**

36 Blue Bulls v FS Cheetahs, 2009 final score 36–24

33 Free State v Western Province, 1976 final score 33–16

33 Free State v Lions, 1994 final score 33–56

33 Sharks v Lions, 1996 final score 33–15

33 FS Cheetahs v Blue Bulls, 2004 final score 33–42

*The match aggregate of 89 points is also a finals record

** The biggest winning margin in a final (30 points)

Five tries or more

7 Lions v Free State 1994

6 Blue Bulls v FS Cheetahs 2004

5 Northern Transvaal v Western Province 1980

5 Lions v Sharks 1999

5 Blue Bulls v Sharks 2003

Northern Transvaal's captain Thys Lourens with his president, Prof. Fritz Eloff as the Light Blues celebrate another Currie Cup title. Lourens was never on the losing side in his eight Currie Cup finals.

20 points or more by a player

26 Derick Hougaard, Blue Bulls v Lions 2002
(1 try, 5 penalties, 2 drop goals)
24 Naas Botha, Northern Transvaal v Transvaal 1987
(4 penalties, 4 drop goals)
Braam van Straaten, Western Province v Sharks 2007
(1 try, 2 conversions, 5 penalties)
21 Gavin Johnson, Lions v Free State 1994
(6 conversions, 3 penalties)
Morné Steyn, Blue Bulls v FS Cheetahs 2009
(3 conversions, 4 penalties, 1 drop goal)
20 Thierry Lacroix, Sharks v Western Province 1995
(6 penalties, 1 conversion)

Six conversions by a player

6 Gavin Johnson, Lions v Free State 1994

Six penalty goals by a player

6 Thierry Lacroix, Natal v Western Province 1994

Four drop goals by a player

4 Naas Botha, Northern Transvaal v Transvaal 1987

40 points or more in finals

138 Naas Botha (Northern Transvaal) 1t, 10c, 20p, 18dg 1977–1991
54 Morné Steyn (Blue Bulls) 6c, 12p, 2dg 2005–2009
53 Willem de Waal (FS Cheetahs) 7c, 13p 2004–2007
45 Calla Scholtz (Western Province) 1t, 4c, 9p, 2dg 1983–1988
44 Derick Hougaard (Blue Bulls) 1t, 3c, 8p, 3dg 2002–2006
41 Joel Stransky (Natal/Sharks) 1c, 13p 1990–1995

Three tries in finals

4 Ettienne Botha (Blue Bulls) 2003–2004
3 Neil Burger (Western Province) 1982–1985
3 Edrich Krantz (Free State/Northern Transvaal) 1976–1980

MATCH RECORDS

More than 110 points

147 Northern Transvaal v SWD (147–8) Pietersburg 1996
113 Free State v SWD (113–11) Bloemfontein 1996
111 Pumas v SWD (111–14) Witbank 2001

Wins by 100 points

139 Northern Transvaal v SWD (147–8) Pietersburg 1996
106 FS Cheetahs v NFS (106–0) Bloemfontein 1997
102 FS Cheetahs v SWD (113–11) Bloemfontein 1996
102 SWD v NFS (102–0) George 1999

Sixteen tries

23 Northern Transvaal v SWD (147–8) 1996
18 Western Transvaal v EOFS (103–9) 1988
16 Transvaal v Far North (99–9) 1973
16 SWD Eagles v NFS (102–0) 1999
16 Pumas v SWD Eagles (111–14) 2001

35 or more points by a player

46 Jannie de Beer (3t, 14c, 1p) FS Cheetahs v NFS 1997
40 Casper Steyn (2t, 3c, 8p) Blue Bulls v SWD 2000
38 Henry Honiball (4t, 6c, 2p) Sharks v Boland 1996
Lance Sherrell (2t, 14c) Blue Bulls v SWD 1996

37 Casper Steyn (2t, 3c, 7p) Pumas v FS Cheetahs 2003
36 Gerald Bosch (1t, 13c, 2dg) Transvaal v Far North 1973
Eric Herbert (3c, 9p, 1dg) NFS v Falcons 1997
Casper Steyn (1t, 7c, 7p) Blue Bulls v Pumas 2000
35 Jacques Olivier (7t) Northern Transvaal v SWD 1996
Kennedy Tsimba (1t, 9c, 4p) FS Cheetahs v Griquas 2003
Braam Pretorius (2t, 11c, 1p) Pumas v Valke 2009

Six tries by a player

7 Jacques Olivier BNorthern Transvaal v SWD (147–8) 1996
6 Buks Marais Boland v NED (33–3) 1952

Fourteen conversions by a player

14 Lance Sherrell Northern Transvaal v SWD 1996
14 Jannie de Beer FS Cheetahs v NFS 1997
14 Nel Fourie Pumas v SWD Eagles 2001

Nine penalty goals by a player

9 Eric Herbert NFS v Falcons 1997
9 Derick Hougaard Blue Bulls v Western Province 2002

Five drop goals by a player

5 Naas Botha Northern Transvaal v Natal 1992

SEASON RECORDS

Seven hundred and fifty points

792 Sharks 15 matches 1996
783 Northern Transvaal 13 matches 1996

One hundred tries by a team

112 Sharks 15 matches 1996
102 Northern Transvaal 13 matches 1996

Two hundred and fifty points by a player

268 Johan Heunis Northern Transvaal 1989
263 Gavin Lawless Lions 1996
252 Casper Steyn Blue Bulls 1999

Fifteen Tries

19 Carel du Plessis Western Province 1989
19 Colin Lloyd Leopards 2006
18 Ettienne Botha Blue Bulls 2004
18 Alistair Kettledas Pumas 2009
16 Jan-Harm van Wyk FS Cheetahs 1997
16 Ryno Benjamin Boland 2006
15 Philip Burger Free State 2006

Fifty conversions

62 Louis Koen Western Province 1997
55 Jannie de Beer FS Cheetahs 1997
54 Braam Pretorius Pumas 2009

Forty penalties

48 Gavin Lawless Lions 1996
47 Willem de Waal Free State 2005
45 Lance Sherrell Western Province 1991
Johan Heunis Northern Transvaal 1987
Cameron Oliver Transvaal 1989
42 Cameron Oliver Transvaal 1990
André Joubert Free State 1989

Twenty drop goals

20 Naas Botha Northern Transvaal 1985

CAREER RECORDS

One hundred matches

142 Helgard Müller Free State 1983–1998
141 Rudi Visagie Free State, Natal & SE-Tvl 1980–1996
136 Chris Badenhorst Free State, Natal & SE-Tvl 1986–1999
128 Burger Geldenhuys Northern Transvaal 1977-1989
Ollie le Roux Free State & Sharks 1993–2007
126 André Joubert Free State & Sharks 1986–1999
125 Eric Herbert NFS & FS Cheetahs 1986–2001
123 Naas Botha Northern Transvaal 1977–1992
118 Willie Meyer EP, Free State & Lions 1989–2002
115 AJ Venter FS Cheetahs, Lions & Sharks 1997–2008
114 Piet Krause Lions, Griquas, Blue Bulls, Valke 1996–2007
112 Louis Moolman Northern Transvaal 1974–1986
108 Eddie Fredericks WP, Leopards, FS Cheetahs, Griffons 1998–2009
106 Martiens le Roux Free State 1973–1986
De Wet Ras Free State & Natal 1974–1986
104 Gerrie Sonnekus Free State 1974–1985
103 Uli Schmidt Northern Transvaal & Transvaal 1983–1994
Albert van den Berg Griquas & Sharks 1996–2009
102 Adolf Malan Northern Transvaal 1983–1992
101 Gysie Pienaar Free State 1974–1987
100 Adi Jacobs Valke & Sharks 2001–2009

One thousand points

1699 Naas Botha Northern Transvaal 1977–1992
1402 Eric Herbert NFS & FS Cheetahs 1986–2001
1213 Willem de Waal FS Cheetahs & Western Province 2002–2009
1210 De Wet Ras Free State & Natal 1974–1986
1165 André Joubert Free State & Sharks 1986–1999
1017 Calla Scholtz Boland & Western Province 1980–1989

Most Tries

77 John Daniels Boland & Lions 1998–2008
70 Breyton Paulse Western Province 1996–2007
65 Chris Badenhorst Free State 1986–1999
58 André Joubert Free State & Sharks 1986–1999
52 Egon Seconds Western Province & Griquas 2001–2009
Stefan Terblanche Boland & Sharks 1994–2009
51 Gerrie Germishuys Free State & Transvaal 1971–1985
Carel du Plessis Western Province & Transvaal 1980–1989
Neil Burger Western Province 1982–1991
Jan-Harm van Wyk Free State & Pumas 1996–2001
50 Eddie Fredericks Western Province, Griffons, FS Cheetahs & Leopards 1998–2009
Fabian Juries EP, FS Cheetahs & NFS 2001–2009
49 Danie Gerber, EP, Free State & WP
46 Ryno Benjamin Lions (13t) & Boland (33t)
42 Ettienne Botha Falcons (20t) & Blue Bulls (21t)
42 Jongi Nokwe Boland (23t/41) matches; FS Cheetahs (19t/20 matches)
42 Justin Swart WP & Sharks
41 Gerhard Mans Free State & South West Africa
41 Adrian Jacobs Valke (20t) & Natal Sharks (21t)
40 Hennie Bekker Boland, WP & Free State
39 John Mametsa Blue Bulls
38 Pieter Hendriks Transvaal
37 Jannie van der Walt Lions
37 Deon Oosthuysen Western Transvaal & Northern Transvaal
37 Dave Prins Griquas
37 James Small Lions, Sharks & WP
36 Gerrie Sonnekus Free State
36 Kallie Grobler EP & Pumas
35 Edrich Krantz Free State & Northern Transvaal

35 Ray Mordt Zimbabwe, Transvaal & Northern Transvaal

Fastest Try after Kick-off

20 seconds: Chris Jack 11/7/2009– Western Province v Sharks: Newlands
29 seconds: Gerrie Britz, 2/8/2003– FS Cheetahs v Pumas: Puma Stadium
39 seconds: Paul de Koker 5/10/2002– Griquas v Blue Bulls: Absa Park
40 seconds: Dale Heidtman 20/7/2002– Pumas v EP, PE Stadium
46 seconds: Juan de Jongh 10/10/2009– Western Province v Lions: Coca-Cola Park
54 seconds: Riaan Swanepoel 17/7/2009– Sharks v Boland Cavaliers: Absa Stadium

Fastest Drop Goal after kick-off

22 seconds: Willem de Waal 22/9/2007 FS Cheetahs v Western Province: Newlands

More than 200 points in a season

268 Johan Heunis Northern Transvaal–15 matches 1989
263 Gavin Lawless Lions–15 matches 1996
252 Casper Steyn Blue Bulls–13 matches 1999
230 Kennedy Tsimba FS Cheetahs–14 matches 2003
228 Kennedy Tsimba FS Cheetahs–10 matches 2002
227 Calla Scholtz Western Province–14 matches 1988
224 Louis Koen Western Province–14 matches 1997
217 Cameron Oliver Transvaal–13 matches 1989
212 Willem de Waal FS Cheetahs–17 matches 2007
212 Willem de Waal FS Cheetahs–15 matches 2006
210 Naas Botha Northern Transvaal–11 matches 1987
200 Chris Maree North West–12 matches 1989
200 Jannie de Beer FS Cheetahs–14 matches 1997

17 points or more in a final

26 Derick Hougaard Blue Bulls v Lions (1 try, 2 drop goals, 5 pen) 2002
24 Naas Botha Northern Transvaal v Transvaal (4 drop goals, 4 pen) 1987
24 Braam van Straaten Western Province v Sharks (1 try, 2 con, 5 pen) 2001
21 Gavin Johnson Lions v Free State (6 con, 3 pen) 1994
21 Morné Steyn Blue Bulls v FS Cheetahs (3 con, 4 pen, 1 drop goal) 2009
20 Thierry Lacroix Sharks v Western Province (6 pen, 1 con) 1995
19 Naas Botha Northern Transvaal v Western Province (2 con, 3 pen, 2 drop goals) 1980
19 Willem de Waal FS Cheetahs v Blue Bulls (5 pen, 2 con) 2005
18 De Wet Ras Free State v Western Province (3 con, 3 pen, drop goal) 1976
18 Henry Honiball Sharks v Lions (3 con, 4 pen) 1996
17 Gerald Bosch Transvaal v Eastern Transvaal (1 con, 2 pen, 3 drop goals) 1972

MOST DROP GOALS

Career

135 Naas Botha Northern Transvaal
69 De Wet Ras Free State & Natal

Season

20 Naas Botha Northern Transvaal 1985
19 Naas Botha Northern Transvaal 1987

Final

4 Naas Botha Northern Transvaal v Lions 1987

3 Gerald Bosch Transvaal v Eastern Transvaal 1972
3 Naas Botha Northern Transvaal v Western Province 1985

Non-final

5 Naas Botha Northern Transvaal v Natal 1992
4 Len Rodriquez Western Province v Griquas 1950
4 De Wet Ras Natal v Western Province 1979
4 Giepie van Zyl Eastern Province v Transvaal 1981
4 Naas Botha Northern Transvaal v Transvaal 1985
4 Naas Botha Northern Transvaal v NFS 1985
4 Naas Botha Northern Transvaal v Transvaal 1987 (at Loftus)
4 Naas Botha Northern Transvaal v Transvaal 1987 (at Ellis Park)

Fastest yellow card after kick-off

43 seconds Derick Kuün Blue Bulls v Sharks Loftus Versfeld 5/7/2008
58 seconds Bakkies Botha Blue Bulls v Western Province Newlands 17/10/2009

Youngest winning captain in a final

22 years 217 days: **Naas Botha** Northern Transvaal 1980

Winning captain, manager and coach in finals

Naka Drotské FS Cheetahs -captain 2005
-manager 2006
-coach 2007

Most successful coaches

Buurman van Zyl Northern Transvaal (9 wins & 2 draws) 1968–1981
Dawie Snyman Western Province (5 consecutive wins) 1982–1986
Ian McIntosh Natal & Natal Sharks (4 wins) 1990–1996
Heyneke Meyer Blue Bulls (3 consecutive wins 2002–2004; 1 draw) 2006

Youngest winning coaches

32 years 351 days: **Rassie Erasmus** (5/11/1972) FS Cheetahs 22/10/2005
33 years 89 days: **Dawie Snyman** (5/7/1949) Western Province 2/10/1982

Club with most players in one final

Shimlas Free State v Western Province 1976:
13 players:
Gerrie Germishuys, Joggie Jansen, Dirk Froneman, Edrich Krantz, De Wet Ras, Barry Wolmarans, Wouter Hugo, Martiens le Roux, Theuns Stofberg, Klippies Kritzinger, Ross van Reenen, Eben Jansen (injured Eben Jansen replaced by a Shimla player Gerrie Sonnekus during the match).

CURRIE CUP INDIVIDUAL RECORDS

Most Currie Cup matches as referee

135 **Jonathan Kaplan** SARU
100 **André Watson** SARU

Tries scored in a season (+12)

19 **Carel du Plessis** Western Province 1989
(*)Colin Lloyd Leopards 2006
18 **Ettienne Botha** Blue Bulls 2004
(*)Allistair Kettledas Pumas 2009
16 **Jan-Harm van Wyk** FS Cheetahs 1997

15 **Phillip Burger** FS Cheetahs 2006
14 **Niel Burger** Western Province 1984
Manie van Vuuren Eastern Province 1994
Jannie van der Walt Lions 1996
Thinus Delport Lions 1999
Kabamba Floors Eagles 2003
John Mametsa Blue Bulls 2007
13 **Agie Koch** Western Province 1977
Cabous van der Westhuizen Sharks 1996
Jan-Harm van Wyk Free State 1996
Joos Joubert Sharks 1996
Hannes Venter Northern Transvaal 1996
Stefan Terblanche Boland 1997
Henry Pedro Eastern Province 1998
Breyton Paulse Western Province 1998
John Daniels Lions 2003
Egon Seconds Western Province 2004
Henno Mentz Sharks 2005
12 **Edrich Krantz** Free State 1978
Pieter Hendriks Transvaal 1992
Chris Badenhorst Free State 1996
Thinus Delport Lions 1997
André Joubert Sharks 1997
Shaun Payne Sharks 1997
Casper Steyn Blue Bulls 1999
Chris Badenhorst FS Cheetahs 1999
Breyton Paulse Western Province 2000
Kennedy Tsimba FS Cheetahs 2002
Giscard Pieters Pumas 2004
(*)**Jan van Zyl** Leopards 2008
(*)**Vuyo Zangqa** Leopards 2008
Jongi Nokwe FS Cheetahs 2009
(*) Currie Cup decided in two Divisions: Lloyd (2006), Van Zyl (2008), Zangqa (2008) and Kettledas (2009) scored their tries in the lower First Division.

Tries scored in a league match (+5)

7 **Jacques Olivier** Northern Transvaal 4/10/96 v SWD Eagles
6 **Buks Marais** Boland 4/6/52 v NED
5 **Piet Maritz** Northern Free State 1982 v South Eastern Transvaal
Justin Swart Western Province 1996 v Northern Free State
Breyton Paulse Western Province 1997 v Falcons
Egon Seconds Western Province 28/8/2004 v Griquas
Andries Bekker Western Province 13/9/2008 v Valke

MOST POINTS BY A PLAYER

Career (+700)

1 699 **Naas Botha** Northern Transvaal 1977–1992
1 402 **Eric Herbert** Northern Free State (1124), Free State (278) 1986–2001
1 213 **Willem de Waal** Leopards (259), FS Cheetahs (811) & Western Province (143)
1 210 **De Wet Ras** Free State (1101), Natal (109)
1 165 **André Joubert** Free State, Sharks 1986–1999
1 017 **Calla Scholtz** Boland (25), Western Province (992)
961 **Kennedy Tsimba** FS Cheetahs (676), Blue Bulls (43), Pumas (26) & Griffons (216) 2000–2004
956 **Robbie Blair** Western Province & Transvaal 1974–1984
954 **Casper Steyn** Blue Bulls & Pumas 1997–2001
879 **Louis Koen** Western Province, Lions 1996–2002
777 **Jannie de Beer** FS Cheetahs (718) & Lions (59)
755 **Giepie van Zyl** Eastern Province 1981–1988
712 **Derick Hougaard** Blue Bulls 2002–2007
708 **Louis Strydom** Griffons (150), Blue Bulls (142), Falcons (266), Lions (120) & Cheetahs (30) 2001–2009
703 **Tjaart Marais** Western & Northern Transvaal 1980–1990
656 **Morné Steyn** Blue Bulls 2004–2009

League match (+30)

46 **Jannie de Beer** FS Cheetahs v Northern Free State Free State Stadium Bloemfontein (3 tries, 14 con, 1 pen) 19/9/1997

40 **Casper Steyn** Blue Bulls v SWD Loftus Versfeld Pretoria (2 tries, 3 con, 8 pen) 28/7/2000

38 **Henry Honiball** Sharks v Boland King's Park, Durban (4 tries, 6 con, 2 pen) 28/9/1996

38 **Lance Sherrell** Blue Bulls v SWD Pietersburg (2 tries, 14 con) 4/10/1996

37 **Casper Steyn** Pumas v FS Cheetahs Witbank (2 tries, 3 con, 7 pen) 2/8/2003

36 **Gerald Bosch** Transvaal v Far North Ellis Park, Johannesburg (1 try, 2 drop, 13 con) 7/7/1973

36 **Eric Herbert** Northern Free State v Falcons North West Stadium Welkom (3 con, 9 pen, 1 drop) 15/8/1997

Casper Steyn Blue Bulls v Pumas Loftus Pretoria (1 try, 5 con, 7 pen) 12/8/2000

35 **Jacques Olivier** Northern Transvaal v South Western Districts Pietersburg (7 tries) 4/10/1996

Kennedy Tsimba FS Cheetahs v Griquas West Absa Park Kimberley (1 try, 9 con, 4 pen) 13/9/2003

Braam Pretorius Pumas v Valke Barnard Stadium Kempton Park (2 tries, 11 con, 1 pen) 5/9/2009

34 **Naas Botha** Northern Transvaal v Rhodesia Loftus Versfeld Pretoria (1 try, 3 con, 7 pen, 1 drop) 12/5/1979

Casper Steyn Blue Bulls v Griffons Loftus Versfeld Pretoria (2 tries, 12 con) 5/6/1999

Kennedy Tsimba FS Cheetahs v Griffons North West Stadium Welkom (1 try, 4 con, 7 pen) 20/7/2002

33 Piet Visagie Griquas v Rhodesia De Beers Stadium Kimberley (2 tries, 9 con, 1 drop, 2 pen) 3/8/1968

MJ Smith Free State v South Western Districts Free State Stadium Bloemfontein (1 try, 14 con) 21/9/1996

Chris Rossouw Western Province v Blue Bulls, Newlands Cape Town (3 tries, 9 con) 13/9/2003

32 **Louis Koen** Western Province v SWD Mossel Bay (2 tries, 11 con) 28/9/1996

Jannie de Beer FS Cheetahs v Northern Transvaal Free State Stadium Bloemfontein (1 try, 6 con, 5 pen) 16/8/1997

Casper Steyn Blue Bulls v Boland Loftus Versfeld Pretoria (2 tries, 6 con, 3 pen) 24/7/1999

André Fourie FS Cheetahs v Griffons Free State Stadium Bloemfontein (7 con, 6 pen) 13/8/1999

Eric Herbert Griffons v Eastern Province Telkom Park Port Elizabeth (2 tries, 2 con, 5 pen) 1 drop 2/9/2000

Kennedy Tsimba FS Cheetahs v Griquas Vodacom Park Bloemfontein (3 tries, 7 con, 1 drop) 24/8/2002

31 **Tjaart Marais** Western Transvaal v Eastern Free State Olën Park Potchefstroom (14 con, 1 pen) 3/9/1988

Eric Herbert Free State v Western Province Springbok Park Bloemfontein (1 try, 1 con, 6 pen, 2 drop) 28/5/1994

Andries Fourie Pumas v Northern Free State Johann van Riebeeck Stadium Witbank (2 tries, 6 con, 3 pen) 3/10/1997

Kobus Engelbrecht Lions v SWD Ellispark Johannesburg (1 try, 7 con, 4 pen) 4/9/1999

Nel Fourie Pumas v SWD Eagles Puma Stadium Witbank (14 con, 1 pen) 18/8/2001

Gaffie du Toit Sharks v Western Province Absa Stadium Durban (1 try, 1 con, 8 pen) 13/10/2001

Naas Olivier Leopards v Pumas Atlantic Park Witbank (2 tries, 6 con, 3 pen) 24/6/2005

30 **Jannie de Beer** FS Cheetahs v Leopards Olën Park Potchefstroom (1 try, 5 con, 5 pen) 13/7/1999

Henry Honiball Sharks v Western Province Kings Park Durban (1 try, 8 con, 3 pen) 21/8/1999
Conrad Barnard FS Cheetahs v Elephants Free State Stadium Bloemfontein (9 con, 4 pen) 18/8/2001
Kennedy Tsimba FS Cheetahs v Blue Bulls Vodacom Park Bloemfontein (1 try, 2 con, 7 pen) 21/9/2002
Derick Hougaard Blue Bulls v Western Province Loftus Versfeld Pretoria (9 pen, 1 drop) 28/9/2002
André Pretorius Lions v Western Province Ellis Park Johannesburg (1 try, 5 con, 5 pen) 12/10/2002
André Pretorius Lions v SWD Ellis Park Johannesburg (1 try, 11 con, 1 pen) 4/10/2003
Willem de Waal Cheetahs v Lions Ellis Park Johannesburg (1 try, 2 con, 5 pen, 2 drop) 4/9/2004
Conrad Barnard Griquas v Valke Bosman Stadium Brakpan (1 try, 8 con, 3 pen) 15/9/2007
Earl Rose Lions v Valke Coca-Cola Park Johannesburg (3 tries, 3 con, 3 pen) 5/7/2008

MOST PENALTIES

Season

48 **Gavin Lawless** Lions 1996
45 **Lance Sherrell** Western Province 1991
Johan Heunis Northern Transvaal 1987
Cameron Oliver Transvaal 1989

Final

6 **Thierry Lacroix** Sharks v Western Province 1995

League match

9 **Jannie Kruger** Northern Transvaal v Western Province 1996
Eric Herbert Northern Free State v Falcons 1997
Derick Hougaard Blue Bulls v Western Province 2001
8 **André Fourie** FS Cheetahs v Griquas 1997
Casper Steyn Blue Bulls v SWD Eagles 2000
Gaffie du Toit Sharks v Western Province 2001

MOST CONVERSIONS

Season

62 **Louis Koen** Western Province 1997
55 **Jannie de Beer** FS Cheetahs 1997

Final

6 **Gavin Lawless** Transvaal v Free State 1991

League match

14 **Tjaart Marais** Western Transvaal v Eastern Free State 1988
MJ Smith Free State v South Western Districts 1996
Lance Sherrell Northern Transvaal v South Western Districts 1996
Jannie de Beer Free State v Northern Free State 1997
Nel Fourie Pumas v SWD Eagles 2001
13 **Gerald Bosch** Transvaal v Far North 1973

Most career matches

142 **Helgard Müller** Free State 1983–1998
141 **Rudie Visagie** Free State, Natal & Pumas 1980–1996

136 **Chris Badenhorst** Free State 1987–1999
128 **Ollie le Roux** Free State, Sharks & Cheetahs 1993–2007
Burger Geldenhuys Northern Transvaal 1977–1989
126 **André Joubert** Free State & Sharks 1986–1999
125 **Eric Herbert** Northern Free State, Griffons & Free State 1986–2001
123 **Naas Botha** Northern Transvaal 1977–1992
118 **Willie Meyer** Eastern Province, FS Cheetahs & Lions 1991–2002
115 **AJ Venter** Western Province, Sharks, Lions & FS Cheetahs 1996–2007
114 **Piet Krause** Valke, Blue Bulls, Leopards, Griquas & Lions 1997–2008
113 **Louis Moolman** Northern Transvaal 1974–1986
108 **Eddie Fredericks** WP, FS Cheetahs & Griffons 1998–2009
106 **Martiens le Roux** Free State 1973–1986
De Wet Ras Free State & Natal 1974–1986
104 **Gerrie Sonnekus** Free State 1974–1985
103 **Uli Schmidt** Northern Transvaal & Transvaal 1983–1994
Albert van den Berg Griquas & Sharks 1996–2009
102 **Adolf Malan** Northern Transvaal 1983–1992
101 **Gysie Pienaar** Free State 1974–1987
99 **Louis Strydom** Griffons, Blue Bulls, Valke, Lions & FS Cheetahs 2001–2009

Most finals

11 **Burger Geldenhuys** Northern Transvaal
Naas Botha Northern Transvaal
9 **Louis Moolman** Northern Transvaal
8 **Hennie Bekker** Free State & Western Province
Tommy du Plessis Northern Transvaal
Thys Lourens Northern Transvaal (on the winning side in every final, four times as captain)
Uli Schmidt Northern Transvaal & Transvaal
7 **Jannie Breedt** Northern Transvaal & Transvaal
Carel du Plessis Western Province & Transvaal
Pierre Edwards Northern Transvaal
Willie Kahts Northern Transvaal
Ollie le Roux Free State, Natal Sharks & FS Cheetahs
Adolf Malan Northern Transvaal
Heinrich Rodgers Northern Transvaal & Transvaal
Theuns Stofberg Free State (win 1976), Northern Transvaal (share with Western Province in 1979, win 1980) & Western Province (win in 1982 & 1983).
6 **Daan du Plessis** Northern Transvaal
Michael du Plessis Western Province & Transvaal
Gerbrand Grobler Northern Transvaal & Transvaal
Martiens le Roux Free State
Rob Louw Western Province
Shaun Povey Western Province
Divan Serfontein Western Province
James Small Lions, Sharks & Western Province
Henning van Aswegen, Free State & Western Province
Pedrie Wannenburg Blue Bulls
5 **Mark Andrews** Natal
Wahl Bartmann Transvaal & Natal
Darius Botha Northern Transvaal
Gary Botha Blue Bulls
Fourie du Preez Blue Bulls
Robert du Preez Northern Transvaal & Natal
Pote Fourie Northern Transvaal
John Knox Northern Transvaal
Johann Lampbrecht Northern Transvaal
Hennie le Roux Transvaal
Victor Matfield Blue Bulls
Dick Muir Sharks & Western Province
Jan Oberholzer Northern Transvaal
Gavin Passens Blue Bulls (2002, 2003, 2004) & Cheetahs (2006, 2007) (on the winning side in every final)
François Pienaar Lions
De Wet Ras Free State
Danie Rossouw Blue Bulls
Pieter Rossouw Western Province
Calla Scholtz Western Province
André Skinner Northern Transvaal & Transvaal

Gerrie Sonnekus Free State
Toks van der Linde Western Province
Moaner van Heerden Northern Transvaal
André van Staden Northern Transvaal
Christo Wagenaar Northern Transvaal

Semi-finalists

Various formats, only one semi-final in certian years

Year Winners Losers Venue

1954 Northern Transvaal 9 Free State 8
Free State Stadium, Bloemfontein
1956 Natal 11 Western Province 10
Newlands, Cape Town
1969 Western Province 13 Boland 11
Newlands, Cape Town
1970 Northern Transvaal 24 Natal 8
Kings Park, Durban
1971 Transvaal 23 Natal 10
Ellis Park, Johanesburg
1972 Free State 19 Western Province 15
Newlands, Cape Town
1973 Northern Transvaal 20 Rhodesia 7
Loftus Versfeld, Pretoria
1974 Transvaal 30 Eastern Province 6
Ellis Park, Johannesburg
1979 Northern Transvaal 16 Eastern Province 6
Boet Erasmus, Port Elizabeth
Western Province 20 Griquas 15
De Beers Stadium, Kimberley
1980 Northern Transvaal 49 SE-Transvaal 6
Loftus Versfeld, Pretoria
Western Province 21 Eastern Province 13
Boet Erasmus, Port Elizabeth
1981 Northern Transvaal 36 Northern Free State 12
Loftus Versfeld, Pretoria
Free State 28 Eastern Transvaal 15
PAM Brink, Springs
1982 Western Province 47 Natal 18
Newlands, Cape Town
Northern Transvaal 24 Northern Free State 21
North West Stadium, Welkom
1983 Western Province 7 Natal 3
Kings Park, Durban
Northern Transvaal 32 Northern Free State 15
Loftus Versfeld, Pretoria
1984 Natal 26 Free State 15
Kings Park, Durban
Western Province 53 Eastern Transvaal 0
Newlands, Cape Town
1986 Transvaal 18 Natal 4
Kings Park, Durban
1987 Transvaal 12 South West Africa 9
National Stadium, Windhoek
1988 Western Province 26 Northern Free State 9
North West Stadium, Welkom
1989 Western Province 71 Western Transvaal 9
Olën Park, Portchefstroom
1996 Sharks 35 Free State 20
Kings Park, Durban
Lions 31 Northern Transvaal 21
Loftus Versfeld, Pretoria
1997 Western Province 38 Lions 18
Newlands, Cape Town
FS Cheetahs 40 Sharks 22
Kings Park, Durban
1998 Western Province 27 Griquas 11
Hoffe Park, Kimberley
Blue Bulls 31 Sharks 17
Loftus Versfeld, Pretoria
1999 Lions 81 SWD 21
Ellis Park, Johannesburg
Sharks 45 FS Cheetahs 8
Kings Park, Durban
2000 Sharks 29 FS Cheetahs 15
Absa Stadium, Durban
Western Province 43 Lions 22
Newlands, Cape Town
2001 Western Province 40 FS Cheetahs 18
Newlands, Cape Town
Sharks 16 Lions 9
Absa Stadium, Durban
2002 Lions 43 FS Cheetahs 29
Vodacom Park, Bloemfontein
Blue Bulls 22 Sharks 19
Absa Stadium, Durban

2004 Blue Bulls 40 Lions 33
Loftus Versfeld, Pretoria
FS Cheetahs 17 Western Province 11
Newlands, Cape Town
2005 FS Cheetahs 16 Western Province 11
Newlands, Cape Town
Blue Bulls 31 Lions 23
Loftus Versfeld, Pretoria
2006 Blue Bulls 45 Western Province 30
Loftus Versfeld, Pretoria
FS Cheetahs 30 Sharks 14
Vodacom Park, Bloemfontein
2007 Lions 19 Sharks 12
Absa Stadium, Durban
FS Cheetahs 11 Blue Bulls 6
Vodacom Park, Bloemfontein
2008 Sharks 29 Lions 14
Absa Stadium, Durban
Blue Bulls 31 FS Cheetahs 19
Loftus Versfeld, Pretoria
2009 FS Cheetahs 23 Sharks 21
Absa Stadium, Durban
Bluc Bulls 21 Wcstcrn Provincc 19
Newlands, Cape Town

CURRIE CUP WINNERS

Various league systems between 1892 and 1936

Winners of league format

1892 Western Province
1894 Western Province
1895 Western Province
1897 Western Province
1898 Western Province
1899 Griquas
1904 Western Province
1906 Western Province
1908 Western Province
1911 Griquas
1914 Western Province
1920 Western Province
1922 Transvaal
1925 Western Province
1927 Western Province
1929 Western Province
1932 Border/Western Province
1934 Border/Western Province
1936 Western Province

Finals from 1939, with three exceptions

Year Winners Losers Venue
1939 Transvaal 17 Western Province 6
Newlands, Cape Town
1946 Northern Transvaal 11 Western Province 9
Loftus Versfeld, Pretoria
1947 Western Province 16 Transvaal 12
Newlands, Cape Town
1950 Transvaal 22 Western Province 11
Ellis Park, Johannesburg
1952 Transvaal11 Boland 9
Boland Stadium, Wellington
1954 Western Province 11 Northern Transvaal 8
Newlands, Cape Town
1956 Northern Transvaal 9 Natal 8
Kingsmead Cricket Ground, Durban
1957–1959 Western Province
Decided over two seasons (1957 and 1959)
No Currie Cup until 1964
1964 Western Province
1966 Western Province
1968 Northern Transvaal 16 Transvaal 3
Loftus Versfeld, Pretoria
1969 Northern Transvaal 28 Western Province 13
Loftus Versfeld, Pretoria
1970 Griquas 11 Northern Transvaal 9
De Beers Stadium, Kimberley
1971 Transvaal 14 Northern Transvaal 14
Ellis Park, Johannesburg
1972 Transvaal 25 Eastern Transvaal 19

PAM Brink, Springs
1973 Northern Transvaal 30 Free State 22
Loftus Versfeld, Pretoria
1974 Northern Transvaal 17 Transvaal 15
Loftus Versfeld, Pretoria
1975 Northen Transvaal 12 Free State 6
Free State Stadium, Bloemfontein
1976 Free State 33 Western Province 16
Free State Stadium, Bloemfontein
1977 Northern Transvaal 27 Free State 12
Loftus Versfeld, Pretoria
1978 Northern Transvaal 13 Free State 9
Free State Stadium, Bloemfontein
1979 Western Province 15 Northern Transvaal 15
Newlands, Cape Town
1980 Northern Transvaal 39 Western Province 9
Loftus Versfeld, Pretoria
1981 Northern Transvaal 23 Free State 6
Loftus Versfeld, Pretoria
1982 Western Province 24 Northern Transvaal 7
Newlands, Cape Town
1983 Western Province 9 Northern Transvaal 3
Loftus Versfeld, Pretoria
1984 Western Province 19 Northern Transvaal 9
Newlands, Cape Town
1985 Western Province 22 Northern Transvaal 15
Newlands, Cape Town
1986 Western Province 22 Transvaal 9
Newlands, Cape Town
1987 Northern Transvaal 24 Transvaal 18
Ellis Park, Johannesburg
1988 Northern Transvaal 19 Western Province 18
Loftus Versfeld, Pretoria
1989 Northern Transvaal 16 Western Province 16
Newlands, Cape Town
1990 Natal 18 Northern Transvaal 12
Loftus Versfeld, Pretoria
1991 Northern Transvaal 27 Transvaal 15
Loftus Versfeld, Pretoria
1992 Natal 14 Transvaal 13
Ellis Park, Johannesburg
1993 Lions 21 Natal 15
Kings Park, Durban
1994 Lions 56 Free State 35
Springbok Park, Bloemfontein
1995 Sharks 25 Western Province 17
Kings Park, Durban
1996 Sharks 33 Lions 15
Ellis Park, Johannesburg
1997 Western Province 14 FS Cheetahs 12
Newlands, Cape Town
1998 Blue Bulls 24 Western Province 20
Loftus Versfeld, Pretoria
1999 Lions 32 Sharks 9
Kings Park, Durban
2000 Western Province 25 Sharks 15
Absa Stadium, Durban
2001 Western Province 29 Sharks 24
Newlands, Cape Town
2002 Blue Bulls 31 Lions 7
Ellis Park, Johannesbrug
2003 Blue Bulls 40 Sharks 19
Loftus Versfeld, Pretoria
2004 Blue Bulls 42 FS Cheetahs 33
Loftus Versfeld, Pretoria
2005 FS Cheetahs 29 Blue Bulls 25
Loftus Versfeld, Pretoria
2006 FS Cheetahs 28 Blue Bulls 28
Vodacom Park, Bloemfontein
2007 FS Cheetahs 20 Lions 18
Vodacom Park, Bloemfontein
2008 Sharks 14 Blue Bulls 9
Absa Stadium, Durban
2009 Blue Bulls 36 FS Cheetahs 24
Loftus Versfeld, Pretoria

Bibliography and Acknowledgements

Albert Heenop, 2001. *Team of the 90s*. Durban. Mundell Media.

Alfred Herbert, 1980. *The Natal Rugby Story*. Pietermaritzburg. Shuter & Shooter.

Andy Colquhoun, 2007. *Hennie Muller: Die windhond*. Cape Town. Don Nelson Publishers.

Chris Greyvenstein, 1977. *Springbok Saga*. Cape Town. Don Nelson Publishers and Toyota SA.

Chris Greyvenstein, 1989. *Naas Botha: Rugby's golden boy*. Cape Town. Don Nelson Publishers.

DH Craven, 1949. *Ek speel vir Suid-Afrika*. Cape Town. Nasionale Pers Bpk.

DH Craven, 1964. *Springbok Annals: 1891–1964*. Johannesburg. Mimosa Publishers.

DH Craven, 1964. *Springbok-annale: 1891–1964*. Johannesburg. Mimosa Publishers.

DH Craven, 1980. *Die groot rugbygesin van die Maties*. Cape Town. Galvin & Sales.

Frikkie van Rensburg, 1986. *Die ontstaan van Griekwalandwes-rugby: 1886-1986*. Kimberley. Noordkaaplandse Drukkers.

Fritz Joubert and Schalk Burger, 1995. *'n Sport vir manne*. Cape Town. Human & Rousseau.

Graham K Jooste, 1995. *South African Rugby Teams: 1919–1995*. Johannesburg. Penguin Books.

Hennie Gerber, 1982. *Craven*. Cape Town. Tafelberg.

Herman le Roux, 1998. *Sportpourri*. Pretoria. JL van Schaik.

Ivor D Difford, 1933. *History of South African Rugby Football: 1875–1932*. Cape Town. The Speciality Press.

Johan Volschenk, 1977. *Die Ligbloues*. Pretoria. TRI-Uitgewers.

John Bishop, 2000. *Mac: The face of rugby*. Cape Town. Don Nelson Publishers.

JT Ferreira, JP Blignaut, PJ Landman and JF du Toit, 1989.*Transvaal Rugby Football Union: 100 years*. Johannesburg. Transvaal Rugby Football Union.

Kim Shippey, 1971. *The Unbeatables: Springboks in Australia*. Unknown Publisher.

Leon Gouws, 1971. *Frik du Preez: Rugbyreus.* Johannesburg. Janssonius & Heyns.

MC van Zyl (ed.), 1988. *Noord-Transvaalrugby 50.* Pretoria. Northern Transvaal Rugby Union.

Reg Sweet, 1990. *Natal 100: Centenary of the Natal Rugby Union.* Durban. Natal Rugby Union.

Richard Bath, 2008. *The British and Irish Lions Miscellany.* London. Vision Sports Publishing.

Shelley Carmichael (ed.), 2003. *112 Years of Springbok Rugby, Tests and Heroes.* Cape Town. Highbury Monarch Communications.

Steve de Villiers, 1989. *Kaviaar vir 'n kameraad.* Johannesburg. Perskor.

Steve de Villiers, 1991. *Kaviaar vir 'n kanniedood.* Johannesburg. Perskor.

Teddy Shnaps, 1989. *A Statistical History of Springbok Rugby.* Cape Town. Don Nelson Publishers.

Wim van der Berg and Gerhard Burger, 2008. *Blue Bulls: 70 years of glory.* Johannesburg. Penguin Books.

Gerhard Burger and Wim van der Berg, 2008. *Lions Tale: 120 years of the red and white.* Johannesburg. Online Communications.

Other sources

Brochures and newspaper and magazine cuttings from the collection of Herman le Roux, former sports editor of *Volksblad* and *Beeld.*

Blue Bulls Rugby Union (BBRU) archives

Golden Lions Rugby Union (GLRU) archives

SA Rugby Annuals, 1953–2009. Various publishers, sponsors and printers.

SA Rugby Publications. Various publishers, sponsors and printers.

Transvaal Independent Rugby Football Union.

The Irish Rugby Football Union literature

www.supersport.co.za/rugby

www.sarugby.co.za

www.genslin.us/bokke

www.planetrugby.com

www.rugby365.com

www.rugbyvaria.com

www.thebulls.co.za

ACKNOWLEDGEMENTS

The author wishes to thank Penguin (South Africa) for their input and guidance during the writing of this book.

My thanks also go to:

Online Publishing for their role as coordinator and facilitator and for procuring much of the material used in this book;

Beeld and Johan Rynners for the use of some of the photos contained in this book

Blue Bulls Company (Pty) Ltd, the Golden Lions Rugby Union, Griqualand West Rugby Union, and SA Rugby Union for their input and assistance;

Jan Schaafsma for the editing;

Zia Fourie for the proofreading;

JJ Harmse for ensuring the factual correctness in the quagmire of scores, dates and scorers;

Piet Ebersohn for the use of his extensive rugby 'library';

Herman le Roux and Gerhard Burger for their substantial contributions;

My wife Alida for her patience and support over many rugby years, and for her advice and input with this book.